T0373389

The Ring of Myths

The Ring of Myths

The Israelis, Wagner and the Nazis

TRANSLATED FROM THE HEBREW BY MARTHA GRENZEBACK
AND MIRIAM TALISMAN

NA'AMA SHEFFI

sussex
ACADEMIC
PRESS
Brighton • Chicago • Toronto

Copyright © Na'ama Sheffi 2001, 2013.

The right of Na'ama Sheffi to be identified as Author of this work has been
asserted in accordance with the Copyright, Designs and Patents Act 1988.

2 4 6 8 10 9 7 5 3 1

First published in hardcover, revised and updated 2013 in paperback by
SUSSEX ACADEMIC PRESS
PO Box 139
Eastbourne BN24 9BP

Distributed in North America by
SUSSEX ACADEMIC PRESS
IIndependent Publishers Group
814 N Franklin St, Chicago, IL 60610, USA

All rights reserved. Except for the quotation of short passages for the purposes
of criticism and review, no part of this publication may be reproduced,
stored in a retrieval system or transmitted in any form or by any
means, electronic, mechanical, photocopying, recording or
otherwise, without the prior permission of the publisher.

Chapter 5 was first published as, "Cultural Manipulation: Richard Wagner
and Richard Strauss in Israel in the 1950s," *Journal of Contemporary History* 34, no. 4
(1999): 619–39. Reprinted by permission of Sage Publications Ltd.

British Library Cataloguing in Publication Data
A CIP catalogue record for this book is available from the British Library.

Library of Congress Cataloging-in-Publication Data
Sheffi, Na'ama.
[Taba'at ha-mitosim. English]
The ring of myths : the Israelis, Wagner and the Nazis / Na'ama Sheffi ; translated
  from the Hebrew by Martha Grenzeback and Miriam Talisman.
pages   cm
Includes bibliographical references and index.
ISBN 978-1-84519-574-8 (p/b : alk. paper)
  1. Wagner, Richard, 1813–1883—Public opinion. 2. Wagner, Richard, 1813–
1883—Relations with Jews. 3. Music—Political aspects—Israel. 4. Public
opinion—Israel. 5. Music and state—Israel. 6. Music and antisemitism. I. Title.
ML410.W19S4513 2013
782.1092—dc23

                                                                2012047408

Typeset and designed by Sussex Academic Press, Brighton & Eastbourne.
Printed and bound by CPI Group (UK) Ltd, Croydon, CR0 4YY
This book is printed on acid-free paper.

Contents

Preface

Since *Kristallnacht*, the anti-Jewish pogrom that took place in Germany in November 1938, Richard Wagner (1813–1883) became *persona non grata* in Israel's concert halls. Several days after the pogrom a work by Wagner was removed from the concert program of the Palestine Symphony Orchestra (which would become the IPO, Israel Philharmonic Orchestra) on ideological grounds. In Israel, Wagner's identification with the racist views of National Socialism and vicious anti-Semitism made his musical oeuvre into one of the explicit symbols of the Holocaust and its atrocities. However, until 2012 no body, from the legislative and judicial authorities to the Board for Film and Theatre Review (the censorship board) and the broadcasting and orchestra institutions, ever publicly banned the performance of Wagner's work.

Since the 1990s Wagner has been the only composer whose perform-ance in Israel has stirred up bitter resentment. The ban on other composers, whom the orchestras and broadcasting authorities refrained from performing, was lifted. Franz Lehar, Carl Orff, and Richard Strauss – all composers who collaborated with the Nazi regime – are included in the programs of Israel's large orchestras, and no longer arouse public controversy. Recordings of performers who collaborated with the Nazis to one degree or another, such as conductors Wilhelm Furtwängler, Herbert von Karajan and Karl Böhm, and sopranos, the German Elizabeth Schwartzkopf and the Norwegian Kirsten Flagstad, are broadcasted. From the outset Richard Strauss was the only musician who generated discontent similar to Wagner. As the founding director of the music chamber in the Nazi Ministry of Propaganda, Strauss was perceived as an ideological ally of the Nazis.

Attempts to play Wagner in Israel at the dawn of the twenty-first century met with bitter resentment. Such was the fate of the endeavours of the Israel Rishon LeZion Symphony Orchestra in late 2000, the encore to the concert of the Staatskapelle Berlin (Berlin State Opera) in the Israel Festival in the summer of 2001, and the initiative of the Israeli Wagner Society and Israeli-born conductor Asher Fisch in the spring of 2012. Concerning the latter event, no public hall could be found from the Tel Aviv University to the Tel Aviv Hilton to host a special performance of the Philharmonia Orchestra and soloists that were commissioned for one Wagner concert in Tel Aviv.

In the early days of the boycott, opposition was fueled by the recentness of the Holocaust; at that time Israelis were categorically united in their total rejection of anything that reminded them of the sinister twelve years of the Third Reich. Over the years, however, the hatred of Wagner seemed to become an obsession that permitted a degree of unity even in a state with a population divided between those who prayed and those who fought, those who labored and those who grew rich, those who wanted both sides of the Jordan River and those who wanted territorial compromise.

At least some of the opposition to Wagner appeared to be motivated by efforts to maintain the social unity of the early years by using the battle over the state's relations with new post-1945 Germany as a rallying point. Perhaps preserving the evil in its original form would make it possible to sustain Israeli society's shared identity? Perhaps clinging to a past sown in the present would keep the precarious social unity intact? Yet that traumatic past was unlikely to foster the sense of social partnership that was so pervasive in the early days of the state. The new millennium is characterized by ever-increasing schisms in Israeli society. The commemoration of the Holocaust plays a major role in the identity of numerous Israelis. Yad Vashem, the state's institution for the documentation and commemoration of the Holocaust, launches numerous projects every year. Teenagers, soldiers, civilians and politicians visit the memorial sites in Poland and throughout Europe. Nevertheless, the frequent use of the Holocaust as a political tool that represents the dangers Israel may face devalues its true moral importance in the eyes of many. Moreover, some sectors are indifferent to the subject, largely the extremists – the ultra-Orthodox group, *Neturei Karta*, a small number of anti-Israel Palestinians, and a small group of racist teenagers, the majority immigrants of Russian-speaking origin.

I doubt that the present account of the social history of opposition to Wagner will be instrumental in moderating the stormy emotions incited by the controversial composer and his rich oeuvre. Whenever the Wagner issue comes up, the numerous articles and letters to the editor attest to the deeply-felt emotions involved. His anti-Semitism and adoption by the Nazis prevents many Israelis from investigating Wagner's music and thought. A German-Israeli conference, "Wagner and the Jews," held in Bayreuth in 1998 aroused criticism within the Israeli academy, while many subsequent discussions – including a one-day symposium held at Tel Aviv University in the winter of 2001 – were received rather peacefully. The latter event, that included chamber arrangements of Wagner's music, drew a great deal of attention. Such was the case of a special demonstrated lecture given by conductor Asher Fisch in the winter of 2011. In August 2011 the Israeli Chamber Orchestra took part in a musical event in the Bayreuth annual Wagner Festival (but not in the festival itself). In Israel reports on the concert were negligible, in contrast to the mayhem it evoked prior to the event. In the autumn of 2010 the festival's newly appointed manager, Katharina Wagner, decided to cancel a press conference announcing the invitation of the Israeli orchestra, a step followed by many offensive op-eds in the Israeli press.

The passage of time cannot obscure the fact that Wagner was a major anti-Semitic theoretician whose essay "Judaism in Music" was the acme of classic anti-Jewish indictment. However, it is also hard to forget a long series of anti-Semitic creative geniuses, as well as all the eminent artists whom the Nazis inducted into the all-German pantheon they sought to build for their loyal subjects.

I take Wagner's adoption by the Nazis very seriously, as I do any political use of a work of art, and more particularly, any attempt to orient art to the dictates of public opinion. But his automatic rejection on political and social grounds has often slipped into the realm of a simplistic emblem. In my view, Israelis have a special duty to be standard-bearers in the struggle against political exploitation of art; they suffered when the books of Jews were burned in the town squares of the Third Reich – a fire that ended by consuming their community. However, observation of Israeli audiences who see Wagner as the basest of artists suggests that the voice of reason is not necessarily the one that will determine this debate. Those who ban Wagner in Israel while utilizing him as a symbol of the Holocaust merely instrumentalize him and thus abuse the memory of the catastrophic event. Yet, criticising them should not diminish the suffering of those for whom the sound of Wagner's music is exceedingly upsetting, reverberating in their ears like the scream of Satan.

The performance of Wagner's works in Israel is an extremely fraught issue, one that is continually batted back and forth between various groups with conflicting agendas. Should greater weight be given to the desire of this or that orchestra to improve its technical virtuosity; or should the musical aspect take second place to the possibility of injury to the feelings of the audience? Should we privilege the general population's right to listen to certain kinds of music in public places, or should we shrink from hurting those Holocaust survivors who are still among us and the growing number of younger Israelis who have assimilated the anti-Wagner message as part of a general worldview? Does one group's right to hear, be that group large or small, take precedence over another group's right to close its ears? Answers to these questions are likely to emerge only gradually, as the Holocaust recedes further into the past. Distance may work in both ways: urge further and wider documentation of the Holocaust and attempts to decipher it, or support relaxation of the efforts to investigate this event. Like the warring sides in the controversy, I too wonder what shape the memory of the Holocaust will take in the decades to come, as the number of survivors among us dwindles; unlike those who oppose the performance of Wagner's music, I do not believe the shape of that memory should be determined by a boycott, be it musical or other. Both the Nazi and the Israeli perceptions of Wagner essentially followed the same process by which Wagner created his mythical world of the Nibelungs. In each case a ring of myths was created, albeit for widely different purposes. The Nazis' aim was to revive the glory of the Teutonic legend by apotheosizing Wagner's artistic work and political thought; the Israelis sought to condemn them. Ironically, however, they ended up creating their own set of myths about Wagner and German culture.

As an Israeli concerned with the way social and governmental norms are created in my country, I see the polemic raging around the Wagner issue as a microcosm of the profound discord that rends Israeli society. Doubtlessly the performance of one musical work or another is not on the same level with cardinal questions concerning the future of the state; but perhaps for that very reason the pseudo-musical controversy may provide a mirror for broader and more critical social and political issues.

I would like to take this opportunity to thank the people who urged me to research the Israeli attitude toward Wagner and to write this book. First of all, I would like to thank my friends and colleagues Professor Raanan Rein and Professor Moshe Zuckermann of Tel Aviv University, who read the original manuscript, made suggestions and helped me clarify the arguments presented. Professor Zuckerman was the force behind the German publication of the book. Other colleagues encouraged me to rethink and refine my arguments and conclusions; I would like to express my gratitude to Professor Patricia Hall of the University of California, Santa Barbara, Professor Alex Lubet of the University of Minnesota, Professor Anita Shapira of Tel Aviv University, and Professor Nicholas Vazsonyi of the University of South Carolina. My editors in Israel and England, Professor Fania Oz-Salzberger of the University of Haifa, and chief editor of Sussex Academic Press, Anthony Grahame, who offered support and good advice. The three translators with whom I worked rendered the original text into foreign languages. I wish to thank Martha Grenzeback for her sensitive, intelligent translation of the original edition of this book, and Miriam Talisman for voicing me accurately in many articles and in the perceptive creation of this revised edition. Liliane Meilinger illuminated other obstacles while thoughtfully translating the German edition. I owe a debt of thanks to Mr. Ephraim Mittelman, Director of the Israel Philharmonic Orchestra Archives, who provided crucial and valuable support as I read the material on Richard Wagner and Richard Strauss. Mr. Gunter Fischer of the Nationalarchiv der Richard-Wagner-Stiftung in Bayreuth was a loyal friend on my visits to his city, and presented me with an extraordinary range of information on musical activity in Bayreuth since the death of Wagner. I am grateful to my academic home, Sapir College, and to my colleagues who were extraordinarily supportive.

Finally, I would like to thank my friend Limor Blatt for being a willing listener, a critical reader and a staunch supporter throughout the years I was researching, writing and revising this book.

Glossary of Political Parties

Mapai *(Mifleget Poalei Yisrael – Israel Labor Party)*: Moderate left-wing party founded in 1930. It led the pre-state Jewish *Yishuv*, and in 1968 provided the basis for the Labor Party, together with Achdut Haavodah (Unity of Labor Party) and Rafi (Israel Workers' List). Beginning in 1965, it ran in elections as part of the Maarach ("Alignment"), a bloc that initially represented Mapai and Achdut Haavodah and, subsequently, Mapai and Mapam. All the different components of the Maarach adhered to a socialist worldview, although they differed on foreign and defense policies. In its various metamorphoses, Mapai was the ruling party until the 1977 elections. Since then the party gradually diminished and in 2011 five members split, forming a new party, Atzmaut (Independence).

Mapam (Mifleget Poalim Meuchedet – United Labor Party): A socialist-Zionist left-wing party representing Hashomer Hatzair (Young Guard) and the National Kibbutz movements. It was a member of several government coalitions until 1969, when it ran for election as part of the Maarach. In 1992 it joined Meretz, another left-wing party.

Herut: A right-wing party established by Menachem Begin in 1948, composed of members of Etzel and the Revisionist Movement. In 1965 it joined the Liberal Party to form Gahal (Herut-Liberal Bloc), and was a member of the 1967–1970 national unity government. In 1973 Gahal combined with a number of smaller political factions to create the Likud. It was the main opposition party until 1977, and is one of the major political parties in Israel today.

Independent Liberals: Formed from a schism in the Progressive Party in 1965, this moderate, centrist party was a member of the Maarach coalitions until 1977. Since 1984 it has been part of the Likud.

National Religious Party (Miflaga Datit Leumit – Mafdal): A religious party that was formed in 1965 from a merge between the Mizrachi movement and the Hapoel Hamizrachi party. It has been a member of almost every coalition – of the left and the right – since the establishment of the state. In 2006 the party ran for the Knesset elections with the right-wing National Union (Ha-Ihud Ha-Leumi) together with two other right wing parties, and two years later integrated with the right-wing national religious party The Jewish Home (Ha-Bayit Ha-Yehudi).

Shinui: A moderate centrist party that was formed in the wake of the 1973 Yom Kippur War. It was a component first of Dash (Democratic Movement for Change) and later of Meretz, cooperating with the left-wing Civil Rights Movement (CRM) and Mapam.

Tehiya: An extreme right-wing party that grew out of a split in the Likud caused by dissension over the 1979 Camp David Accords. It joined the Likud government at the time of the Lebanon war, reintegrating into the Likud in 1992 after it failed to garner sufficient votes for a Knesset seat on its own.

Merkaz: A short-lived party composed of retirees of the Labor, Likud and Tzomet parties (a later metamorphosis of Tehiya). The party was established in 1999 and survived only the 15th Knesset, until early 2002

1

An End that Marked a Beginning

In November 1938, following the decision of the Palestine Symphony Orchestra to cut the prelude of *Der Meistersinger von Nürnberg* from its first concert series of the season, performance of Richard Wagner's music in Palestine, and later, Israel, came to an end over an extended period. From then on, no professional musical body in Israel could play works by this celebrated German composer without creating an uproar; for that cancellation, motivated by a desire to condemn the conduct of the Third Reich and the Nazis' incitement of the *Kristallnacht* pogroms, proved to be the beginning of a taboo that would persist for many years. In Israel the boycotted composer became one of the most prominent and problematic symbols of the Third Reich's legacy. Wagner's exclusion from Israeli repertoires in succeeding years was the basis for a long series of disputes marking the beginning of a complex and intriguing public debate. As a sort of invisible presence, Wagner became a central figure in a process of cultural controversy which at times even seemed manipulative, extending far beyond the boundaries of the musical world.

The Wagner affair became one of the most interesting junctures between art and politics in Israeli society. In its early stages the political aspect seemed dominant. Members of the *Yishuv* (the small Jewish community) in Palestine received news of distressing developments in Europe in general and in Germany in particular, but were not always able to grasp its significance. When matters came to a crisis – or at least what seemed at the time to be the apex of brutality – the political leadership in Palestine could do little in response. The *Yishuv* was small and ruled by another power – the British Empire; the *Yishuv's* influence in the international order that had been violated by the rise of dictatorial regimes in Europe was slight indeed. Thus, even if the Zionist leadership considered taking some sort of action, its only real option was propaganda, which would be disseminated primarily among Jews rather than other, more important and influential, leaders.[1]

However, in the cultural sphere the leadership of the *Yishuv* found compensation for its political impotence. Although on both the political and cultural levels any response was essentially directed inwards, toward Jewish society – and particularly Palestinian Jewish society – gestures in the cultural field were perceived as having a wider impact. Moreover, the means used to express protest made it seem more of a public statement, and heightened the Jewish community's sense of internal solidarity by uniting the different sectors of the *Yishuv*. The Jews of Palestine themselves, at least, could see some sort of trenchant statement in their modest response. Their cultural protest served largely as an outlet for political steam and the emotions that had built up with respect to the Nazis.

The cancellation of Wagner's piece, which was one of those most popular with the leaders of the National-Socialist party, was only one element in the cultural struggle against the Third Reich. The same aversion to German sounds applied to the German language, and as a result the first victims of the opposition to the Third Reich's outrages were in fact Jewish immigrants from Central Europe who had chosen to settle in Palestine. Their continued use of the German language made them a target for the ridicule of the veteran community, and their mother tongue a focus of nationalistic opposition.[2] At the same time, selective restrictions were imposed on the import of German culture to Palestine, one of the most conspicuous examples being an embargo on German-language films.[3] Another major change was in the kind of books translated from German to Hebrew. From the beginning of the 1930s to the establishment of the state, the translation of German works into Hebrew increasingly provided a means of expressing opposition to Nazi ideology. The main trend in the translation sphere at that time was a very calculated, ostentatious discrimination in favor of writers whose works the Nazis sought to eliminate – Jews and other opponents of the Nazi regime – and a complete disregard of literature admired by the Third Reich.[4]

What began as a political statement and a struggle over the image of modern Hebrew culture became a vehicle for perpetuating and shaping the cultural heritage after World War II and the establishment of the State of Israel. As the true dimensions of the Holocaust began to emerge, and the Nazi-inflicted physical and emotional scars of the survivors were revealed, the Israeli perception of German culture became a channel for expressing horror, rage, and hate. Initially there was a sweeping opposition to German culture as such. However, over the years the scope of the rejected culture narrowed dramatically until it comprised only isolated cultural items, most notably the music of certain German composers – especially Richard Wagner.[5]

The evolution of the resistance to Wagner's music in Israel encompasses far more than the history of a modern Israeli cultural repertoire. Doubtlessly many people are familiar with the main points of the affair, either from personal memory or from having noticed Wagner's absence from the musical repertoire in Israel; others have learned about the turbulent attitude toward Wagner through the drawn-out dispute. The development of the complex relationship between the State of Israel and the Federal Republic of Germany – as well as between Israeli and German society – is also well known. However, conjoining the two subjects may shed additional light on the construction of nationality in Israeli society, and on the ways in which that society has dealt with its past and with the creation of its collective memory. An integrated study of the three sides of the triangle formed by state, society, and culture offers broader insights than the usual treatment of the Wagner affair. By elucidating the different stages of the controversy's development and by adopting a methodology that incorporates more than one level of research, the present work puts the opposition to Wagner into the context of Israeli reality and explains it more fully. From this perspective the Wagner affair reflects certain aspects of the formation of a modern civil–secular Israeli nationality that has, to some extent, cut itself off from the obsolete practices of the Diaspora.[6] Nonetheless, the 2012 finding that 80 percent of the Israelis believe in God – from "to some extent" to full orthodoxy – suggests that the society is undergoing a significant change.[7]

With each new discussion of Wagner or other musicians who were perceived as inspirations for or collaborators with the Nazi regime, emotions boiled over again in Israel. The main argument against these composers' music, and the one that kept recurring for several decades, was the absolute impossibility of accepting anyone who had served the satanic regime that had cut short the lives of millions of Jews. At first this argument was voiced most often by those who had experienced the horrors of the Holocaust themselves or who had lost family members in the concentration camps. However, as the years passed it became etched on national memory, a code of conduct and response unrelated to the actual proximity to the Holocaust of individuals in Israeli society.

The different inflections of each successive public debate on the topic – debates that together formed one multifaceted controversy – show that the issue was not purely cultural, or even a clash between cultural needs and political views. The opinions expressed in the course of all the debates over the "forbidden" musicians suggest that historians who see the affair as an intersection of culture and politics may be adopting too narrow a view. The controversy should rather be perceived as a meeting of culture, politics, and social and national integration, since in it the head-on collision of culture and politics gave rise to an ideology that served broad sectors of society.

Among all these highly charged, intersecting issues, certain common lines connected the different phases of the controversy. Since the Wagner affair gave the politicians an axe to grind, its general political features are easily identified. The most prominent of these was its instrumentality. Every sector that pronounced on the issue found Wagner a handy vessel in which to pour ideologies with varying aims. Thus, in the 1950s and 1960s Wagner was an important argument for the factions opposing the restoration of ties with Germany; in the 1970s he was a vehicle for the anger of intellectuals at what they termed Israeli hypocrisy; in the 1980s he was a key figure in the struggle over the preservation of the memory of the Holocaust; in the 1990s he served the national ultra-Orthodox religious ideology which calls on Israelis to content themselves with Hebrew culture and stop copying the ways of the Gentiles; at the dawn of the twenty-first century, Wagner functions mainly as a common emblem that Israelis cannot deny.

However, since the debate was both emotional and rational, attitudes on the Wagner issue did not follow conventional political lines. In general terms, the political right supported the taboo against Wagner and musicians who had collaborated with the Nazis, this being part of their general opposition to any sort of relations with the Federal Republic of Germany. Parts of the center and the left advocated lifting the boycott in the name of ideological pluralism and separation between the ideology of the regime and the professional and ideological decisions of artistic bodies. This attitude may have been fostered to some extent by the spectacle presented by the totalitarian regimes established in the early twentieth century – including the Nazi regime, which had made all cultural institutions subject to the governmental apparatus of the Third Reich. Nonetheless, some members of the right took a moderate view of the affair, while, conversely, even more members of the left – particularly those who had lived through the Holocaust – were vehemently opposed to any lifting of the boycott, out of consideration for the feelings of those who had survived the death camps. At the beginning of the twenty-first century it seems that most politicians prefer to either avoid the sensitive subject or express fierce objection to public performances of the only boycotted artist, Richard Wagner. In short, even the customary characterization of the right as anti-Germany and the left as defenders of freedom of expression does not apply – or less consistently, at least – to this affair.

The process by which politicians became involved in the affair was interesting not only in the context of each particular flare-up of the controversy, but also as a continuing evolution over time. At first their intervention typically consisted of formal statements about the neutrality of the political bodies and the right of every orchestra to make its own artistic decisions. Behind the scenes, however, many political influences were busily at work trying – successfully – to prevent local musicians from shaping their repertoire and the country's musical life in the European image familiar to them. Hence, in many respects the Wagner affair was conducted much as other cultural and educational issues were at the time: with a great deal of governmental authoritarianism. Nonetheless, Wagner was never formally censored in Israel. All governmental bodies – the Ministry of Education, the Knesset Education and Culture Committee, and the Tel Aviv District Court – all ruled for freedom of expression of musical bodies.

During the first decades of the controversy, government intervention was limited to covert pressure while the Ministry of Education and

Culture repeated the litany: If the musical bodies in question were to ask our advice, we would counsel refraining from public performances of works by composers who had collaborated with the Nazis in any way. Only in the last phases of the dispute, when the governing coalition included people who had been vociferous opponents of breaking the taboo in the 1950s and 1960s, and their successors, was there any open attempt to explicitly interfere in the orchestra's artistic decisions. And even then the Ministry of Education refrained from actually imposing the views of the coalition majority on any musical institution. Yet, in 1994 the Knesset Education and Culture Committee released an appeal "from the heart," requesting the cultural institutions to refrain from performing the works of anti-Semitic composers, as these might hurt the feelings of the public.[8]

The theoretical possibility of governmental intervention in the establishment of the repertoire exposes one of the legal problems still existing in Israel with respect to civil rights. Until 1992, human rights were not recognized by the Basic Laws, the closest thing to a constitution that Israel has; and even after the enactment of Basic Law: Human Dignity and Liberty, many gaps remained that, while making the law more flexible, also emasculated it. Moreover, freedom of speech was still subject to ad hoc decisions by the court system.[9] Since the issue of performing Wagner in Israel never actually came up in a court of law, it was hard to know whose freedom was deemed more important in the eyes of the judiciary. Was an audience's right to hear music, any music, paramount, or should consideration of a particular sector's offended sensibilities take precedence? In Israel, there were no hard and fast rules to sanction the infringement of the former or the disregard of the latter. The recurring disputes concerning the performance of Wagner's music in Israel were possible in part because of the hazy legal status of civil liberties.

Despite similarities between the successive rounds of the controversy over the musical ban, each stage of the dispute had unique aspects that reflected the spirit of the times. During the 1950s, the opposition to Wagner – and, in some cases, to other German music – was fueled by other burning issues of the day. The recent discoveries of what had taken place during the Holocaust and the highly controversial signing of a reparations agreement with the Federal Republic of Germany were central to the debate over cultural affairs. The same arguments that had not prevented the government from concluding a political alliance served as important ammunition in the battle against public performances of music by composers favored by the Nazis; and just as the political struggle against the reparations agreement had given rise to attacks on Ben-Gurion's policy from both the right and the left, so the cultural dispute, too, created unusual rifts in the leftist camp. The same motives underlying the institutionalization of public commemoration of the Holocaust through the inauguration of a Holocaust and Ghetto Uprising Remembrance Day

(1951), the establishment of the Yad Vashem institute to document the Holocaust (1953), and the legislation of the Day of Remembrance of the Holocaust and Heroism (1959) also served the interests of those who opposed any manifestation of German culture in Israel. In other words, the need to preserve the national trauma as a perpetual outrage worked on several cultural levels, from the establishment of the national pattern of commemoration to the codification in art of what was desirable and what was loathsome.

In the following decade opposition to the "forbidden" musicians continued strong, but on slightly different grounds. The Eichmann trial publicly exposed the pain of the survivors and focused public attention on the events of the Holocaust and concentration-camp survivors' difficulty in living with fears of the past. The trial's significance for Israeli society and that society's perception of the Holocaust in all its horror remain controversial. Some claim that the public disclosures made by survivors did not materially change the attitude to the Holocaust, because awareness of the Holocaust had developed earlier; others assert that putting the subject on the public agenda in this revelatory way eliminated the shame associated with the Holocaust and facilitated a rapprochement between those who had "been there" and other Israelis.[10] It was now easier and more acceptable to evoke the horrors of the Holocaust as grounds for rejecting German culture. The revelation at the beginning of the 1960s that the Germans were providing financial assistance for the development of Egyptian missiles lent support to those who claimed that there was no such thing as "another Germany," and that consequently neither forgiveness nor concessions could be extended. This particular issue remained part of the overall opposition to Germany, although ultimately it proved to be a mountain made out of a molehill. The establishment of diplomatic relations with West Germany in 1965 was grist to the mills of both opponents and proponents of German culture. The opponents saw the cultural issue as the last barrier to the relinquishment of Israel's anti-German bias, whereas the proponents could now portray their adversaries' adherence to the cultural taboo as unnecessary and facile niggling that flew in the face of the economic and political ties Israel was developing with Germany.

The political, economic, and social changes that Israel underwent in the decade between the Six-Day War (1967) and the Likud's rise to power (1977) substantially altered the tenor of the arguments that characterized the next phase of the controversy. Although the dispute that broke out in the spring of 1974 – a moderate one, overshadowed by the trauma of the Yom Kippur War (1973) – appeared to be the last chapter of the controversy, the renewal of the affair at the end of 1981 showed that what had been a convenient tool for political attacks in the 1950s and 1960s could also serve the interests of different sectors of the public 20 or 30 years later.

In 1981 controversy erupted over the first actual attempt by the Israeli Philharmonic Orchestra (IPO) to play (rather than simply declare an intention to play) a short excerpt from Wagner's *Tristan und Isolde*. The pandemonium in Tel Aviv's Mann Auditorium was the beginning of six weeks of fierce wrangling which received full coverage in the press: Reports, interviews, and commentary filled the print and electronic media. Two figures played particularly prominent roles this time around: the IPO's music director, Zubin Mehta, and the deputy minister in the Prime Minister's Office, Dov Shilansky. Shilansky's suggestion that Mehta return to his native land, India – a piece of advice he later explained as simply a request to the maestro to leave the Israelis to deal with the Wagner affair in their own way – was interpreted by many as racist. Some of the public endorsed the remark, giving proof both of the vulgarity of public discourse during the 1981 elections and the large dose of xeno-phobia (usually directed against Arabs) that was the corollary of mounting nationalism. Another sector of the public was embarrassed by Shilansky's words, and used them as conclusive proof of the obscurantism spreading through the country and what they saw as the trampling under-foot of pluralistic values.

Ten years passed before the conductor Daniel Barenboim tried to breach the wall that had risen still higher following the 1981 brouhaha. Although he was a man who considered himself Israeli in every respect, he, like Mehta, failed to make a dent in public opinion, and was forced to settle for a private concert. From then until the summer of 1998 no real effort was made to break the taboo, and the only times Wagner was played on a public stage – aside from a modest series of piano recitals – were in rehearsal or during educational activity in music academies.

Since late 2000 actors outside the IPO entered the fray of breaking the taboo on Wagner. In October 2000 the Rishon LeZion Symphony Orchestra, the first to play Strauss in public in 1990, included *Siegfried Idyll* in a Friday matinée. Unlike the quiet reaction in 1990, the Wagner concert drew attention even before it actually took place. Two Holocaust survivors appealed to the court demanding a permanent injunction instructing the orchestra to refrain from performing any musical pieces by Richard Wagner or Richard Strauss. The judge refused in the name of cultural pluralism. Six months later, in the spring and summer of 2001, the Knesset Culture and Education Committee was called to deal with the matter. Daniel Barenboim and the Staatskapelle Berlin were invited to perform in the Israel Festival, and intended to incorporate a piece by Wagner. Although tickets sold well, the Knesset Education and Culture Committee requested the Festival management and Barenboim to refrain from playing Wagner. They agreed, but at the end of the concert, which was also the Festival's finale, Barenboim sug-gested an encore which was the *Liebes Tod* from *Tristan und Isolde*. Some members of the audience left the hall, and others listened quietly.

The Education and Culture Committee announced Barenboim "a cultural *persona non grata*."[11]

Small scale attempts took place in the following decade. Yet the one that drew a great deal of attention was the endeavor of the Israeli Wagner Society with Israeli conductor Asher Fisch, who gathered a philharmonic orchestra and singers for a special Wagner event in the spring of 2012. The plan never materialized as Tel Aviv University cancelled the rental of its Smolarz Auditorium and a consequent attempt to rent the Tel Aviv Hilton's hall failed as well. This time the objection to Wagner was quiet but fierce; no institution in Tel Aviv was willing to touch this hot potato. It seems that the answer to the Wagner question is becoming clear: it is hard to expect such attempts to end peacefully.

Unlike the accepted steady resistance to Wagner, from the mid-1980s and particularly during the 1990s, a strange and interesting change took place. The boycott against German musicians who had shared Wagner's pariah status among Israelis, composers such as Richard Strauss, Carl Orff, and Franz Lehar, was lifted. This change began quietly, in the musical periphery. Orchestras smaller than the Philharmonic began to perform their works, and state radio stations began playing ever longer excerpts of their music. The IPO – the then only musical body in the country named for the state – followed the example of other orchestras and gradually included in its repertoire the three composers whose cooperation with the Nazis was publicly known. Only Richard Wagner, who had died 50 years before the Nazis ever came to power but who was considered a great source of inspiration for their deeds, was still banned. Yet his music, too, was performed before small audiences such as a 1998 piano recital, a 2001 chamber arrangement, and a 2011 lecture which included a few *Lieder*. The first sign of weakening was the unvoiced agreement to allow his works to be played on the state radio and recordings from his operas to be broadcast on cable television.

This is the place to clarify the special role that the electronic media have played in the Wagner affair. In the early stages of the conflict their participation was negligible. Israel lagged behind the rest of the Western world in developing the infrastructure for electronic media; the only such medium already operating in the country up to the end of the 1960s was the radio, and even that was limited to three Hebrew networks, augmented by broadcasts from any foreign stations in range, mostly Arab. Some of those stations – for example, Radio Ramallah – were very popular with Israelis. At that stage radio coverage of the Wagner issue appeared mainly in laconic reports on the affair and its ramifications. In the 1970s, when the various stations' broadcasting hours had been expanded and new state channels had been inaugurated, the radio stations increased both their reports on the Wagner affair and their own active participation in it. Some of the networks began to use the controversial music for illustrative purposes in documentary programs, and in the

1980s attempts were being made to integrate excerpts from Wagner's works into the regular broadcast listings. Such attempts became progressively frequent in the 1990s, to the point that the boycott no longer had any significance – at least not on the Voice of Music (*Kol Hamusika*) the state classical-music station. In the pluralistic climate of Israeli radio broadcasting of the time, the networks would be hard-pressed to limit broadcasts of works considered problematic; the large number of local broadcasting stations, both legal and pirate, made it impossible.

Television's entry into Israeli cultural life at the end of the 1960s also brought a gradual change in the perception of Wagner as abhorrent. Television, in fact, underwent more or less the same process that the radio had. Initially it served as a medium for reporting developments in the affair, but little by little these reports began to express opinions as well. Seemingly neutral reports on Wagner festivals in Bayreuth marked the beginning of the boycott's erosion. The establishment of companies providing cable services further undermined the television's boycott. The national cable packages included Channel 8, a science and culture channel that made no secret of its intentions; from the beginning it broadcast the operas of Richard Strauss, who had headed the musical department of the Third Reich in its early years. Attempts to broadcast Wagner's works were tentative at first, but recordings from the Bayreuth Festival captured television screens in the summer of 1997, and the summers that followed. Moreover, most of the cable packages available in Israel included the German cultural channel 3-SAT, and some of them also offered the European cultural channel Arte, both of which broadcast, several times a year, operas and other pieces composed by those perceived in Israel as Nazi collaborators.

In short, the struggle waged over the image of modern Israeli culture necessarily presents a different aspect at the beginning of the twenty-first century. The facility of communication and Israeli society's residency in the global village created by international channels knocked down some of the bulwarks that had been feasible in the more closed world of the print media in the years when Israeli society seemed nearly monolithic. Increased travel abroad by Israelis was merely one more factor that contributed to the breakdown of the relative cultural isolation that characterized the country in its early years. Nonetheless, it seems that the early 2000s saw a decline in the number of such public broadcasts. This may have to do with the less pluralistic and tenser political and social climate in Israel, as well as the tightening supervision of the state channels by government officials.

Anyone who is not fully acquainted with the evolution of the Wagner affair in Israel may be astonished at the powerful influence it exerted over so many decades. After all, Israelis had plenty of reasons for political, social, and cultural controversy. What, then, made this particular dispute, focusing on a form of culture that appealed to a very narrow sector of the public, so unusually popular? Firstly, it is possible that the circumstances that first triggered the whole dispute – the need for a significant cultural and political response that would unite all Israelis – was what tied all the different phases of the controversy together. The persistence of the dispute may also be attributable to the prolonged, uncompromising opposition to the pragmatic political necessity of accepting Germany as a legitimate member of the world community. Perhaps the rage provoked by the Nazi attempt to cleanse Europe of Jews inflamed passions anew each time. Or the involvement of politicians and intellectuals may have increased the affair's importance in the eyes of many Israelis. Yet another possibility is that the intensive media coverage – particularly the print media – drew into the struggle a much wider sector of Israeli society than simply classical music aficionados.

The press's involvement in the Wagner affair merits special mention. To begin with, it should be noted that since the days of the *Yishuv* the country had been rich in daily newspapers, weeklies, and various other periodicals – in short, dozens of publications intended for a public that initially did not number more than a few hundred thousand people. Thus, the scope for expressing different viewpoints was enormous relative to the actual population. In addition, the breakdown of press attitudes to the Wagner affair and the "forbidden" composers in general reflected traditional political divisions. This correlation derived partly from the party affiliations of many newspapers, as well as the active participation of Holocaust survivors and heirs of the Revisionists in a significant sector of the private press. The attacks from both left and right on the establishment of relations with Germany were also reflected in the anti-German cultural bias. Yet as an extremely general rule of thumb, it may be said that papers like the labor-affiliated *Davar* advocated the elimination of the ban; liberal papers like *Haaretz* insisted on the need to anchor intellectual pluralism in Israeli cultural life; and right-wing papers like *Herut* and *Maariv* – as well as the socialist *Lamerhav* and *Al Hamishmar* – were vehemently opposed to anything that gave off a whiff of Germanism. As the years passed the deep divisions between the papers became blurred, and the attitude of any particular paper was determined largely by the views of its individual reporters. The members of Achdut Haavoda (Unity of Labor Party) passed on, the last of the Revisionists had retired, and so it transpired that a new generation with different values and interests conducted the debate during the 1980s and 1990s. Those decades and the first decade of the twenty-first century saw another important change: most of the party-oriented newspapers were shut down due to minimal readership and financial deficits. Others were established but were mostly financially oriented. Moreover, the birth of the Internet altered the old-time polite letters to the editor, rendering them Internet TalkBacks, whose rude tone is rather common in Israel. The Wagner affair, of course, drew many aggressive Internet responses.

However, it is clear that for long years the dispute was about much more than simply Wagner and his fellow pariahs. The conflict over the supposedly musical issue was nothing other than one more battle over the shaping of modern Israeli culture, a battle that largely reflected the development of Israeli society itself and the consolidation of its identity and political concepts. In this case, this intersection of music, society, and state created a channel for more than one simple decision about an orchestra's musical repertoire. The evolution of the Wagner affair reflected the struggles of a society under construction, and its uphill efforts to accept its past and form a collective national memory for itself.

In terms of nation building, the dispute over music attests to the need of post-Holocaust secular Israelism to define itself. For the Israelis, the debate opened a channel through which they could express their feelings toward Germany, Germans and German culture – be it hatred or admiration. Gradually, the "Wagner controversy" became a code which everyone could decipher, just like any other national code or tradition. It meets Eric Hobsbawm and Terence Ranger's definition of national tradition as a main common denominator; it plays a uniting role of a community as characterized by Benedict Anderson; it is employed in accordance with Anthony Smith's explanation of the role of an ancient emblem known to all; and it has become a common symbol which complies with Michael Billig's concept of "banal nationalism."[12]

During all the years of the controversy both those who favored the boycott and those who wanted to put an end to it presented arguments about the role the "forbidden" musicians had played in the Nazi regime. Obviously, each of the warring sides had its own truth, a truth based at times on historical documentation and at times on scraps of more or less reliable information embraced on an ad hoc basis for the purposes of the argument. The fragments of justification for rejecting the banned composers were stitched together in the course of the efforts to shape a collective national memory – a national memory that reserved an important niche for Germany's role as an enemy of the Jews and for the Holocaust as a central axis for the unification of the nation in the modern age.

Until a very late stage Israelis did not attempt any in-depth analysis of the evolution of the Wagner affair and the underlying reasons for the cancellation of the performance of *Die Meistersinger von Nürnberg* in the fall of 1938. It was not until 1984 that a book was published in Israel about this fascinating and complex piece of history.[13] Since then the subject has not returned to the center of the historical–cultural debate, but has only been mentioned indirectly. This is why the present work begins with two chapters (2–3) of historical background, presenting a short review of those aspects of Wagner's work that made him controversial in Israel and the story of his adoption by the Nazi regime. Although these chapters are no substitute for the wealth of professional literature that has been written on these two fertile topics, without them it would be difficult to understand the source of Israeli hostility toward this prolific and special creator.

Chapters 4–10 describe the ban imposed on Wagner and its extension to other creators and performers who cooperated with the Nazis. Chapter 4 recounts the event that laid the foundation for the Israeli attitude to Wagner and other artists, detailing the reasons for the opposition to his music and other items of German culture. The succeeding chapters describe and analyze in chronological order the various permutations of the public debate on the subject in the five decades from the 1950s to the early 2000s. Each new flare-up was rooted in contemporary political and social events in Israel, and on each occasion the three-way intersection between Wagner, Israeli–German relations, and Israeli culture came up in a new configuration.

The methodology adopted in this research interweaves archival documentation of the details of the Wagner affair with analyses of the political and social processes affecting the State of Israel and its citizens at the time. This approach provides a broad view of the Wagner affair based on more complete data than the testimony of the contemporary press. I am hopeful that such a view will facilitate a more penetrating examination of the relationship of Israeli society to Germany and Germanism.

Notes

1 Chaim Weizmann was one of the few leaders who had any success in convincing European leaders to encourage easing the immigration rules. See J. Reinharz, *Chaim Weizmann: the Making of a Statesman* (Oxford, 1993).

2 Opposition to the German-speakers who immigrated to the *Yishuv* in the 1930s is widely documented in the contemporary press. See, for example, S. Eisenstadt, "To Our Cultural Action among German Immigrants [Hebrew]," *Hapoel Hatzair* (4 Aug. 1933): 8; W. Jurgrau, "On the Action among Immigrants from Germany [Hebrew]," *Hapoel Hatzair* (3 Feb. 1939); and A. Ben-David, "Toward German-Speaking Immigrants [Hebrew]," *Hapoel Hatzair* (24 March 1939): 11–12.

3 On the reluctance in the *Yishuv* to patronize German films, see Y. Davidon, *Love under Duress* [Hebrew] (Tel Aviv, n.d.), p. 170; on the actions of the Brit Habiryonim ["Alliance of the Toughs"] against the embassy of the Third Reich in Jerusalem, see Y. Ornstein, *In Chains: Memories of a Fighter* [Hebrew] (Tel Aviv, 1973), p. 61.

4 See N. Sheffi, *Von Deutschen ins Hebräische: Übersetzungen aus dem Deutschen im jüdischen Palästina, 1882–1948* (Göttingen, 2011), pp. 137–216.

5 Following a drop in the translations from German into Hebrew in the first two-three decades of statehood, the Israeli market became more open to German literature. Since the late 1990s, German children's literature is particularly popular in Israel. See N. Sheffi, "Between Germanophobia and Germanophilia: Israelis read German Literature," *Trumah* (forthcoming).

6 For an instructive discussion of the building of historical traditions and

pseudo-traditions based on isolated historical facts, see E. Hobsbawm, "Introduction: Inventing Traditions," in *The Invention of Tradition*, ed. E. Hobsbawm and T. Ranger (Cambridge, 1992), pp. 1–14. See also B. Anderson, *Imagined Communities: Reflections on the Origin and Spread of Nationalism* (London, 1990).

7 See A. Inbari, "The End of the Secular Majority [Hebrew]," *Haaretz*, 3 Feb. 2012.

8 D. Lahav, "Background document on the subject: Performing Wagner's music at the 2001 Israel Festival [Hebrew]," submitted to the Knesset Education and Culture Committee, 7 May 2001, p. 3.

9 Until human rights were explicitly established by law, Israeli courts rendered precedent-setting judgments that established the general principles governing situations in which a conflict of interest arose between different rights. The best known example in this respect was the right to know about security-related incidents versus the theoretical possibility of compromising state security. See A. Rubinstein and B. Medina, *The Constitutional Law of the State of Israel* [Hebrew] (Jerusalem and Tel Aviv, 1997), 2: 999–1010.

10 Classic examples of various analyses include that of Hanna Yablonka, who does not see the trial as a turning point in the Israelis' attitude to the Holocaust: H. Yablonka, "The Law for the Punishment of Nazis and their Collaborators: Another Aspect of the Issue of Israelis, Survivors, and the Holocaust [Hebrew]," *Cathedra* 82 (Jan. 1997): 135–52. Anita Shapira is a proponent of the view that the Holocaust was always on the public agenda: A. Shapira, "The Holocaust: Private Memory and Public Memory," *Jewish Social Studies* 4, No. 2 (Winter, 1998): 40–58. Tom Segev, in contrast, upholds the view that the trial played a central role in reconciling Israelis to debate on the issue of the Holocaust. See T. Segev, *The Seventh Million: Israelis and the Holocaust* (New York, 1993), especially pp. 211–52.

11 Minutes no. 316, meeting of the Knesset Education, Culture and Sport Committee, 24 July 2001.

12 See E. Hobsbawm, "Introduction," *The Invention of Tradition*, pp. 1–14. B. R. Anderson, *Imagined Communities*. A. D. Smith, *National Identity* (London, 1991), especially pp. 19–70. M. Billig, *Banal Nationalism* (London, 1995).

13 See R. Litvin and H. Shelach, eds., *Who's Afraid of Richard Wagner: Different Aspects of the Controversial Figure* [Hebrew] (Jerusalem, 1984). The affair has also attracted a certain amount of interest abroad. See, for example, P. L. Rose, *Wagner: Race and Revolution* (New Haven and London, 1992), pp. 189–92; and M. A. Weiner, *Richard Wagner and the Anti-Semitic Imagination* (Lincoln and London, 1997), pp. 349–53.

CHAPTER

2

Legends, Tribes, and Anti-Semitism: Ideas and Issues in Wagner's Work

With his range of talents and unique personality, Richard Wagner (1813–1883) became a figure that both attracted and repelled fairly early in life. At the age of 16, after attending a performance by the soprano Wilhelmina Schröder-Devrient, Wagner decided that his greatest desire was to become a musician, and he began to study music. By the age of 21 he was already the musical director of orchestras in Magdeburg and Bad Läuchstadt. After years of wandering around Germany during which he began to compose music of his own, he was appointed conductor of the Dresden Opera House, the last position he held before turning to full-time freelance composition. Once he took this step, his work began to expand into increasingly far-flung artistic and intellectual directions: He composed musical works – from his *Lieder* to unusually long operas; he invented musical instruments that were especially suited to the type of sound he wanted to achieve in his musical works; he wrote the librettos for his operas, revealing an unusually well-developed linguistic sense; he wrote theoretical essays on both the arts and general topics. Besides all this, Wagner was an eccentric, intriguing figure who took controversial political positions and never hesitated to exploit the good nature, emotions, and financial resources of his lovers, admirers, and acquaintances.[1]

Although Wagner left his mark on several cultural spheres, each of them a worthy subject in its own right, the focus of this chapter is limited to aspects of two kinds of work that occupied much of his time: his operas and his theoretical writings. In both these fields he achieved great emotional and charismatic heights, and in both he not only demonstrated his intellectual and lyrical ability, but also revealed the basic lines of his social and political philosophy. Just as he used the artistic stage as a platform for presenting social and political ideas, his participation in the political world fueled his artistic activity. In his youth a large part of his work was inspired by his involvement in the political life of the German-speaking regions, and in later years he enjoyed massive financial support from King Ludwig II of Bavaria.

Wagner was never loath to express his opinions about society and the proper way to run things. He believed that citizens should be integrated into the political process, and he seemed to lean toward a sweeping economic and political democratization of the stratified society in which he lived. These ideas and his connections with such persons as the Russian anarchist Michael Bakunin did not stop him from enjoying a flashy, hedonistic lifestyle that was incongruous with the socialist ideology he had supposedly embraced.

Wagner was in fact both revolutionary and reactionary, a paradox that was only one of a long series of contradictory characteristics, behaviors, and views.[2] Thus, for example, the composer who vilified Jews preferred to work with the conductor Hermann Levi, the son of a rabbi, as well as a long list of Jewish performers. The man who was unfaithful to his women and ridiculed some of them wrote works about strong women and unreliable men. Although he was a rational theoretician and researcher, he was hurt by the biting criticism of his works and his ideas. His protean ability to move between extremes did not at all dull the brilliance of his artistic talents, and certainly did no harm to his reputation. Although the asymmetry of his personality is an important key to understanding why a sizable sector of the public initially rejected him, it was also a factor in the deep adoration he inspired in musicologists, political elites, and ordinary people.

This is the moment to address a point that will come up more than once in the discussion of Wagner's legacy: Even if Wagner himself did not intend to accord his various writings political or social overtones, as soon as he published them he lost all exclusivity over their interpretation. From that point on, whatever implications others might perceive in his work were completely legitimate interpretations. Nonetheless, some of the meanings attributed to his works over the years may have been tendentious, specifically tailored to substantiate theses that Wagner himself neither conceived nor supported.

Frequently we may divine Wagner's opinions on current affairs by carefully reading between the lines of his theoretical writings on music, which incorporate – inadvertently or deliberately – fairly clear indications of Wagner's overall views on political and social issues. The same is true of his creative writing – that is, his opera librettos, most of which were based on old European folk tales that he researched and revised to suit his needs. The ancient societies, whether they had actually existed at one time or came to life only on stage, served overtly or covertly as political allegories. He was not, of course, the first person to link these legends with contemporary political events; such links had been made throughout the hundreds of years that they had been known as village folk tales. Although he had a unique way of planting the seeds that produced connections between events on stage and events in the political arena, he was not the only nineteenth-century composer to use historical events as the basis for a libretto inspiring ideological identification. This sort of identification underlay the writing of some of the major German creators and thinkers 50 years before Wagner began to create his own works. The end of the eighteenth century, for example, saw the publication of plays such as *Emilia Galotti*, by Gothold Ephraim Lessing, and *Die Räuber* (The Robbers), by Friedrich Schiller, which called for radical social reform. In contrast, nineteenth-century opera-writers who based their plots on specific historical events emphasized romantic and entertaining stories to create emotional identification, while obscuring the ideological aspect of the plot – if there even was one.[3]

The 11 operas that Wagner composed were unusual for his time, although his melodies did not break any new ground until he created the combination of tones that gave rise to the "Tristan chord" that has been identified with Wagner's music since he composed the *Wesendonck Lieder* in the years 1857–8 and particularly since he composed the opera *Tristan und Isolde* (which debuted in 1865). From that time on his works moved away from the conventional forms of the day – forms that had been established in the century of musical composition spanning Wolfgang Amadeus Mozart, Ludwig van Beethoven, and Robert Schumann. Wagner broke a few norms that were considered standard in music: He did not keep to eight-bar periods, but broke them up as he wished; he deviated from the commonly accepted chord and harmony structures, bending and stretching them in previously unknown directions.[4] As for his librettos, only a small portion of them conform to the categories of the time, namely the grand opera, the comic opera, and the lyric opera.

Doubtlessly, Wagner was not the only composer of complex tragedies; his contemporaries, too, appealed to the emotions, transporting audiences with crowded, spectacular scenes. Some consider Wagner as the German parallel to the Italian Giuseppe Verdi, who, like him, created a genre of his own, with influence from German Romanticism and reflecting a great deal of the Italian nationalism of his day. And yet Wagner was clearly unique. First of all, most of his operas involved a larger number of characters than usual, linked by intricate relationships that were difficult to follow. Another common feature in his librettos was the adaptation of medieval European tales that Wagner had researched extensively in order to write new versions, versions that remained close to the original yet invited interpretation in the context of current social and political issues.

An outstanding example of this updating of medieval tales is Wagner's greatest work, *Der Ring des Nibelungen*, which consists of four parts, *Das Rheingold* (The Rhine Gold), *Die Walküre* (The Valkyrie), *Siegfried*, and *Götterdämmerung* (The Twilight of the Gods), lasting 14 hours all together.[5] *Der Ring des Nibelungen* is a good introduction to Wagner, providing a microcosm of his esthetic ideas and artistic conception. For one thing, in the same period that Wagner began laying the foundations of his tetralogy, he was also engaged in writing some of his most important esthetic and intellectual essays – "Kunst und Revolution" (Art and

Revolution, 1849), "Das Kunstwerk der Zukunaft" (The Art Work of the Future, 1850), and "Das Judentum in der Musik" (Judaism in Music, 1850) – all basic elements of Wagner's overall intellectual formation. Furthermore, the complexity of *Der Ring des Nibelungen*, the many responses to it, and the varied interpretations it elicited, make it a particularly convenient framework of reference for Richard Wagner's musical and artistic approaches and general philosophy. However, it should be emphasized that the short explanations of *Der Ring des Nibelungen* provided here are intended solely to indicate the complex and varied facets of a controversial figure, not to substitute for the many thick tomes that analyze Wagner's personality and works; they are merely a basis for my discussion of the way this composer has been accepted and rejected in Germany and Israel.

The Nordic legend embodied in the plot of *Der Ring des Nibelungen* had been adopted in the Germanic regions back in the Middle Ages and its heroes associated with the golden age of the early Germanic tribes, so it was easily converted into one of the figurative and artistic apogees of German history. These circumstances left a clear national imprint on the modern versions of the story in general and Wagner's version in particular; in some respects, this is Wagner's most "German" work, together with his tale of a sixteenth-century competition between the itinerant singers known as *meistersinger*.

Almost certainly Wagner's use of the Nibelung legend was linked to the development of a broader ideological trend that was discernible in Europe for close to a century. From the mid-eighteenth century, interest in tracing national roots was popular in Europe in general and in England and Germany in particular. In England this interest took the form of seeking clues to British origins in ancient texts that would show both the thinking and the history of the modern Englishman's forebears. Some commentators associate this quest with the scientific biology of the founder of evolutionary theory, Charles Darwin; humanistic researchers also seemed to be looking for the evolutionary bases of the society they lived in.[6]

German-speakers showed the same interest in discovering their ancient past. From the beginning of the eighteenth century, German literati tried to uncover early texts and rekindle interest in them, like their counterparts in England; but the German quest had an added significance. Here researchers were seeking not merely sources to explain the cultural and social development of German-speakers, but also – and later mainly – a cultural infrastructure that would provide a suitable platform for the unification of German-speakers into an integrated nation and state. Thus it happened that the pioneers of German philological research prepared the ground for the growth of German nationalism as well – though not necessarily with any national awareness on their part – even before the Germans began to move toward a national unity designed to stem the French tide that was sweeping over Europe. Along with academic research on the Sanskrit origins of the Germanic and other ancient languages, publishers issued new editions of old folk tales and historical legends. The most notable manifestations of this new focus included the folkloric borrowings by the writers of the Romantic stream; works by the *Sturm und Drang* authors which reflected their interest in the roots of German literature; and the work of the brothers Wilhelm and Jacob Grimm, who in 1815 published two thick volumes of collected folk and fairy tales (*Kinder- und Hausmärchen*).[7]

Among the other discoveries of this period, various versions of the Nibelung legend came to light. This legend, which derives from a northern folk tale, shows clear traces of true historical events, including the marriage of Attila the Hun (Eztl or Etle in the Nordic and Germanic sources) to a Burgundian woman (called in later versions Kudrun, Gudrun, or Kriemhilde) who in real life murdered him in 453. Besides historical vestiges of this kind, the various versions of the plot contain not only elements of folk tradition or mythology, but also glimmers of the characters and customs of various medieval rulers.

The legend was widely disseminated – similar versions surfacing even in Britain (*Beowulf*) – apparently by traveling merchants and itinerant singers. Although the basic plot of the *Nibelungenlied* had been written down as of the second half of the twelfth century, the legend continued to spread primarily as an oral tradition, while local rulers appropriated its basic ideas for their own purposes: Through the medium of the story, power struggles between different political groups found pertinent expression in the context of current events. Written versions appeared at the same time in various formats, one of the best known the 1557 rendering by the great *meistersinger* Hans Sachs of Nuremberg, who was the model for the main character in Wagner's *Die Meistersinger*. Interest in the legend petered out around the fifteenth century, however, flaring up again only in the eighteenth century, with the upsurge of nationalist and philological interest in the history of the Germanic tribes.[8]

In 1726 *Das Lied vom hürnen Siegfried* (The Tale of Horn-Skin Clad Siegfried) was published anonymously, subtitled "a beautiful story about the famous Siegfried; the amazing adventures of this faithful knight; to be remembered and read with joy." Another manuscript of the *Nibelungenlied* came to light in 1755, and a pair of researchers concluded at the time that it was a German correlate of early Greek poetry. Although the publication of these obscure texts did not arouse any great interest at the time, toward the end of the century researchers were galvanized by the inauguration of the first periodical for the study of German and Nordic literature, *Bragur*, in Leipzig. Within a few years, literary researchers were defining the *Nibelungenlied* as a national myth and comparing it with Homer's work. The poem gained currency, eventually winning a place in the curricula of various principalities of the German-speaking regions.

The legend, which recounts the story of the struggles between different principalities, in this case took the form of an allegorical representation of the Napoleonic wars of the early nineteenth century: Its message was that a people must oppose and fight off any foreign, invading ruler seeking to impose his heritage on regions that are not his own. However, concerned that the masses would interpret the story as sanctioning opposition to all rulers in general, the authorities removed the legend from the books offered to students in the German principalities. This was followed by a reduction in the hours devoted to Germanic studies in the schools and universities, and the medieval tale lost its importance in popular literature. From then on the various renderings of the story became collector's items and objects of interest for linguists, historians, and social elites. Researchers believed they had found the Nordic equivalent of the Achilles story; historians saw the legend as the basis for pan-Germanism; while anyone who could afford it could buy a prestigious facsimile edition of one of the adaptations of the legend, or play cards with a deck that depicted the legendary characters.[9]

When Wagner set out to create his own version of the legend, he took its sources very seriously, examining at least 10 different historical renderings before coming up with his own finished product.[10] In his time, the sources were accessible, since the subject attracted many intellectuals; a few dozen of the plays published in the first half of the nineteenth century were based on the old legend, although only one of them, Ernst Raupach's *Die Nibelungenhort* (The Nibelung Hoard), written in 1828, achieved any real success. The appeal of Raupach's play lay not only in its quality, but also – in fact, mainly – in its political implications. It was published at a time when nationalist musical dramas were being produced in France and Italy, in the period around the 1830 wave of political upheavals. At the time, however, the play was not perceived as directly relevant to the ideas guiding the German revolutionaries of the time, and enjoyed a revival only during the 1848 revolutions, when the opponents of the regime looked upon it as a national symbol. This interpretation was reinforced by Friedrich Engels, who claimed that Siegfried, the hero of the piece, represented "German youth."[11]

Most likely the play's renewed popularity in the context of the 1848 revolutions also influenced the reception of Wagner's work. In his case, however, the link with the revolution was even more complex. Wagner began to sketch in the main lines of *Der Ring des Nibelungen* around the time of the revolutionary ferment, in which he was involved himself. His political activity had begun a decade earlier, when he joined the Young Europe and Young Germany movements as an expression of his cosmopolitan philosophy in which the German principalities were merely "a very small part of the universe," as he put it. In later years, Wagner's version of the Nordic legend was interpreted as a classic expression of the nationalist spirit that had characterized the German-speaking region since the days of Johann Gottfried Herder, a spirit that grew until it achieved fruition in the unification of Germany in 1871. At the beginning of February 1848 Wagner published a leaflet supporting the new generation revolutionaries, in which he developed the idea that the world should be run on the basis of profound faith rather than reliance on political bodies. These views laid him open to criticism no less than did his artistic work.[12]

Forced by both political indiscretions and bad debts to flee to France, Wagner suffered the bitterest insults of his career there, but later on became the critics' pet. One of them believed that *Der Ring des Nibelungen* was the truest artistic rendition of the 1848 revolution.[13] This view was shared by Friedrich Nietzsche, Wagner's good friend who became his intellectual rival. Nietzsche said: "Half his lifetime Wagner believed in the Revolution as only a Frenchman could have believed in it. He sought it in the runic inscriptions of myths; he thought he had found a typical revolutionary in Siegfried."[14]

Indeed, anyone leaning toward this interpretation will find more than a few revolutionary overtones in Wagner's work. The original story, focusing on a dauntless hero, Siegfried, who establishes peace and order in the lands where he wanders, ends in tragedy: Siegfried is murdered after his wife reveals the only weak spot in his body, between his shoulders. In most of the early versions of the story, the murder is described as a base exploitation of Siegfried's innocence and his wife's naïveté, although Siegfried himself is clearly part of a dark world in which conspiracies abound, enveloped in a web of lies and counter-lies. On the way to his tragic end, Siegfried is accompanied by a host of legendary characters: people who become animals, a horrible dragon, birds whose language he understands, dwarves and giants – all the usual denizens of medieval stories. Wagner gave the plot a twist by putting in its center the leader of the gods, Wotan, with the other characters falling into three main categories: human beings, gods, and hybrids. The integration of the original fiction into the new structure gave Wagner the latitude to move between the old form of the story, which made the most of the protagonists' superhuman powers, and an allegorical commentary on his own era, the tyranny of government, and the corruption of leaders.

Wagner began the libretto for *Der Ring des Nibelungen* in late 1848, writing *Siegfrieds Tod* (Siegfried's Death) at a time when Europe was in a furor over demands for constitutional change. The main character, Siegfried, appeared as an ideal hero who embodied nearly every noble virtue. In subsequent years, Wagner revised this work five times, and instead of making Siegfried the center of the plot, as in the folk tales, he had the story revolve around Wotan, the leader of the gods, who, with his daughter Brunhilde, led the mythological world he had built to the brink of destruction because of the terrible mistakes the gods had made and the lies they had been forced to tell as a result. This new plot focus made it necessary to lengthen the text, since Wagner insisted on clarifying all the new meanings in the story and pointing out its underlying messages. Ultimately the work became an unusually long tetralogy.[15]

It was produced for the first time in 1876, inaugurating the theater (the Festspielhaus, or Festival Theater) built especially for Wagner in the quiet Bavarian town of Bayreuth. King Ludwig II, who had put up the money to build the theater, was present at the debut on 1 August. Next to him sat critics who could not praise the unique new work enough – only 15 years after they had torn Wagner and his complex works to pieces. The audience that had once slung mud was now ready with a laurel wreath. Paradoxically, it was Wagner's most complex composition that established him in the regard of German public opinion.

The medieval legend's transformation into a musical tetralogy marked a high point in the composer's steady progress toward public favor, a process that had already been clearly underway in the late 1860s. His new popularity allowed Wagner to inculcate the esthetic and intellectual principles he championed more easily. The most conspicuous change that he made in his work was to return to the early Nordic sources that described the destruction of the world as a liberation from futility and lies and a doorway to the creation of a new, purer and better, world. In the context of the time, Wagner was obviously transmitting a revolutionary message: the world of decadent aristocracy was over, and the system – and if necessary its architects – had to be destroyed to make way for a new world.

To this fundamental principle he added another, separate idea, adumbrated in the early versions of the legend: Love and power could not be bedfellows. He went on to suggest an unequivocal solution to the constant tension between these two elements, a tension emphasized throughout the opera. Every individual had to choose either one or the other and adhere to that choice: one might choose fabulous wealth (Rhine gold), or sources of power (a ring and a magic cape), but that choice would preclude any future possibility of living in the world of love. Efforts to integrate the two would necessitate frequent lies; and the exposure of those lies would undermine the whole world.

The characters who embodied these messages on the stage fell, as mentioned, into three main categories: gods, humans, and hybrids. All three coexisted with giants and dwarves, and the entire assemblage offered opportunities for unending speculation concerning Wagner's overt and covert intentions. Did he remain faithful to the familiar social stratification, merely replacing the aristocracy, the bourgeoisie, and the working class with three new classes? Did he have a racial division in mind? Who were the creatures on the periphery, the dwarves and the giants? Heroic beings and miserable mutations? Members of particular ethnic groups? The complexity of Wagner's thinking, which had already been expressed in some of his esthetic and political writings, only fueled the proliferation of guesses and assumptions about the identity of his characters.

Wagner's essay about the 1848 revolution is the key to understanding his oeuvre in the context of contemporary political events.[16] It is possible that when he began composing *Der Ring des Nibelungen* he was indeed thinking about the break-up and replacement of the familiar European political infrastructure. However, by the time the work was publicly performed for the first time, the political world around him had changed significantly. The aristocracy of Western and Central Europe was being forced to share power with increasingly larger numbers of citizens, and residents of the German-speaking regions were living in new political frameworks. Prussia's war against France in 1870 proved to be the catalyst for the unification of Germany and the establishment of its neighbor to the south, the Austro-Hungarian Empire. When unification finally took place, Wagner was too comfortable to revolt.

However, even before that the circumstances of his life were clearly at variance with the ideas he expressed in his essays. About 20 years before the political changes that reshaped the face of Europe, Wagner had become one of the most famous revolutionary composers of the Bavarian court. His rebellious nature and self-absorption, which kept him from holding down a regular job, together with the huge resources he invested in each new composition, made him an ideal protégé for rich patrons. The Bavarian King Ludwig II, an eccentric and extravagant aristocrat, became the main backer of Wagner's highly expensive creative flow. His connections with the king and constant quest for public favor to ensure his operas' success almost completely eroded Wagner's revolutionary spirit and his opposition to the exploitative ruling classes, although he continued to express his criticism of society in his letters.

One of the main outlets Wagner found to vent his disgust with the existing social structure was his attitude toward a small and flourishing ethnic minority that lived in his country, where it enjoyed a complete political equality that it had never before known in Europe. The Jews, with whom Wagner made friends and maintained a productive musical dialogue, were the scapegoats for his social ideas, and every now and then he directed various accusations at them. Some of these were recorded over the years in his personal writings and in the diaries of his second wife, Cosima, and others were interwoven in writings published on the occasion of the musical festivals held in Wagner's Festspielhaus in Bayreuth.

His most famous diatribe against the Jews appeared in his essay "Judaism in Music." This article was printed twice during Wagner's lifetime: the first time in 1850 under the pen name K. Freigedank (meaning "freethinker"), when Wagner was still an impoverished, persecuted revolutionary, and the second time in 1869, under his own name, when he was well known and appreciated. This article was in fact the first place that Wagner openly revealed the anti-Semitic side of his personality. The main focus of the article was an attempt to prove "Jews' natural lack of [musical] talent" through an analysis of Jewish music – primarily music from Ashkenazi synagogues. In the course of his argument, Wagner described a process of *Verjüdung* ("Judaization") – a German term he apparently invented himself – that he claimed had corrupted the arts in general and music in particular.[17] His "evidence" for the Jews' alleged lack of talent in the musical field consisted of racist, negative comments about Jewish behavior, dress, and external appearance. He concluded the article by calling for the redemption of the Jews through *Untergang* (destruction). This harsh pronouncement, which was extreme even in the context of the anti-Semitism prevalent at the time, established Wagner in the front ranks of Jew-haters. It was also the most notable assertion linking Wagner's anti-Semitic theory with the racist philosophy endorsed by the National Socialists, who unlike him were also proponents of the mass elimination of Jews. The statements Wagner made in this essay pigeonholed him as a classic anti-Semite, a presumption further validated by the fact that his associates also tended to express themselves in racist terms in general and anti-Semitic terms in particular.

The shudder that his words elicited in every Jewish reader – and, of course, in other readers who saw people rather than labels – justifies Wagner's classification as an anti-Semitic extremist. Moreover, the militant quality of the essay explains why Wagner is perceived as a significant contributor to the development of modern anti-Semitic ideology and a proto-Nazi theoretician. Yet it must be remembered that in Wagner's time many individuals and groups were pronouncing explicitly anti-Semitic views; so although Wagner may have been intemperate, his attitude was generally consistent with the atmosphere prevailing in certain intellectual circles. We have only to examine the nationalist philosophy that the founder of modern gymnastics, Friedrich Ludwig Jahn, instilled in his pupils, or the views of the intellectuals Friedrich Hegel, Karl Guzkow, Bruno Bauer, and Ludwig Feuerbach, to apprehend the anti-Jewish intellectual atmosphere that must have been familiar to Wagner. Some commentators claim, however, that Wagner expanded on these anti-Semitic views and incorporated them in his music, which is filled with conspicuously anti-Jewish elements.[18]

Wagner's specific comments on two Jewish composers of his own time, Felix Mendelssohn Bartholdy and Giacomo Meyerbeer, reinforce the impression that at least the article "Judaism in Music" was conceived not as a general attack against Jews, but rather as a convenient medium for a personal attack, a way of "settling accounts." Wagner had borrowed, inter alia, a chord in his opera *Parsifal* from Mendelssohn (who, though a grandson of the Jewish philosopher Moses Mendelssohn, was himself born a Christian); yet he wrote that Mendelssohn's creative power was declining, forcing him to openly appropriate details of form unique to the predecessors whom he took as models. In particular, he accused him of plagiarizing Bach. Meyerbeer, castigated just as severely as a musical trickster who attracted light-minded audiences to the opera houses, was mentioned in the article only by implication due to – some claim – the intensity of the jealousy and contempt he inspired in Wagner. Yet none of this was enough to cause Jews living in the German-speaking countries to turn their backs on the many-faceted composer. For years they were considered a sympathetic and enthusiastic audience of Wagner's works, and continued to attend productions of Wagnerian music for decades after the composer's death.[19]

Wagner's negative attitude toward Jews was a major part of the social analysis reflected in *Der Ring des Nibelungen*. In fact, his social views as expressed in "Judaism in Music" served – and still serve – as the ideological cornerstone for any analysis of *Der Ring*. Some have claimed that the characters who provoke ridicule in the work, the dwarves, are the on-stage portrayals of Jews. Their expressed avarice lent force to this kind of association, since at that time Jewish financiers were kingpins in German economy (providing the basis for the literary character of Jew Süss as well).[20] A critical and pro-Jewish reading of Wagner's writings is likely to uncover increasing numbers of ridiculous or money-grubbing characters who appear to be Jewish, and many Wagner researchers, Jewish and non-Jewish alike, have undertaken such readings.

However, this kind of approach does not necessarily reveal the qualities that Wagner himself sought to give his characters. It seems to me that intensive use of this prism not only attributes too much importance to Wagner's anti-Semitic essay "Judaism in Music," but also clearly reflects both an uncritical acceptance of contemporary nineteenth-century racist interpretations of Wagner's works, and, especially, complete faith in the assumption that this work was one of Hitler's favorites. Such interpretations are likely to interfere with the capacity to properly understand the libretto, and will possibly reveal more about the reader's own views and the way he or she sees Wagner than about the composer's original intentions. In other words, the focus on racist ideas – some of which did in fact express Wagner's outlook – is apt to obscure the different levels of the work. It is interesting, for example, that the avarice of those characters forged in a more "German" mold has not been generally perceived as a Jewish attribute.

Similarly, the complex power relations depicted in the work – between men and women and between other groups – have not, in most cases, been analyzed satisfactorily. A sufficiently keen examination of the portrayal of the various groups as interlocutors or adversaries would probably invalidate some of the claims concerning Wagner's stratified and perhaps racially based approach to the characters he created. A serious discussion of the relationship between men and women in the work would reveal the sage image and prophetic perception Wagner attributed to the women on his stage, an image reflecting a great deal of appreciation on the part of its creator – even though he humiliated the women in his own life more than once. Given the complexity of the work and the contradictory aspects of its creator, *Der Ring des Nibelungen* can be

analyzed from different and varied – sometimes even opposing – perspectives.

After Wagner's death the dam burst and German periodicals were
flooded with interpretations of his operas. However, even then most critics
failed to examine the less predictable parts of the text. The vast majority
settled for drawing parallels between Wagner's public persona and his
works, treating the man and the oeuvre as an ideological whole. Many
critics interpreted Wagner's works in the spirit of their own time, thereby
jettisoning some of the composer's original layers of meaning. Such interpreters, by adapting Wagner's "real" intentions to suit their own
philosophies, made Wagner into putty in the hands of publicists and
archivists, all of whom were happy to appropriate the ideas and persona
of someone who was considered one of the pillars of modern German
culture.

Wagner's idiosyncratic social stratification and revolutionary
approach were not the only reasons for the great interest in the composer
and his work. In *Der Ring des Nibelungen* Wagner maximized his unconventional use of music so that it served the text and gave it added meaning.
This musical conception incorporated several musical elements: frequent
use of the leitmotif, the creation of an innovative tonality that permitted
the linking of chords and melodies once considered incompatible, and the
composition of musical phrases that did not conform to the current standard forms.

Wagner made intensive use of the leitmotif, a concept already known
before his time, by assigning musical themes to most of the characters,
emotional responses, wonders of nature, and things and events described
in the opera.[21] Their purpose was to evoke events and characters even at
times when they did not appear physically on the stage. For example, in
Der Ring des Nibelungen, the leitmotif for "twilight of the gods" – an
idea associated with the last part of the plot – appears first in the intro-
ductory act, *Das Rheingold*, while the Siegfried motif is first heard even
before the hero's birth. Such motifs, which in fact constitute a series of
symbols brought to the spectator's attention at different times, have over
the years become one of the most intensively researched aspects of
Wagnerian studies.

Robert Donnington has explained that throughout *Der Ring des
Nibelungen* some of the characters externalize attributes that are
perceived by the spectator as collective symbols. He also maintains that
Wagner used this device purposely to activate latent areas in the minds of
the spectators. Thus, through clever use of music and a deliberate appeal
to the subconscious, Wagner created a level of emotional identification in
his audience that they would not have reached through the medium of the
text alone.[22]

If such was indeed his intention, Wagner achieved the perfect consum-
mation of his own stage concept, known as *Gesamtkunstwerk* (total work

of art). According to this concept, which was the focus of several of Wagner's esthetic essays, all aspects of the stage work contribute to the achievement of the whole.[23] In Wagner's view, the creation of an opera did not end with the completion of the score and the libretto; the stage set, the costumes, the acting, and, of course, the musical emphases all constituted integral elements of the complete work. This explains why Wagner, unlike other opera composers of his time, insisted on writing his own words for the operas he composed; why his scripts included instructions concerning conducting, directing, and stage sets; and why he preferred that his works be called "music dramas" rather than operas. Thus, Wagner labored to create a full concordance between the music and the linguistic accents and syllabic combinations of the words that conveyed the plots he devised. The leitmotif was part of a broader concept that viewed the work as a whole, made up of a collection of perfectly integrated textures. This full scope approach is, in my opinion, Wagner's most significant influence on the political thought of the first half of the twentieth century. The idea of complementary components which form the whole is the foundation of many totalitarian regimes, including National Socialism.

However, despite its exceptional importance, this holistic worldview was overshadowed for a long time by Wagner's unique approach to musical composition. Not only did his unconventional tonal combinations – based on modifications of the Tristan chord – draw attention, but the works he composed, by ignoring the contemporary norms of musical phrasing, initially aroused rage and scorn. The music was different and irritating to someone who had been raised in the classical and romantic traditions, and the libretto usually ended with a shocking tragedy. Among the Wagnerian commentators who did not forgive his special approach to the world of music was the philosopher Friedrich Nietzsche. "Wagner is a great corrupter of music," Nietzsche said in 1888. "With it he found the means of stimulating tired nerves – and in this way he made music ill [. . .] He is the master of hypnotic trickery, and he fells the strongest like bullocks."[24]

Before he died Wagner broke through the barriers of hostility erected against him, but the musical analyses and rather simplistic insights concerning his intentions continued to direct attention away from the uniqueness of his librettos. Although he became one of the luminaries of modern German culture, his profound ideas were ruthlessly plundered and torn into little scraps of predictable, sometimes even empty, pronouncements that he may not ever have intended to express. Occasionally these scraps were used to substantiate and validate the theses of others, presumably giving them the authority of "the divine word." Thus, while some writers were busy making serious analyses of the complex aspects of Wagner's oeuvre, other persons and bodies claiming some kind of connection to Wagner's spirit were appropriating his works for their own ideological and political purposes. There was only one common denominator to all the interpretations: Even those who rejected Wagner's musical system outright – Nietzsche, for example – could not ignore his outstanding talent and unique ability to bend music into new forms with new content. Consequently, no one tried to deny his artistic importance; at most, critics underscored those aspects of his work that were perceived as dark, threatening, or difficult to absorb.

The many analyses of Wagner's artistic work and expository writing make it challenging to determine exactly what Wagner actually intended, and what attitudes may have been unjustly imputed to him. His many anti-Semitic remarks, documented in his letters, his writings, and his wife's diaries, reinforce the impression that his works, too, contain at least an echo of these ideas. His appropriation by confirmed racists, from Houston Stewart Chamberlain (who married Wagner's daughter Eva in 1908, 25 years after the composer's death), to Adolf Hitler, complicates still further any attempt to examine his attitude toward Jews, although some maintain that his own declarations are sufficient evidence of the depth of his anti-Semitism.[25] Nor does the great admiration for him expressed by other artists, beginning with Thomas Mann, make the task any easier. As we will see later, most critics see a large measure of conscious, deliberate anti-Semitism in Wagner, basing this presumption on Wagner's cozy reception by proclaimed anti-Semites. In response, however, I will argue that this thesis is difficult to verify. The circumstances of Wagner's turbulent life do not facilitate attempts to examine his character; despite every effort to categorize him according to conventional social and political mores, the impulses of this rebel must, in my view, remain a riddle. Finally, however anti-Semitic he may have been, he cannot be classified with aggressors who actually carried out violent acts against Jews – and he should certainly not be turned into the classic symbol of German anti-Semitism.

Notes

1   Much can be learned about Wagner's life from collections of his articles and other writings: R. Wagner, *Gesammelte Schriften und Dichtungen* (Leipzig, 1872). Other important sources include the diaries of his second wife, Cosima – C. Wagner, *Die Tagebücher* (Munich, 1982) – and the many biographies and articles dealing with different aspects of his works and personality. The biography that is still considered definitive today is E. Newman, *Wagner as Man and Artist* (New York, 1914). See also: R. W. Gutman, *Wagner – The Man, His Mind and His Music* (New York, 1972); J. Köhler, *Der letzte der Titanen. Richard Wagners Leben und Werk* (Munich, 2001).

2   For a detailed discussion of this issue, see M. Zuckermann, "Richard Wagner, the Revolutionist and Reactionist [Hebrew]," *Zmanim* 12 (Summer, 1983): 60–73; and the references in Rose, *Wagner*, pp. 73–88. On the relationship between politics and artistic expression in Wagner's work, see U. Bermbach,

Blühendes Leid. Politik und Gesellschaft in Richard Wagners Musikdramen (Stuttgart and Weimar, 2003).

3 Contemporary reviews indicate that Wagner was exceptional for his time. See, for example, E. Hanslick, "Wagner Cult," in *The Attentive Listener: Three Centuries of Music*, ed. L. Haskell (Princeton, NJ, 1996), pp. 170–4 (originally published in *Neue Freie Presse*, 1882); and an enthusiastic article by F. Filippi, "Wagner's Musical Voyage in the Land of the Future," in *The Attentive Listener*, pp. 156–60 (originally published in *Preseveranza*, 1870). For background on opera-writing throughout Europe during Wagner's time, see the well-known D. J. Grout and C. V. Palisca, *A History of Western Music* (New York and London, 1996; 1st edn. 1960), pp. 625–51. For further general information about Wagner's work, see T. S. Grey (ed.), *The Cambridge Companion to Wagner* (Cambridge, 2008).

4 This unconventional and demanding use of the musical scale and the unusual phrasing caused great problems when the work was performed, causing Wagner considerable worry. In a letter to a friend in May 1851, he wrote: "The more the thought of seeing my Siegfried's Death performed on the stage occupied my mind, the more distinctly I faced the difficulties it would present to our singers, unused to such a task, and to the public, unused to such a plot." See J. N. Burk, ed., *Letters of Richard Wagner: The Burrel Collection* (London, 1951), pp. 492–3.

5 See R. Wagner, *Der Ring des Nibelungen* (various editions), or the summary in *Bayreuther Festspiele 1957* (4 Programmhefte) (Bayreuth, 1957). Another useful work is C. Osborne, *The Complete Operas of Wagner* (London, 1992), pp. 179–261. See also M. Geck, "Wagner's 'Ring' – The Sum of a Philosophy of Life?" in *Programmhefte der Bayreuther Festspiele 1973*, Heft vii, pp. 13–27. On the medieval versions, see M. L. Goodrich, *Medieval Myths* (New York, 1977), pp. 126–54. On the ancient versions, see D. A. MacKenzie, *Teutonic Myth and Legend* (London, 1912).

6 These researchers tended to leap to conclusions concerning the Britons' putative Hellenic roots, and to invent a past designed to fill those gaps still veiled in obscurity. The most famous instance of this was the publication of "Ossian's poems," which had supposedly been rediscovered by James Macpherson, although suspicion arose immediately after their publication in the 1760s that Macpherson had made them up himself. On English romanticism and its ideas, see, for example, M. Gaull, *English Romanticism: The Human Context* (New York and London, 1988); and H. A. Beers, *A History of English Romanticism in the Eighteenth Century* (New York, 1968; 1st edn. 1899). Extracts from Ossian's poems are quoted toward the end of the plot of Johann Wolfgang von Goethe's *The Sorrows of Young Werther*, an epistolary novel originally published in 1774.

7 On the national concept in Germany, see G. G. Iggers's instructive work, *The German Conception of History: The National Tradition of Historical Thought from Herder to the Present* (Middletown, 1968). On German romanticism, see E. Behler, *German Romantic Literary Theory* (Cambridge, 1993). On philological research in Germany and the part played by adherents of the Sturm und Drang trend in encouraging such research, see R. Pascal, *The German Sturm und Drang* (London, 1953). Tales by the Brothers Grimm are available in various editions and translations from the original.

8 Although this legend contains many elements linking it with actual events that took place in different parts of Europe and at different times, it should not be viewed as a literary documentation of historical events. On these links, see H. Reichert, *Nibelungenlied und Nibelungensaga* (Vienna and Cologne, 1985); and N. Benevegna, *Kingdom on the Rhine: History, Myth and Legend in Wagner's Ring* (Harwich, 1983). The legend's popularity apparently declined with the rise of the nation-states in Europe, a development that was incompatible with the tribal notions embodied in the legend.

9 On the legend's dissemination and on the fears of dangerous interpretations, see L. von Saalfeld, "Die ideologische Funktion des Nibelungenliedes in der Preussisch-Deutschen Geschichte: von seiner Wiederentdeckung bis zum Nationalsozialismus" (Ph.D. diss, Freie Universität Berlin, 1977), especially pp. 2–8, 26–7, 58–64; and O. G. Bauer, "The Nibelungen Saga in the 19th Century," in *Götterdämmerung: Programmheft IV* (Bayreuther Festspiele, 1976), pp. 19–25. On the facsimile edition and other stories inspired by the Nibelungen, see W. Wunderlich, "Der Schatz des Drachentödters: Materielen zur Wirkungsgeschichte des Nibelungenliedes," *Literaturwissenschaft-Gesellschaftwissenschaft* 30 (1977): 11–22. On different forms of art inspired by the legend, particularly paintings, see Bauer, *Nibelungen*, p. 24.

10 The sources Wagner used were: *Der Nibelungen Not und die Klage* (ed. Lachmann); *Zu den Nibelungen* (Lachmann); Grimm's *Mythologie*; *Edda – Heldenlieder* (v.d. Hagen); *Die nordische Volsunsaga* (v.d. Hagen); *Wilkina und Niflungasaga* (v.d. Hagen); *Das deutsche Heldenbuch* (old and revised editions, 6 vols.); *Die deutsche Heldensaga* (W. Grimm); *Thidreksaga* (v.d. Hagen); and *Heimskringla* (translation by Mohnike). This list is from J. Bertram, *Mythos, Symbol, Idee in Wagners Musik-Dramen* (Hamburg, 1957), p. 137.

11 On Raupach's play, see L. Mackensen, *Die Nibelungen: Sage, Geschichte, ihr Lied und sein Dichter* (Stuttgart, 1984), pp. 233–4.

12 R. Wagner, "Das Künstlertum der Zukunft (ab 1848)," in *Richard Wagner: Mein Denken*, ed. M. Gregor-Dellin (Munich, 1982), p. 163.

13 This critic was Henri Malherbe, who took this line in an article entitled "Richard Wagner, Absolute Revolutionary," cited in H. Kohn, "Wagner and His Time," chap. 9 in *The Mind of Germany: The Education of a Nation* (New York, 1960), p. 191. The same attitude was expressed decades later by one of Wagner's most fascinating critics, Theodor Adorno. See T. Adorno, *In Search of Wagner* (Norfolk, 1985), especially pp. 11–27.

14 F. Nietzsche, "The Case of Wagner," in *Complete Works*, ed. O. Levy, trans. J. M. Kennedy (New York, 1964), 8:9. On another aspect of the intellectual dialogue between the two men, see Y. Yovel, "'Nietzsche contra Wagner' und die Juden," in *Richard Wagner und die Juden*, ed. D. Borchmeyer et al. (Stuttgart, 2000), pp. 123–43.

15 In 1856, Wagner replaced *Siegfried's Death* with *Götterdämmerung* ("The Twilight of the Gods"), and preceded it with a prologue explaining the climax of the work: the destruction of the entire world. He also rewrote *Der junge Siegfried* ("The Young Siegfried"), putting the stage character of Siegfried in

the shadow of the god Wotan, who occasionally appears disguised as a vagabond. The new section of *Siegfried* was written in several stages between the years of 1856 and 1871. The entire work included two more acts: *Die Walküre* ("The Valkyrie"), which was written in June 1852, and the relatively short prologue, *Das Rheingold* ("The Rhine Gold"), which was written between September and November of 1852. At the end of the 1980s, another part of Wagner's work was discovered, and researchers believe it to be authentic. This fifth act describes the salvation and recovery of the world that had been sacrificed to Wotan's power plays and the loathsome battles involved therein – an optimistic ending that was also typical of the Nordic legends.

16 See R. Wagner, "Die Kunst und die Revolution," in *Gesammelte Schriften und Dichtungen* (Leipzig, 1972), III: 9–50.

17 See J. Katz, *Richard Wagner: Verbotene des Antisemitismus* (Königstein, 1985), pp. 59–79. For further information and interpretation of the anti-Semitic essay and its impact on the social-political discourse of the time, see J. M. Fischer, *Richard Wagners 'Das Judentum in der Musik,' Eine kritische Dokumentation als Beitrag zur Geschichte des europäischen Antisemitismus* (Frankfurt am Main, 2000).

18 On the views common in Wagner's day, see Rose, Wagner, pp. 6–22. On Wagner's anti-Semitism, see Weiner, *Richard Wagner*, pp. 261–306. See also F. Busi, "Wagner and the Jews," *Midstream* 32, No. 2 (Feb. 1986): 37–42. On anti-Semitic overtones in his music, see H. Zelinsky, "Richard Wagner 'Kunst der Zukunft' und seine Idee der Vernichtung," in *Von kommenden Zeiten: Geschichtsprophetien im 19. und 20. Jahrhundert*, ed. J. A. Knoll and J. A. Schoeps (Stuttgart and Bonn, 1984), pp. 84–105.

19 This attitude continued outside the State of Israel. See, for example, E. Brody, "The Jewish Wagnerites," *Midstream* 32, No. 2 (Feb. 1986): 46–59. See also an article by Joseph Horowitz about Wagner's reception in the large Jewish community in the United States: J. Horowitz, "Wagner und der amerikanische Jude – eine persönliche Betrachtung," in *Richard Wagner und die Juden*, ed. D. Borchmeyer et al., pp. 238–50.

20 The best-known story about Jew Süss was written by a Jew, Lion Feuchtwanger, who used it for both a play and a novel. See L. Feuchtwanger, *Jud Süss* [the novel] (Frankfurt a.M., 1959), and L. Feuchtwanger, *Jud Süss* [the play] (Munich, 1918). The play was written first, and only some years later did Feuchtwanger write the more wide-ranging novel, in which he placed greater emphasis on the Jewish aspect and anti-Semitism. The Nazis used the plot for a virulently anti-Semitic film, *Jud Süss* (1940), which was produced under the aegis of the Ministry of Propaganda headed by Joseph Goebbels. On the various uses of Süss's biography, see N. Sheffi, "Jews, Germans and the Representation of Jud Süss in Literature and Film," *Jewish Culture and History* 6, No. 2 (Winter, 2003): 25–42.

21 Wagner exploited this system to the full in *Der Ring des Nibelungen*, which contains no fewer than 106 motifs. For a better idea of their clever use, it is

helpful to read the libretto containing the annotations governing the motifs and their transitions while listening to the words sung on stage. See, for example, R. Wagner, *Der Ring des Nibelungen: Text mit Notentafeln der Leitmotive* (Mainz and Munich, 1988; 1st edn. 1913).

22 Many articles have been written on the significance of Wagner's musical motifs. On the psychological delusion of the audience, see R. Donnington, *Wagner Ring and Its Symbols: The Music and the Myth* (London, 1963); D. Borchmeyer, *Drama and the World of Richard Wagner* (Princeton, 2003), pp. 212–37. Compare also P. McCrelless, *Wagner's Siegfried: Its Drama, History and Music* (Michigan, 1981), and B. Perl, "Drama and Music in the Work of Richard Wagner [Hebrew]," in *Who's Afraid*, pp. 170–200. Approaches of this kind were typical in analyses of Wagner's works even in earlier years. Already at the beginning of this century the claim was made that Wagner's works were built around psychological cycles that produced a stream of conscious and unconscious associations in the audience. See A. O. Lorenz, *Das Geheimnis der Form bei Richard Wagner* (Berlin, 1924).

23 This idea is explained in a comprehensive article that Wagner wrote as a guide to some of his opera librettos (*Tannhäuser*, *Lohengrin*, and *Tristan und Isolde*). See R. Wagner, *The Art-Work of the Future and Other Works*, trans. W. A. Ellis (Lincoln and London, 1993), pp. 69–213.

24 Nietsche, "The Case of Wagner," p. 14.

25 Katz, *Richard Wagner: Verbotene des Antisemitismus*, pp. 59–79.

3

Racism, Music, and Power:
The Nazification of Wagner

In the last quarter of the nineteenth century, beginning shortly before Wagner's death, the controversies that had punctuated the early period of his work remained an intellectual and occasionally academic issue. In the opera halls, boos were heard less and less frequently, and only a handful of spectators still publicly demonstrated their distaste for the music by leaving the concert hall in the middle of a performance. Directors and conductors sought to bring out previously hidden facets of the operas and to vary the stage productions, even at the cost of ignoring some of Wagner's meticulous instructions. Music critics sought new ways to illuminate Wagner's works, which were now viewed with approbation. Wagner's musical philosophy became a guiding light for other composers, including, most notably, the members of the "Vienna School" (Arnold Schönberg, Alban Berg, and Anton Webern), who at the beginning of the twentieth century worked on expanding and modifying the Wagnerian tonal concept. At the same time creators in the plastic arts, the Impressionists, continued Wagner's innovations through other artistic media.

The friendlier attitude toward Wagner's work was shared by several critics and fans who steered the composer's ideas into channels that, although not alien to Wagner's thinking, henceforth gave it a very radical turn. Such interpreters, headed by Wagner's admirer who later married the composer's daughter, Houston Stewart Chamberlain, opened the door – wide – to the National Socialists' appropriation of Wagner a few decades after the latter's death, before they formed their own parliamentary party and became the totalitarian body that established the Third Reich.

In the years following Wagner's death, the composer's widow, Cosima Wagner, ruled the Festspielhaus in Bayreuth with a firm hand, trying to preserve her husband's legacy as completely as possible. In general her ideas were welcomed by the public and warmly supported by Chamberlain, who believed that her activities helped advance his own purposes. Some people, however, took a dim view of the Wagner family's total monopoly of what went on in the Bayreuth opera house, and tried to suggest that this valuable asset should be transferred to the public domain. In 1888, only five years after the composer's death, there were proposals to nationalize both the theater and Wagner's private home. An article published in the daily *Berliner Tageblatt* just before the opening of the Bayreuth Festival – which was and still is a Wagner festival – complained that the composer had been cut off from the society around him, and protested against the private, elitist use of the theater. The author of the article argued that the German princes should make Bayreuth a national monument that would serve the needs of the nation, instead of maintaining it in its present role as a purely Wagnerian theater.[1]

Other voices echoed these complaints. One critic explained in an article published before the 1905 Festival that Wagner's work in Bayreuth and the legacy he had left behind him were analogous to the spiritual assets that the eighteenth-century intellectual Friedrich Schiller had bequeathed to the German people (mainly his major writings on esthetics). In other words, given its enormous significance for the entire German nation, Wagner's Festspielhaus could not be considered a private or family asset, or maintained as an elitist institution.[2]

However, such comments were overshadowed by the articles dedicated to Wagner and his works that were published in the magazine he had founded himself, *Bayreuther Blätter*, and by the mainstream of ideological interpretation represented by Chamberlain. The latter zealously decoded his father-in-law's thinking, emphasizing the nationalist background apparent in Wagner's various writings and weaving his own opinions into the composer's original essays. Wagner had been on close terms with his son-in-law. The English Chamberlain, upon marrying Wagner's daughter Eva, had embraced his wife's nationality and undergone a rapid process of "Germanization." A well-to-do intellectual, he devoted most of his time to researching the new ideas that were emerging in the second half of the nineteenth century. He pored over the writings of Charles Darwin, trying to guess whom the renowned nature researcher had been thinking of when he developed his idea of "the survival of the fittest."[3] Chamberlain, like other secular people of the time, did not interpret the term "fittest" in the way that Darwin had originally conceived it – the adaptation of a certain element in nature, whether animal or plant, to its environment – but solely in human terms, as a ranking of human beings according to their attributes. His manifestly high estimation of the German race did not come from Darwin's work but was based on his own views, which were influenced by the racist ideas prevalent throughout Europe at the time.

Chamberlain's sources of inspiration were, of course, the same intellectuals who had contributed to Wagner's own ideological frame of reference. Among these, the leading influence was, interestingly, the least significant theorist, the educator and right-wing philosopher Friedrich Ludwig Jahn, better known as "Father Jahn," who in the second half of the nineteenth century had established two German associations that would have a far-reaching impact on the concept of the Aryan race: the Language Purification Society and the gymnastic clubs known as Deutsche Turnerschaft. Both groups extolled the German race, its purity, and its outstanding abilities. Underlying the idea of gymnastic societies was an anti-Napoleonic attitude and the belief that physically healthy young people would better serve the goals of national unity. Father Jahn, who also supervised the young gymnasts' spiritual education, urged them to listen to lectures on the *Nibelungenlied* during those times when they were not engaged in physical training.[4]

Chamberlain's other theoretical sources – more eminent intellectually than Father Jahn – included the French political philosopher Count Joseph Arthur de Gobineau, who had met Wagner in 1873 and exchanged ideas and opinions with him. The Count's intellectual heirs in Germany, in particular Ludwig Schermann, established a society called the *Gobineau Gesellschaft* in order to disseminate this French aristocrat's racist worldview. Another influential figure was the German philosopher Karl Stein, who in 1883 published *Helden und Welt* (Heroes and World), a book expressing views that were a direct continuation of Gobineau's ideas. Stein, who passed away in his prime, had also been personally acquainted with Wagner, who wrote an introduction for Stein's book just before his own death.[5]

Besides these intellectuals, in the last years of the nineteenth century a number of politicians were also busily trying – with some success – to introduce ideas bordering on blatant anti-Semitic racism into the parliaments of Wilhelmine Germany and the Austro-Hungarian Empire. Two such politicians were the German Adolf Stöcker and the Austrian Georg von Schönerer, whose parties were later associated with the beginnings of the wave of anti-Semitism that swept through the German-speaking regions in the twentieth century. Doubtlessly, an anti-Jewish atmosphere also pervaded other countries, notably France, where anti-Semitism led to the notorious trial of the Jewish army officer Alfred Dreyfuss on trumped-up evidence.[6]

Chamberlain's writings indicate that the ideas current among racist politicians of his generation were present in his mind when he wrote his books. The two Chamberlain works most germane to our subject were his historical study of the nineteenth century, *Die Grundlagen des neunzehnten Jahrhunderts* (The Foundations of the Nineteenth Century), published in 1899, and a biography of Wagner, published in 1896. In his general analysis of Wagner, Chamberlain also tried to explain Wagner's political views. He claimed that Wagner had championed the institutions of absolute monarchy on the assumption that such a monarchy would ultimately emancipate the nation, and that he had disapproved of the Church institutions, since they subverted true religious faith.

Wagner himself would probably not have endorsed this shallow interpretation. Although he was financially dependent on the king of Bavaria, both his artistic and philosophical writings undermined and sometimes ridiculed absolute rulers and the corrupt tyranny that was the inevitable consequence of their power. Similarly, in view of his writings on pagan worlds, his contempt for Judaism, and his lax adherence to basic religious values such as the sanctity of marriage, it is doubtful whether Wagner ever gave any deep thought to the issue of religious faith. Chamberlain's key remarks on Wagner's philosophy, however, concerned Wagner's vision of Germany as a strong, independent body within the borders envisioned in the "Greater Germany" plan (that is, the unified Germany of 1871 with the addition of parts of the Austro-Hungarian Empire).[7]

This view perfectly matched the way Chamberlain presented Germany and the Germans in his book on the nineteenth century, in which he unequivocally asserted the Germans' superiority to other peoples. Both books discussed here, *Die Grundlagen des neunzehnten Jahrhunderts* and the Wagner biography, contained the basic elements of the racist interpretations that would henceforth be attributed to Wagner. As noted earlier, these interpretations were not taken out of the context of Wagner's own writings, nor did they contradict them in any way. However, they strongly emphasized lines that in Wagner's thinking had been part of a larger whole – one that did not necessarily tend to racism but rather to a comprehensive social and political debate. In any case, that part of Wagner's philosophy that saw Jews as a repulsive element of society was not expressed on the personal level, since he was friendly with many representatives of what Chamberlain considered "the inferior races." Moreover, although Wagner's writings reflected contempt for those the composer considered less talented than himself, he did not go to the extreme of making absolute generalizations about the quality of Germans compared with other people, nor did he portray them as a superior race, even though he did show signs of considerable xenophobia. As for Wagner's concept of sanctity, Chamberlain himself remarked that the composer displayed reverence only for artistic creation.[8]

Since Chamberlain had conversed often with Wagner and remained in Bayreuth as part of the family that was now guarding Wagner's spiritual legacy, his words carried the authority of an official interpretation. In addition to his own writings, occasional pieces by other writers appeared in the *Bayreuther Blätter* expressing racist views that the authors considered to reflect the spirit of Wagner.[9] In the context of the pronouncements by both Wagner's contemporaries and his heirs in Bayreuth, it is understandable that later thinkers should attribute similar ideas to the composer himself. From the beginning of the twentieth century, however, all such interpretations came under the influence of a single admirer who turned the celebrated composer into a symbol of the most extreme racist movement that the modern world has ever known. It was Adolf Hitler's feelings about Richard Wagner that retroactively pointed up the composer's racist ideas and established Wagner as a perfect artistic symbol of National Socialism.

The true measure of Hitler's appreciation of Wagner will probably never be known, but many works on both Wagner and Hitler contain the assessment that Hitler idolized Wagner and saw him as a prophet and his writings as an ideological standard.[10] Nonetheless, it is worth noting that the frequent playing of Wagner's music in concert halls in general, and at Nazi party conventions in particular under the Third Reich may be attributable not only to Hitler's personal admiration and the composer's popularity (which was conspicuous under the Weimar Republic, too), but also to Wagner's perfect all-German image.

Hitler was exposed to Wagner's works early in life. In 1901, at the age of 12, he attended a performance of one of Wagner's operas, *Lohengrin*, and was spellbound. The short Wagnerian-style opera he tried to compose in honor of the great composer was only the beginning of a more complete identification with his idol. In the early 1920s, at the outset of his career, Hitler developed a close acquaintance with the Wagner family, awakening interest among those of the clan who wished to preserve the composer's memory as a philosopher of racist ideas. Hitler's introduction to Chamberlain's philosophy was merely one little step in the ideological rapprochement between the young politician and Wagner.

The other side of the equation, which became particularly significant, was the Wagner family's deep appreciation of Hitler. The date of Hitler's first visit to Bayreuth is in some dispute, being variously estimated as sometime in 1923 or at latest 1924. The most interesting asseveration is that of Wagner's granddaughter Friedelind, the daughter of Siegfried and Winifred Wagner, although her testimony is particularly problematic – she was only five years old when Hitler first visited "Wahnfried," the family estate. As she remembered it, Hitler had come to the house for the first time in May 1923, and, clearly one of Winifred Wagner's idols, was presented as the man who "would be Germany's savior." As a young woman during World War II Friedelind herself chose to leave her country and go into exile, publishing an autobiographical book in the United States in which she expressed her deep antipathy toward those family members who had embraced the Nazi ideology, particularly her mother.

Winifred, who married Wagner's son Siegfried – himself a successful conductor – was a member of the Nazi movement from its beginnings, and an enthusiastic spectator of Hitler's march in Munich at the time of his attempted putsch in the fall of 1923. Although her presence there had been purely fortuitous – her husband happened to be conducting a concert that evening in a nearby auditorium – a few days later Winifred published a manifesto in the daily *Oberfränkische Zeitung* supporting the instigators of the putsch. At that time, as Germany labored under the burden of sky-high inflation and the sequels of its defeat in World War I, she believed that Hitler was the political leader the nation was waiting for.

By her daughter's account, some of Winifred's great affection for Hitler may have been due to his agreeable manner. Friedelind Wagner remembered Hitler as a "good uncle" who used to visit her family in the quiet little town where they lived, a pleasant man who corresponded with her brothers and herself. When he was sentenced to prison in Regensburg for his part in the putsch, Winifred Wagner collected food and clothing for the other families involved, but sent Hitler himself writing materials – which, researchers believe, he used to write *Mein Kampf*.[11]

The Munich putsch also provided material for an additional link between Hitler and Wagner. The painter Georg Grosz – a member of the Spartacist opposition who later became one of the most prominent activists against the Nazi regime – drew Hitler marching along clad in leather and carrying a spear, the image of the legendary Siegfried. Although Grosz was alluding to German mythology, he was probably influenced by the prevailing conceptualization of plot details which had been transformed into a series of allegorical terms familiar to everyone. The most prominent example of this was the adoption of the name Siegfried as a nickname for the German line of defense on the banks of the Rhine in World War I. It can reasonably be assumed that Grosz's drawing was influenced not only by the well-known legend, but also by the strong impression made by the Wagnerian stage figure. The *Niebelungen* image continued to prevail even after Germany's collapse in World War I: German leaders compared the defeat to a knife in the back by the other European countries, the same fate met by innocent, honest Siegfried. Nor were images from the medieval repertoire limited to the plot of the *Niebelungen*; in another cartoon from the early days of Hitler's career Viennese *Simplicissimus* artists drew him as a medieval knight riding a horse into modern Berlin while his servants decimated figures dressed in dinner jackets.[12]

Hitler's actions upon completing his prison term reinforced his bond with the Wagner family. As soon as he was released from prison he went to visit Wagner's grave, and in the following months he became a regular visitor at the Wagner home. The family's affection for him was clear. Winifred gave the new son of the house published editions of all Wagner's writings and a page from the original manuscript of *Lohengrin*. Hitler's regular visits to the annual festival soon converted him into a patron of the event who did everything he could to disseminate Wagner's writings throughout Germany. Although during those years his main interest was in strengthening his movement and turning it into a political party, he spared no time or effort to promote Wagner's spiritual and artistic legacy.[13]

The 1920s saw considerable efforts to expand the audience for Wagner's writings and musical works. In 1926, the German Richard Wagner Society (Deutsch-Richard-Wagner-Gesellschaft) was formed, an organization inspired primarily by Nazi followers' readings of Wagner's texts. Although political bodies sought to give the composer a proto-Nazi image, the general public had increasing opportunities to discover other facets of this versatile artist's work, thanks to the rapid development of mass communications in those years. The *Niebelungen* plot enjoyed yet another revival when it was retold in a film directed by Fritz Lang in 1924, without Wagner's music but definitely inspired by Wagner's work. Seven years later, in August 1931, music from the Bayreuth opera house was heard for the first time in other parts of the world: In the first radio transmission of its kind, a performance at the Bayreuth Festspielhaus was broadcast to 200 locations throughout Europe, America, and Africa, a clear rebuttal to claims that the festival was a closed, elitist affair and that the Wagner family were snobs. The sounds of the festival, previously enjoyed only by the wealthy, were now to be accessible to all.[14] Yet Wagner's works were already familiar even among the less well-to-do, and in the provincial towns. At that time Wagner's operas were the most frequently performed throughout Germany, closely followed by the operas of Giuseppe Verdi and Giacomo Puccini, with the works of Wolfgang Amadeus Mozart plodding far behind.[15]

The growing appreciation of Wagner received an additional boost shortly before the Nazis took power. About three weeks before the Nazi party garnered close to half the German vote and established a narrow coalition, Wagner's admirers commemorated the fiftieth anniversary of the prolific composer's death. One of the main speakers at the ceremony was the celebrated writer Thomas Mann, who had received the Nobel Prize for literature and was considered one of the greatest contemporary humanist intellectuals; Wagner's works had provided him more than once with the outlines for entire novellas or parts of novels. In his speech, Mann mentioned several of the characteristics that had made Wagner a great creator and a dangerous philosopher at the same time:

> On the subject of Wagner the psychologist a whole book could be written, dealing with the psychological art of the musician and the poet (in as much as one can distinguish between the two in his case). The device of musical reminiscence, already used on occasion in the old operatic tradition, was gradually developed by him into a subtle and masterly system that made music, to a degree never before realized, into an instrument of psychological allusion, elaboration and cross-reference.[16]

Mann's words illuminated two aspects of Wagner. The first was his great originality, which inspired admiration and even adoration from major artists such as Mann himself. Although there was nothing here to indicate that Wagner would become so sweepingly popular, Mann's remarks showed that Wagner's works were appreciated by moderate humanist intellectuals as well as extremists. The other aspect was the propagandist potential of Wagner's works: His operas propagated ideas that reverberated through the memories of the listener-spectators each time their senses focused on a particular leitmotif. In short, Mann clearly delineated the same features that the Nazi propagandists would discover in using Wagner's works to their own advantage, as well as the psychological principles that they would later borrow from him in order to inculcate their ideas.

The Nazis' appreciation of Wagner went further than Hitler's personal admiration and the development of the ideas stressed by Chamberlain. From the moment the Nazis gained power, Bayreuth became one of the main centers of their activity. *Die Meistersinger von Nürnberg*, an opera that described the difficult singing competitions of the sixteenth century, was one of the works most often played at Nazi party conventions. Possibly the call by the aging singer Sachs for a strong and creative Germany encouraged the Nazis to adopt the whole opera as a sort of anthem. More generally, however, any glory linked to the magnificent past of the German tribes, especially in the Middle Ages, clearly appealed to the ideologues of the party, who exalted the historic "golden age." This attitude was the target of sarcastic jibes from the opponents of Nazism – in and out of Europe – who ridiculed this yearning for the past in cartoons. One such caricature, printed in April 1933 about a month after the Nazis came to power, showed Hitler as a generously proportioned woman leading Germany into the Dark Ages.[17]

During the early months of their reign, the Nazis strove to identify themselves with Wagner. The music critic of *The New York Times*, quoting an article published earlier in a local paper, noted that Bayreuth had become a symbol of the Third Reich: "Bayreuth is the symbol of the Third Reich. National Socialism sees in the works of Richard Wagner something related to it in the essence and in the spirit."[18] This identification was so complete that the Nazis dared to replace the souvenir portraits of Wagner sold during the festivals with portraits of the stalwart new leader, Hitler. The Chancellor also held a special reception for festival participants, a festive event that became an institution in the following years. Hitler increased his involvement still more by organizing financial assistance for the festival in the years 1933–40. After World War II broke out, he arranged free transport to Bayreuth for wounded soldiers so that they could convalesce to the strains of Wagner's music.

Hitler's close relations with Winifred Wagner also opened the way to exemptions from the rigid laws enacted by the Nazis. The music department of the Ministry of Propaganda and Education controlled the strict ban on "degenerate" (*entartete*) music – that is, music considered "not Aryan" – and the hiring of performers for orchestras and choirs. Hitler, at his own discretion, authorized the participation of 40 to 50 Jewish performers in Bayreuth Festival productions to avoid compromising productions that had already been planned. The personal involvement of Nazi party figures in the arts also led to the performance of works by

Richard Strauss, the first head of the music department (dismissed after one year) – works that featured lyrics by the well-known Jewish author Stefan Zweig, although written under cover of a pen name.[19]

The interest Nazi party leaders took in the German arts was also evident in other fields: architecture, literature, and the plastic arts. They maintained firm control over the artistic and literary repertoires offered to the citizenry. They also "adopted" a number of other favorite musical pieces, most notably Beethoven's *Ode an die Freude* (Ode to Joy) with lyrics by Friedrich Schiller, which was often played during World War II at moments of exultation over new conquests. An extract of Franz Liszt's *Préludes* was played to signal the beginning of news broadcasts; and Carl Orff's bombastic, accessible work *Carmina Burana* was played at Nazi party conventions. Orff was on close terms with the party leaders, and conductors such as Wilhelm Furtwängler and Herbert von Karajan were happy to embark on comfortable careers under the aegis of the Nazi party. They and others benefited from the voluntary exile of many artists from the Third Reich, advancing at meteoric speed to the status of leading conductors. For company they had such well-known performers as the German soprano Elisabeth Schwarzkopf and the Norwegian soprano Kirsten Flagstad, who consented to enliven the leisure hours of senior party members with special concerts.[20]

Wagner, however, remained, in the hands of the Nazi party leaders, a unique artistic tool that could also be used to express concrete political opinions. The propaganda minister, Joseph Goebbels, extolled the composer's contributions to the nation in a speech that was published in a professional music journal.[21] The fact that his remarks were published is indicative not only of the pressure exerted on professional journals to publish articles by Nazi party members, but also of the proliferation of analyses presenting Wagner as a proto-Nazi. Since the Nazis' accession to power, intellectual discussion of Wagner in Germany had mainly involved assessing his role as the spiritual father of National Socialism.

Nonetheless, among the wealth of articles seeking to pour Wagner's philosophy into Nazi molds there were also interpretations focusing on other theoretical aspects of his work, such as his revolutionary tendencies both as a composer and in the political and social spheres.[22] Although Wagner's non-conformism, so antithetical to the norms that the totalitarian Nazi party sought to impose, would eventually become a double-edged sword in the hands of Wagner's admirer, Hitler, Wagner was still the composer whose music was most frequently played in the first years of the Nazi regime, and Hitler's office was decorated with pictures of scenes from *Der Ring des Nibelungen*.[23] With the outbreak of World War II, the Nazis reinforced their link with Wagner once more as they made increasing use of the *Nibelungen* images, stimulating raw memories of national defeat and humiliation in their efforts to revive the heroic aspirations that had been so drastically eroded by World War I. The desire to show the same heroism as their ancestors permitted a revival of the old concepts; thus, the Siegfried Line was resurrected by the Aryan citizens of the Third Reich.

Wagner's other great admirer, Thomas Mann, could not remain indifferent to the Nazi–Wagner symbiosis. About four years after regretting his original willingness to accept the Nazis as a legitimate ruling party, he admitted, as World War II raged, that he found clear traces of proto-Nazism not only in the composer's controversial essays, but also in his music – although Mann had loved his works and was still deeply moved by certain musical passages.[24]

Nevertheless, an end came to both Wagner's great popularity and the conversion of his legacy into an artistic and ideological resource for the Nazis. Wagner's position as the opera composer whose works were most often performed in Germany was eroded during World War II, particularly in the provincial towns. In those years none of his works was among the 10 most frequently heard operas in the German part of the Third Reich.[25] The reason for this decline can be found in documents left not by the Nazis but by Allied theoreticians and propagandists. Apparently at the outset the Nazis had paid attention only to the parts of Wagner's works that called for revolutionary changes in society, without noticing that Wagner in fact advocated a complete destruction of the existing society. This oversight was compounded by a superficial understanding of the Wagnerian savior figures, apparently stemming from a cursory and tendentious reading. Many of Wagner's works do indeed present saviors as sinless heroes who develop a sense of social responsibility and a fair share of personal sensitivity. Yet as often as not, at the climax of such a work these heroes prove to have lied, sinned, or become corrupt, and are punished by a bitter end.

The repeated theme of the Wagnerian hero who is caught up in the vanities of this world and doomed to death is perfectly clear to anyone who is even partially acquainted with Wagner's librettos. Accordingly, it is difficult to understand why Hitler, who knew Wagner's works well, did not perceive the concept of sin and punishment so characteristically associated with Wagner's heroes, and why he did not show greater alertness to the anarchist, even nihilist, overtones of Wagner's creations. Failing to understand the Wagnerian microcosm, Hitler actually embraced the composer's radical ideas, proposing perfect order or complete destruction.[26] But he had not perceived the rigid laws that Wagner laid down in his works: perfect order, complete purity, could be achieved only through total destruction of the existing institutions – an idea that reached its full potential in *Der Ring des Nibelungen*. In other words, the destruction that Hitler saw as the alternative to be sought only after the attempt to establish a perfect system failed was for Wagner mandatory, the sole possibility of creating that perfect, pure structure.

Another explanation for the precipitous decline in Wagner's popularity was the Allies' use of his works for purposes of propaganda. Present-day researchers claim that the *Götterdämmerung* segment of *Der Ring des Nibelungen* was played constantly on BBC counter-propaganda broadcasts, together with warnings that Germany's end would be the same as that of the world of gods presided over by Wotan: complete destruction, and the ruin of the Third Reich, in order to permit the creation of a pure new world. Ironically, that was indeed the Nazis' goal, although, according to Britain, it could be achieved only through their own destruction. There is no direct confirmation of this in the archives of the British Broadcasting Corporation, but other evidence indicates that the Nazis had a rational reason for withdrawing their enthusiastic support of Wagner.[27] *Der Ring des Nibelungen* was performed at the 1942 Bayreuth Festival, but from then on, until the resumption of the festival after the war, this opera was not seen on a public stage. *Die Meistersinger von Nürnberg*, in contrast, was produced a few more times, although the festival gradually sank into decline as Germany's situation on the various fronts deteriorated.

The last nail in the strange edifice that the Nazis built around Wagner was hammered in during the death throes of the Third Reich. The rumor is that before committing suicide Hitler listened to the very work that had served the counter-propaganda effort, *Götterdämmerung*. Although there is no proof whatsoever of this – the Soviets testified that they found the Führer and his mistress, Eva Braun, already dead – surely a more perfect ending could not have been invented for the love affair between the Nazis and Wagner. Hitler may have considered himself unjustly humiliated and scorned, as Wotan was portrayed onstage – a betrayed god who was paying the price for his subjects' crooked behavior.

As soon as World War II ended, intellectuals began trying to dissociate Wagner from his Nazi connections, for fear that the creative giant would be relegated to oblivion if he was identified with the dark side of the modern Western regimes. In general, their efforts were fruitful; Wagner's works continued to be performed on stages throughout Germany and the entire world – except for one country, which made no secret of its opposition: Israel. The usual grounds for Wagner's rejection – his own views and the Nazification of his works – were reinforced by another factor in Israel: the testimony of Holocaust survivors, who reported that Wagner's music had been played in the concentration camps. As in other cases of evidence destroyed during the war, documentation is problematic. And clearly the categorical rejection of Wagner in Israel was not solely attributable to the putative performance of his works in the concentration camps, but also to perceptions of his views and the assumption that Hitler felt a strong bond with him. Yet in my view a close examination of the Wagner affair in Israel will show that its focus was not the composer alone, but much broader and more comprehensive issues.

Notes

1 See H. Ehrlich, "Das Wagner Theater in Bayreuth als deutsches National-Eigentum," *Berliner Tageblatt* 367 (26 July 1888), quoted in S. Grossmann-Vendrey, ed., *Bayreuth in den deutchen Presse: Beiträge zur Rezeptionsgeschichte Richard Wagners und seine Festspiele. Dokumentenband 3,1: Von Wagners Tod bis zum Ende der Äre Cosima Wagner (1883–1906)* (Regensburg, 1983), pp. 68–9.
2 See M. G. Conrad, "Bayreuth in die deutsche Kultur," *Die Propyläen: Literarisch-belletristische Halbwochenschrift der Münchener Zeitung* 74 (30 June 1905), quoted in Grossman-Vendrey, *Bayreuth in der deutsch Presse*, p. 205. The author of the article was referring to Schiller's well-known essays on esthetics: F. Schiller, *On the Aesthetic Education of Man*, trans. R. Shell (New York, 1965; 1st edn. 1954).
3 Darwin raised this idea for the first time in 1859, in a book he wrote after returning from a long sea voyage on the Beagle to the southern hemisphere. His theory created a sensation in academic circles, and 13 years later Darwin published a new edition, in which he responded to all his critics. See C. R. Darwin, *The Origins of Species by Means of Natural Selection* (various editions). In 1871, Darwin also aroused the anger of the Church, which viewed his book on the origins of man as a challenge to the secrets of the divine creation. See C. R. Darwin, *The Descent of Man, and Election in Relation to Sex* (various editions).
4 On the beginnings of German nationalism, see P. Viereck, *Metapolitics: The Roots of the Nazi Mind* (New York, 1961), pp. 77–80. On the relationship between physical education and nationalist concepts in Germany, see H. Kohn, "Father Jahn and the War against the West," Chap. 4 in *The Mind of Germany*, pp. 69–98. In a way, Father Jahn developed the basic idea that Jean-Jacques Rousseau had introduced in his famous *Emile* (1762). Rousseau claimed that a good intellectual spirit could be brought up only in the right environment – one that combined physical and intellectual exercise.
5 On the appropriation of Wagner's legacy in the years after his death, see D. C. Large, "Wagner's Bayreuth Disciples," in *Wagnerianism in European Culture and Politics*, ed. D. C. Large and W. Weber (Ithaca and London, 1984), pp. 72–133. On racist views in the years before the advent of Nazism, see Viereck, *Metapolitics*.
6 On the anti-Semitic atmosphere in Germany that led to the blatant racism culminating in the activities of the Nazi party, see U. Tal, *Christians and Jews in Germany: Religion, Politics and Ideology in the Second Reich, 1870–1914* (Ithaca and New York, 1974).
7 See H. S. Chamberlain, *Richard Wagner* (Munich, 1896). His comments on the significance of "Greater Germany" can be found on p. 112. It should be noted that the Nazis, too, believed that Wagner had a complete religious philosophy, and imposed a ban on performances of his last opera, Parsifal, in 1939, on the grounds that it contained too much Christian content. See Y. Cohen, "Wagner Nonetheless," [Hebrew], in *Who's Afraid*, p. 293.
8 On Chamberlain's anti-Semitic opinions, see, for example, H. S. Chamberlain, "Die Bayreuther Festspiele," *Die Zukunft* 16, No. 3 (1896), quoted by Grossmann-Vendrey, *Bayreuth in der deutsche Presse*, pp. 145–56. On the significance of these opinions, see D. C. Large, "Ein Spiegel des

Meisters? Die Rassenlehre von Houston Stewart Chamberlain," in *Wagner und die Juden*, ed. D. Borchmeyer et al. pp. 144–9.

9   On the nature of the periodical and its anti-Semitic overtones through the years, see A. Hein, *"Es ist viel Hitler in Wagner": Rassismus und antisemitische Deutschtumsideologie in den Bayreuther Blättern (1878 bis 1938)* (Tübingen, 1996).

10 A comprehensive work on the subject has been published. See J. Köhler, *Wagners Hitler: Der Prophet und sein Vollstreker* (Munich, 1997). Köhler suggests a genuinely symbiotic link between Hitler and Wagner, seeing the nineteenth-century composer as a critical source of inspiration for Hitler specifically and for the Nazi regime in general. On the absence of references to Wagner in Hitler's writings, and on the significance of that absence, see S. Friedländer, "Bayreuth und der Erlösungsantisemitismus," in *Wagner und die Juden*, ed. D. Borchmeyer et al. pp. 8–19.

11 On the Wagner family's relations with Hitler, see F. Wagner and P. Cooper, *Heritage of Fire: The Story of Richard Wagner's Granddaughter* (New York and London, 1945). Evidence for Friedelind Wagner's assertions can be found in the introduction Ralph Giordano wrote for a book by Gottfried Wagner, the composer's great-grandson. See G. Wagner, *Wer nicht mit dem Wolf heult: Autobiographische Aufzeichnungen eines Wagner-Urenkels* (Cologne, 1997), pp. 11–28. Gottfried Wagner also calls for an open discussion regarding the composer's worldview. See G. Wagner, "On the Need to Debate Richard Wagner in an Open Society: How to Confront Wagner Today Beyond Glorification and Condemnation," in *Richard Wagner for the New Millennium*, ed. M. Bribitzer-Stull, A. Lubet and G. Wagner (New York, 2007), pp. 3–24. On Hitler's conception of art as a propaganda instrument to serve the cause of the Nazi movement, see A. Perris, *Music as Propaganda: Art to Persuade, Art to Control* (Connecticut and London, 1985); and R. S. Wistrich, *Weekend in Munich: Art, Propaganda and Terror in the Third Reich* (London, 1995). On the putsch in Munich, see K. D. Bracher, *The German Dictatorship: The Origins, Structure and Consequences of National Socialism* (Middlesex, 1985; 1st edn. 1969), pp. 122–58.

12 On Grosz's drawing, see G. Grosz, "Illustration zum Titelblatt der 'Pleite', November 1923," in *Die Nibelungen*, ed. W. Storch (Munich, 1987), p. 254. On the widespread political use of concepts from the *Nibelungen* legend, see H. Münkler, "Mythischer Sinn: Der Nibelungenmythos in der politischen Symbolik des 20. Jahrhunderts," in *In den Trümmern der Eigen Welt: Richard Wagners "Der Ring des Nibelungen,"* ed. U. Bermbach (Berlin and Hamburg, 1989), pp. 251–66. On the medieval cartoon, see "Hitler Einzug in Berlin," *Simplicissimus*, Munich, 1 April 1924, in Hitler in der Karikatur der Welt, ed. E. Hanfstaengl (Berlin, 1935), p. 19.

13 On Hitler's increasingly close relations with the management of the Bayreuth festival, see Köhler, *Wagner's Hitler*, pp. 347–82; and also R. G. L. Waite, *The Psychopathic God: Adolf Hitler* (New York, 1978), p. 265. On Hitler's ceaseless preoccupation with the issue of Wagner and Bayreuth, see the interesting testimony of the "house director" of the Nazi propaganda bureau, Leni Riefenstahl, *Memoiren* (Munich and Hamburg, 1987), p. 159.

14 On Lang's film, see F. Tomburg, "Faschismusverständnis im Schatten Richard Wagners," *Dialektik, Beiträge zu Philosophie Wissenschaften:*

Antisemitismus 7 (1983): 202–23. On the first radio broadcasts from the festival, see O. G. Bauer, "Das sichtbare und unsichtbare Theater: Zur Geschichte von Funk, Fernsehen und Schallplate im Festspielhaus," in *Bayreuth 1980: Rückblick und Vorschau* (Bayreuth, 1979), unnumbered pages.

15 For full statistics on opera performances throughout Germany, including provincial towns, see F. H. Köhler, *Struktur der Spielpläne Deutschsprachiger Opernbühnen von 1896 bis 1966*, pp. 53–6, lecture delivered at the Schul- und kulturstatistik conference in Koblenz, 16–17 May 1968.

16 T. Mann, "The Sorrows and Grandeur of Richard Wagner," (10 Feb. 1933), in *Thomas Mann: Pro and Contra Wagner*, trans. A. Blunden (London and Boston, 1985), pp. 96–7. See also R. Wagner, "Judaism in Music," in *Stories and Essays*, trans. C. Osborne (London, 1973), pp. 23–39; and Katz, *Richard Wagner*, pp. 59–79.

17 On the Nazis' cultural ideology, see G. L. Mosse, *Nazi Culture: Intellectual, Cultural and Social Life in the Third Reich* (New York, 1981; 1st edn. 1966). The cartoon appeared in *The New York Times* on 2 April 1933, and has been reprinted in *Hitler in der Karikatur der Welt*, ed. Hanfstaengl, p. 144.

18 Quoted in G. G. Windell, "Hitler, National Socialism, and Richard Wagner," in *Penetrating Wagner's Ring: An Anthology*, ed. J. L. DiGaetani (New Jersey and London, 1974), p. 227.

19 On Hitler's personal involvement in the cultural life of the Third Reich, see K. Backes, *Hitler und die bildenen Künste: Kulturveständnis und Kunstpolitik im Dritten Reich* (Cologne, 1988). On the Nazi party's involvement in cultural life in general and the musical world in particular, see H. Hinkel, ed., *Handbuch der Reichskulturkammer* (Berlin, 1937); and E. Kroll, "Verbotene Musik," *Vierteljahrhefte für Zeitgeschichte* III (July 1959): 310–17. On musical life in the Third Reich, see E. Levi, *Music in the Third Reich* (London, 1994).

20 Cohen, "Wagner Nevertheless," p. 294; R. Grunberger, *The 12-Year Reich: A Social History of Nazi Germany, 1933–1945* (New York, Chicago, and San Francisco, 1971), pp. 406–12; G. L. Mosse, *Nazi Culture*; and J. Petropoulos, *Art as Politics in the Third Reich* (Chapel Hill and London, 1996).

21 See "Reichsminister Dr. Goebbels Huldigt Richard Wagner," *Die Musik* XXV, No. 12 (Sept. 1933): 952–54.

22 See, for example, E. Valentin, "Richard Wagner politischer Glaube: Eine Beweisführung aus Zeit und Werk," *Bayreuther Blätter* 60, No. 1 (1937): 12–13.

23 The opera statistics are cited in Köhler, *Struktur der Spielpläne*, p. 54. On Hitler's office decor, see Münkler, "Mythischer Sinn," p. 262.

24 T. Mann, "To the Editor of Common Sense (January 1940)," in T. Mann, *Wagner und unsere Zeit: Aufsätze, Betrachtungen, Briefe* (Frankfurt a.M., 1983), p. 158.

25 J. Köhler, *Wagners Hitler*, pp. 54–6.

26 See Hitler's speech in the Reichstag: *Führerbotschaft an Volk und Welt: Reichstagrede vom 20. Februar 1938* (Zentralverlag der NSDAP, Munich, 1938), p. 7.

27 See Cohen, "Wagner Nevertheless," p. 293. Some evidence for such references to Wagner's works and especially "the Siegfried idyll," can be found in

the BBC archives: "BBC Internal Memo: Copyright Music by Enemy Alien Composers," 24 April 1941, in BBC Archives, London. The activities of the counter-propaganda stations in the war have been well-documented. On the working methods the British passed on to their American allies, see L. C. Soley, *Radio Warfare: OSS and CIA Subservice Propaganda* (New York, Westport, and London, 1989).

4

Music, Politics, and Morality: The Beginning of the Boycott in Palestine

One of the first direct links between Richard Wagner and the *Yishuv* in Palestine was a 1908 article titled "Richard Wagner and the Jews" published in the Jerusalem newspaper *Hashkafa*, edited by Eliezer Ben-Yehuda. While explaining the main themes of Wagner's "Judaism in Music," the author, music ethnographer Avraham Zvi Ben Yehuda (Idelson), argued that Wagner had sensed the desire of assimilated Jews to unite and revive their ancient nation. He ends his interpretation hoping that the anti-Semitic essay would be distributed among all Jews, as propaganda against assimilation and in favor of the adoption of their true identity.[1] This publication attests to the fact that some Jews realized the danger and potential impact of Wagner's anti-Semitic writing. Nevertheless, in 1928, 20 year later, a Hebrew translation of a children's version of *Lohengrin* based on Wagner's libretto was published. By that time Wagner was well known among the *Yishuv* intellectuals as one of the geniuses of modern German culture. Up to the 1920s, at least, his musical oeuvre was deeply appreciated in Palestine, and his admirers downplayed and even ignored his anti-Semitic remarks, so the publication of the *Lohengrin* retelling was perfectly natural.[2] Ten years later, when the Nazi noose was tightening around the necks of the Jews, the *Yishuv* still viewed Wagner as a cultured German. Only two and a half months before *Kristallnacht* a Jewish publicist in Palestine saluted German culture, which he described as "full of geniuses," saying among other things, that "Nietzsche and Wagner are the last representatives of glorious Germany"[3] – the same Germany that the *Yishuv* saw as an emblem and model that was turning bad before their very eyes.

The positive images of Germany were integrally linked to the ascendancy of German culture throughout Europe in the last years of the nineteenth century and the early years of the twentieth. They also represented direct continuation of the general appreciation Jews had felt for German culture since the period of the Enlightenment. The first cultural contacts between Jews and Germans had been established back in the latter half of the eighteenth century, when intellectual dialog between the eminent philosophers of the Enlightenment had been stimulated by the German Jew Moses Mendelssohn and his German colleagues, particularly Gotthold Ephraim Lessing. Their exchange of ideas about religious tolerance and the integration of Jews into the European citizenry laid the foundations for the special bond that would develop between the two sides. Examining the issue of the integration of the Jews as European subjects with equal rights, Mendelssohn turned to his coreligionists on the continent, particularly in the large Jewish communities of Eastern Europe and the German principalities. He advised (or rather commanded) them to make an unequivocal choice between their traditional Jewish cultural life and a more complete assimilation into the civil life around them. The aim was intellectual freedom and emancipation from the state of limbo, in which they preserved their own culture and embraced the local culture in which they lived – a situation epitomized by the use of the hybrid Yiddish language as the main language in the Jewish ghettoes.[4]

Obviously, different groups of Jews dithered over the question of their cultural and national character up to the nineteenth century, and their wide-ranging discussions on the subject did not reach any final conclusions until the turn of the century or later. Meanwhile Jewish attachment to German culture rapidly grew stronger. In addition to increasingly close ties with German intellectuals, acquaintance with German culture in general expanded through at least two channels. The German principalities gave Jews free access to universities – although upon completing their studies graduates were confronted with an employment system that preferred non-Jewish workers. The German policy differed from that of the Eastern European academic bodies, which set quotas (*numerus clausus*) to limit the number of Jews benefiting from higher education. Thus, under the circumstances of the times, German universities were the natural place for the Jews of Eastern and Central Europe to study, and Jewish students subsequently took back to their communities of origin both what they had been taught and the cultural inflections they had absorbed in the course of their studies. In this way young Jewish scholars became agents of German culture throughout Europe, especially among the large Jewish population in Eastern Europe.[5]

Another way in which Jews became acquainted with German culture was through emigration. The German principalities were the first to grant emancipation to the Jews, acting on the constitutional principles of the German Second Reich, which had been developed in Prussia even before German unification. As a result, modern Germany became the favored destination of Jewish emigrants from Eastern Europe, whether they were merely seeking relief from a life of hardship and persecution, or complete assimilation in Central Europe. Although such immigrants were not always welcomed and did not necessarily strike roots, they were strongly influenced by German culture. Moreover, since they had chosen to move to Germany in the first place, they were probably favorably disposed toward the country and its culture from the outset.[6]

This deep, long-term assimilation of German culture was expressed even after some of Europe's Jews fulfilled their nationalist dreams by immigrating to Palestine; the influence of German ideas was evident in many aspects of activity in the Jewish settlement in Palestine. German views were reflected in the processes of urban and rural settlement, German thinking characterized many of the educational and social welfare institutions and financial bodies, and many cultural bodies bore a German imprint. The extensive influence of German ideas was attributable not only to widespread familiarity with German culture in Europe, but also to the complex cultural structure of the *Yishuv*. This structure offered a variety and scope that were enormous in relation to the immediate needs of the meager Jewish population; it was based on the European model most familiar to the newly arrived immigrants.[7]

At the beginning of the 1920s, the *Yishuv* in Palestine numbered some 80,000 Jews. Despite the community's limited size and the Spartan pioneer living conditions in some areas, a rich and extensive cultural life developed. In the 1920s, after the temporary silence imposed by World War I, the *Yishuv* enjoyed a cultural renaissance. In the new cafés a range of locally published and imported newspapers and magazines were read; and during the 1930s, as silent movies were joined by "talkies," some were subtitled for Hebrew audiences. On improvised stages ever-growing professional theatrical efforts could be seen, while the writers, translators, and editors streaming into Palestine turned it into the new Hebrew literary center. A Jewish opera company was founded in Palestine, and chamber music concerts became increasingly common.

However, in the late 1920s the economic boom in the *Yishuv* began to die down. The 1926 depression was compounded by the 1929 Riots, which were the result of the Arab community's fear of Jewish financial dominance.[8] The unrest in the economic and security spheres might have been expected to moderate cultural expansion in the *Yishuv*, but in fact the commercial crisis had a fairly limited effect on the cultural scene, and innovations flourished in the arts and in intellectual life. The opera company founded by Mordechai Golinkin began functioning on a modest scale, existing theaters continued operations, and others were founded – albeit some, such as the Eretz-Yisrael Theater, left the country on educational tours to Europe. Meanwhile Palestine became the world center of Hebrew literature.

On the face of it, the scope of cultural activity was astounding and excessive, since the Jewish population was small and the number of consumers of Hebrew culture within it even smaller. But the leaders of Hebrew cultural life in Palestine – intellectuals, writers, musicians, theater people – were apparently trying to establish a cultural infrastructure based on the model they remembered from Europe. Thus, for example, during the years of the *Yishuv* a variety of theaters were founded – classic, proletarian, avant-garde, and satirical; publishing houses began to specialize in different genres – novels and poetry, plays, socialist ideology, sciences and textbooks; a few musical bodies were set up and began performing a wide repertoire ranging from chamber music to opera; and the press expanded in various directions – news, politics, and special interests. All of these offered consumers not only an impressive array of cultural options, but also helped to sharpen their critical senses.[9]

The effort to create a cultural life modeled on the European one – although this goal was not completely achieved for various reasons – engendered a constant demand for up-to-date information on the cultural developments in the countries of origin of the Jews in Palestine. The general admiration of Germany inspired particularly strong interest in German culture – not only among immigrants from Central Europe, but also among those from the eastern part of the continent. Both the daily papers and various other periodicals helped keep the population abreast of new developments; besides daily news from Europe, the press printed reports and critical essays on the cultural activity on the continent. Special-interest weeklies and other publications devoted considerable space to European cultural life and its institutions, often comparing them to equivalent institutions in Palestine and evoking the special needs of the evolving community. These periodicals included not only artistic and literary magazines, but publications, such as party organs, that were not specifically oriented toward cultural interests. The pages of these publications reveal the extent to which the Jews in Palestine regarded themselves Europeans, ignoring the geographical and demographic conditions in which they lived.

The accelerated local cultural development, together with the close watch kept on cultural developments in Europe in general and Germany in particular, opened the way to debates on Wagner and his oeuvre in the Hebrew press. Together with their warm approval of the cultural heritage that the Germans had bestowed upon the Western world, Hebrew publicists showed an impressive alertness to the new political involvement in cultural spheres in Germany – including in Bayreuth. Most probably their specific interest in the cultural sphere – and their response to the developments there – stemmed from the way the Jewish population in Europe originally viewed German culture. The Jews of Europe, particularly the large Jewish population of Eastern Europe, had long seen the Germans as the shapers of Europe's most successful cultural model, and so it was only natural that when the familiar institutions of the German state came under fire, Jews were concerned about the fate of the specific model that was their cultural guide. The members of the *Yishuv*, who at the time were largely of East European origin, showed special interest in the intellectual developments taking place in Germany.

Their awareness was particularly remarkable given the political impotence of the leaders of both the *Yishuv* and world Zionism when
confronted with Nazism. Journalistic disapproval of the nationalist views
of German artists fueled the generally militant response of Hebrew culture
toward the political and social developments in Germany. Journalists
directed their general opposition to Nazi ideas through cultural channels,
and Bayreuth was their special target. They perceived German
Gleichschaltung (uniformity) largely through a cultural lens, and this
focus may have blinded them somewhat to this characteristic's significance in the political sphere.

However, even before the National Socialist Party took up the reins of
government in Germany, Jewish intellectuals in Palestine had begun to
develop a sensitivity that Jews had previously lacked vis-à-vis the racist
and nationalist interpretations of Wagner's writings. One example was
their new view of a German writer much admired at the time, both in the
Yishuv and throughout the Western world: Nobel Prize winner Thomas
Mann. Around the time that Mann received the prestigious award, the
publicist Rabbi Benjamin (Yehoshua Radler-Feldmann) published a series
of articles on Mann's works, including interesting insights regarding the
link between Wagner and aberrant nationalist ideas. In the second article
in the series Rabbi Benjamin spoke of one of Mann's artistic idols, Richard
Wagner, and described the way Mann had listened to a performance of
Siegfrieds Tod in the Piazza Colonna in Rome:

> His knees give way in his excitement, but he does not applaud, since the
> pressure of the crowd makes it impossible for him to move his hands;
> he does not join in the shouts, for his throat is tight; but as the *Notung*
> motif [the sword motif in *Der Ring des Nibelungen*] builds, tears run
> down his cheeks, he smiles, and his heart beats with the turbulence of
> youth [. . .]. The name of that young man was Thomas Mann [. . .]
> in the days of the [First] World War [. . .] he turned out to be a nation-
> alist German. He mistakenly thought that Germany's politicians were
> right. Later on in the war this position was considered an enormous sin
> among the intelligentsia.[10]

This criticism of Thomas Mann, rather than of the Nazis or the attitudes expressed by Wagner which pleased the Nazis, may be indicative of
a profound familiarity with Mann's writings and with the interesting
triangle constituted by Mann, the Nazis, and Wagner. The yearning for
and attraction to Wagner – which the *Yishuv* may also have been familiar
with from Mann's short stories and novellas – was associated with the
nationalist tendencies in Europe in general which were viewed as an ideological sin.[11] Some three years later, the theater monthly *Bama*, published
by Habima Theater, printed an account of the impressive eulogy Mann
delivered on the anniversary of Wagner's death. The editors of *Bama*

stressed parts of the eulogy that focused on Wagner's important role in German culture, and on that culture's central role in the essence of modern life, Wagner's psychological insights and honest, revolutionary approach to the world.[12]

Although this short report from Bayreuth was printed in May 1933, it failed to include one important fact: The eulogy was delivered at Munich University five days after the last democratic elections in the Weimar Republic at the beginning of February 1933. Despite the fact that this omission may be interpreted as evidence of the separation of art and state, it is still rather peculiar. If the Jews in Palestine were indeed sensitive to the issue of German nationalism and Wagner's link to it, surely they would have emphasized the Nazis' rise to power in their periodicals. But the press of the 1930s reflected both a fear of what was to come and an uninterrupted and unrestrained predilection for German culture.

About six months before the National Socialists emerged from the elections as the largest party in the Reichstag, the last Bayreuth Festival to be held under a democratic regime took place. In October 1932, about two months after the annual festival, when the National Socialist Party was still in the opposition but by then held about a fifth of the seats in the Reichstag, the critic Menashe Rabinovich (Rabina) commented in Palestine on the ominous appropriation of the Wagner Festival. Although his remarks were somewhat late, some seven years after Bayreuth's adoption by Hitler and the Nazi movement, his uneasiness at the sight of the Nazis appropriating a cultural institution clearly reflected his recognition that Bayreuth was only the tip of the iceberg of Nazi efforts to subordinate similar institutions to their own ideological system. In other words, some six months before the National Socialist Party raked in nearly half of all German votes, it was clear to Hebrew publicists that culture was unlikely to remain separate from politics in Nazi Germany – as Rabinovich explained to the readers of the literary journal *Moznaim*:

> Winifred [Wagner] treats the Bayreuth Theater as her own. She chose her advisors not from among musicians, but from among party officials. Hitler's name is sometimes mentioned in allusion to the widow Wagner. The swastika is often seen on the clothing of the critics. Bayreuth, that obscure corner that had only music to bring it fame and glory, threatens to become an impediment to music in its subordination to non-musical purposes.[13]

For the time being, Rabinovich's apprehension focused solely on the politicization of a cultural institution – understandably enough, since the Nazi movement was still busy shifting to the center of political life in Germany; only a clairvoyant could have predicted what was to come. Yet Rabinovich's remarks anticipated the approach the Nazis were to later adopt. They saw culture and its institutions as prime instruments for cleansing Germany of harmful elements and replacing them with the militant "Aryan" ideas they admired.

However, in the years when the National Socialist Party was climbing to power, the vague concern initially inspired by Nazism gradually turned into a sense of real threat. The immediate injury to the Jews of Germany prompted a wave of emigration out of the German-speaking region in general and the Third Reich in particular, but only ripples reached Palestine. Paradoxically, at the outset the Nazi threat to Jews encouraged cultural development in Palestine. This peculiar situation was a result of the social class of the new immigrants: unlike earlier immigrants, a substantial proportion of the new arrivals were well-educated members of the liberal professions. Their presence in the *Yishuv* made it possible to establish not only new organizational infrastructures requiring skilled workers, but also one of the major cultural bodies of the *Yishuv* (and later the State of Israel): an orchestra.[14]

The creation of the Palestine Symphony Orchestra in 1936 was largely the result of country's attraction for Central European musicians seeking a safe haven – a haven where they could continue to work in their profession without having to go through the usual throes of immigration. Unlike members of other liberal professions, they began working immediately and postponed study of the local language to a later stage. Moreover, contrary to other institutions in which employment depended on knowledge of the Hebrew language, the Palestine Symphony Orchestra imposed no linguistic conditions, since the founder, the Polish Jewish violinist Bronisław Huberman, wanted to get the orchestra functioning as soon as possible – with the assistance of the best international artists.[15]

Huberman achieved his goal, managing to import talented and experienced musicians to Palestine and procuring distinguished conductors and soloists, some of them Jews, who at the time constituted an important part of the core of top musical talent in the world. Yet Huberman also encountered a significant complication: None of the great names in the music world would accept the post of musical director in a place that was not yet a country and where there was no concert hall worthy of its name. As a result, the orchestra's early repertoire was designed by several conductors and Huberman himself.[16]

In their concert programs the European conductors included the best of the European musical tradition. As might be expected, the repertoire also incorporated a few works by Richard Wagner, who was considered one of the great German composers of the nineteenth century and whose work was a cornerstone of the repertoires of many Western orchestras. In 1938, for example, three conductors included works by Wagner on concert programs in Palestine: in April Arturo Toscanini conducted the preludes to the first and third acts of *Lohengrin*; in June and July the orchestra played the overture to *Tanhäuser* under the baton of Jascha Hornstein; and the orchestra's first violinist, Bronisław Szulk, who conducted one of the July concerts, chose to include the overture to *Der fliegende Holländer* (The Flying Dutchman).

The case of Toscanini is worth closer investigation. Toscanini had gone into voluntary exile from Fascist Italy, unable to stomach the new regime. Germany's Nazi leaders did not believe that Toscanini would allow his political views to dictate his career, and invited him more than once to participate in musical events in the Third Reich. In this respect, Toscanini established one clear-cut rule of conduct: he adamantly refused to appear anymore at the Bayreuth Festivals, claiming that the Festspielhaus had become a party center in every respect. Reiterating the arguments he had voiced in his own homeland, he expressed opposition to all dictatorial regimes on principle and insisted that art should not be identified with politics. However – and perhaps because of this insistence – the celebrated maestro continued to incorporate orchestral pieces by Wagner in the concerts he conducted around the world, and to this day those concerts are considered to have been particularly interesting interpretations.[17]

The concerts of the Palestine Symphony Orchestra held in the Tel Aviv fairgrounds (the old exhibition grounds) and movie theaters in Jerusalem, Haifa, and Ramat Gan, were received with a great deal of enthusiasm. At this point no one expressed any objections to Wagner as the author of an anti-Jewish indictment; no apprehensions concerning the situation in Bayreuth were evident; and no one commented on Wagner's status as the composer most closely identified with the Nazi regime. Any reservations about Wagner's work related only to the great difficulty of performing it— and, indeed, the Wagnerian repertoire in Palestine consisted exclusively of overtures. At that point it was clear that even a cooperative effort between the opera house founded by Golinkin and the new orchestra would not prove equal to the task of putting on such large and complex productions; and, moreover, Palestine did not yet have a concert hall suitable for such an endeavor.[18]

The extensive repertoire of the orchestra was ideologically challenged following the organized pogrom against Germany's Jews on the night between November 9th and 10th 1938. Within a day reports on the events of *Kristallnacht* reached the Jewish *Yishuv* in Palestine. It was these pogroms that jolted the leaders of the *Yishuv* into taking a firmer line in their attitudes towards European policy in general, and Nazi Germany in particular; they now spoke for the first time of a *Shoah* (Holocaust) rather than pogroms.[19] Although the local press had addressed the dangers presented by the Nazi regime before, *Kristallnacht* was immediately perceived as a point of no return, the beginning of a new national catastrophe comparable to the expulsion of the Jews from Spain and Portugal in 1492.[20]

The opening concert in the series was planned for the following Saturday evening, November 12th. It may well be that the total silence of the German intellectuals prompted the orchestra's founder, Bronisław

Huberman, to respond immediately by removing the prelude to *Die Meistersinger von Nürnberg* from the program. As a political personality, Huberman was aware of the negative changes that had affected German Jews since the Nazis' rise to power. He refused an invitation sent by Wilhelm Furtwängler to appear in Nazi Germany and wrote him harsh letters in 1933. After the Nazi race laws came into effect in February 1936, he published an open and critical letter to German intellectuals in *The Manchester Guardian*. The orchestra he had established in Palestine became the home of Jews who had previously performed in well-known European orchestras and had decided to leave their country due to anti-Semitic persecution and the enforcement of Germany's racist laws.

The circumstances were obvious: the plot of *Die Meistersinger* was associated with medieval German culture, now compared with the belligerent Nazi regime of the time; the composer, Richard Wagner, was a renowned member of anti-Semitic circles despite the fact that he was helped by Jews in his work.[21] The chairperson of the orchestra's executive, Moshe Chelouche, one of Tel Aviv's notable figures, approached Eugen Szenkár who was to conduct the concert that evening. Szenkár could easily relate to the sentiments as he was on the list of 108 artists who had been banned by the Nazi Propaganda Minister, Joseph Goebbels.[22] He replaced Wagner's piece with the overture to *Oberon*, written by an earlier German composer, Carl Maria von Weber, who was, inter alia, the object of Wagner's admiration.

The affair ended relatively quietly, and was reported as a minor news item rather than a major ideological issue. The news reports printed in Cairo, Alexandria, Istanbul, and London, related for the most part to the opening of the season, although they all mentioned the influence of the political events in Germany on the concert and on the removal of the Wagner piece from the program. Only one Italian newspaper saw the Wagner affair as central – perhaps because the reporter himself lived under a regime that used art for political purposes.[23] The full significance of the cancellation was realized only years later, after the State of Israel had been founded and Wagner had been converted into a symbol of Nazism. Since the change was decided on only at the last minute, the programs were not revised.

Apparently, consideration for the feelings of the *Yishuv* audience was not in the nature of a real political declaration, since a few months after this incident, in February 1939, Szenkár himself conducted pieces by Wagner (the preludes to the first and third acts of *Lohengrin* and the overture and the Bacchanalia of *Tanhäuser*) during the orchestra's tour of Cairo and Alexandria. But in Palestine itself, the removal of a Wagnerian work from the program of one concert marked a permanent change in the orchestra's repertoire. From the cancellation in 1938 until the end of the period of the *Yishuv*, the orchestra never again played any Wagner compositions. No one could have imagined that the single cancellation would turn into a permanent one. Moreover, it was impossible to expect that Wagner would be put to use as a component of Israeli identity in years to come, and finally as a common symbol of the Holocaust and its commemoration. In future years "Wagner" became a concept that bonded Israelis of various cultures.[24]

As time passed and more and more reports were received concerning the nature of the Nazi regime, it became clear that this form of political opposition to Nazism was too little and too late. The way the Nazi regime used the Festspielhaus in Bayreuth only added to the feeling that the removal of the Wagner piece from the concert had been justified and represented an approach that was eminently reasonable if not imperative under the circumstances. Taken off the repertoire for political reasons, Wagner could not be reinstated as one of the major nineteenth-century German composers. He remained taboo, and the stain that adhered to him as an accomplice to the sinister deeds of the Nazis expanded even further.

If the Jews in Palestine needed further justification for the cancellation, they might have found it in Wagner's popularity among Nazi party officials. From early on in the Third Reich Wagner was one of the Nazi leaders' favorite composers – not only because of the quality of the music but also – and primarily – because some of Wagner's writings on intellectual and esthetic subjects could be interpreted as nationalistic, if not racist. Thus, as mentioned earlier, parts of his quintessentially German work *Die Meistersinger von Nürnberg* were played at Nazi party conventions, and Hitler kept proclaiming his admiration for Wagner, even making frequent use of the *Nibelung* images that were so closely identified with the composer. Wagner's works were used in several scenes in pro-Nazi and anti-Semitic movies. Concert interludes appeared in Leni Riefenstahl's film, *Triumph des Willens* (Triumph of the Will), which documented the National Socialist Party convention in Nuremberg in 1934; much later, in November 1940, a passage from "Judaism in Music" was quoted in a frightening and preposterous propaganda film, *Der Ewige Jude* (The Eternal Jew), which dehumanized Jews. Another propaganda feature, *Jud Süss* (Jew Süss, September 1940), drew a sharp contrast between the pure German *Lieder* and the mumbling in the synagogue – a theme that probably reflected Wagner's comments in "Judaism in Music."[25] Yet until *Kristallnacht*, *Yishuv* intellectuals continued to separate their attitude toward Wagner's political views in the Nazi context and their great appreciation for his music and its significance in the modern musical world.

The revised approach to Wagner that began in the 1930s reflected the ambivalent attitude of the Jews in Palestine toward Germany and its culture, and their responses to the Third Reich on various levels. This ambivalence had been perceptible in Palestine as early as the beginning of the century, although obviously without the Nazi context. As mentioned earlier, many of the infrastructures established in the *Yishuv* were originally based on familiar German norms. However, at the same time the

German Jews' deep involvement in some of the more prestigious educational institutions in Palestine and their efforts to impose the use of the German language there engendered profound resentment among the rest of the population that felt that this coercion would hinder the formation of a national Zionist entity in Palestine. Matters had reached a head over the "language war" (1914) generated by resistance to the universal instruction in German in the institutions of the *Hilfsverein der deutsche Juden* (Association for Aid to German Jews) and in the Technion (Institute of Technology) in Haifa.[26]

In the 1930s, the years of the great waves of immigration from the German-speaking countries, resistance to the widespread use of German reappeared with a vengeance. The trouble new immigrants from Central Europe seemed to have in learning Hebrew led various bodies, from the Histadrut (General Federation of Labor) to the newspaper publishing committee, to tighten requirements concerning Hebrew fluency, and to be stricter with educated new immigrants who proved recalcitrant. The Association of German Immigrants, an independent organization set up to assist immigrants from German-speaking countries to strike roots in Palestine, encountered strong opposition to what was perceived as separatism.[27]

At the same time, Germany continued to provide a significant proportion of the cultural offerings available to the denizens of the *Yishuv*. Concert programs were studded with works of German composers; plays originally written in German – often by Jews – were translated into Hebrew and formed the core of theatrical repertoires; and editors and translators rendered German works by both Jews and non-Jews into Hebrew.[28] In short, German culture played several roles in the *Yishuv*; it was both a model for various social patterns, and a tool in the resistance to domination by those patterns.

Only when the true nature of the Nazi regime in Germany became apparent – for the Jews in Palestine the moment of truth was *Kristallnacht* – did the adoption of German culture turn into a weapon. The ambivalence toward German culture disappeared and was replaced by determined opposition, although limited to specific matters. From now on works by people admired by the Nazis, including Wagner, were carefully scrutinized, and musicians who worked in the Third Reich of their own free will were considered taboo by the *Yishuv*. It is worthy of note that other musicians, who, like Wagner, were no longer living but whose works had been adopted by the Nazis – notably Beethoven and Liszt – did not disappear from the concert programs in Palestine. In the world of translation, the *Yishuv* went one better: Works by writers whom the Nazis perceived as harmful elements, whether Jews or opponents of the regime, were zealously translated into Hebrew. In this way works banned in the Third Reich were preserved, allowing the *Yishuv* to feel that it was at least responding in some way to the perverse deeds of the Nazis despite the enormous difficulty of taking any real political action. At the same time, however, those writers perceived as major German thinkers continued to be accepted as such by Jewish intellectuals in Palestine. An interesting example was the translation and publication of some of Wagner's epigrams in the theater monthly *Bama*, which printed a selection of quotations from great thinkers and creators in all the 1940 issues.

During the years that German culture was employed to send subtle political signals, its contribution to the cultural inventory in Palestine grew by leaps and bounds. Its centrality, however, could not protect it from political hostility, a hostility that began to overshadow accepted artistic criteria for judging the quality and significance of the works imported to the *Yishuv*. In the context of Palestine, it was obvious from the end of the 1930s, and even more so during the 1940s, that German culture had become another victim of the Nazi regime. Works were judged on the basis of the Nazis' attitude toward them, and as a result, entire cultural categories were rejected. The negative attitude toward the German language, which had begun with the desire to eradicate multilingualism in the *Yishuv*, became genuine revulsion toward everything the Nazis represented.

At the end of World War II a few significant changes occurred in attitudes toward Germany and, by the same token, its culture. On the practical, political level, revenge squads was formed that sent members to Europe to "settle accounts" with the Nazis – in fact, to locate and kill those senior officials of the regime who were still living. In Palestine, efforts were made to take in refugees from the death camps – an enterprise that lasted well into the 1950s – and many resources were devoted to commemorating the communities that had been destroyed.[29] In the cultural sphere several very different steps were taken. For one thing, the years between the end of the war and the foundation of the State of Israel were peak years for the translation of books from German to Hebrew, particularly books by Jews – an undertaking that had served as a weapon in the tenacious war against the Nazi book bans. At the same time, the written testimony of Holocaust survivors, translated from various languages, was being published, the most famous example being the translation of *Salamandra*, by Yehiel Dinur (K. Zetnik), first published in 1947.

Another substantial change in the attitude to German culture stemmed from reports by refugees and concentration camp survivors that Jews had been marched off to the gas chambers to the strains of Wagner's music (among others). The undeniable evidence of Wagner's sweeping popularity among members of the Nazi Party was now bolstered by other indictments. In the absence of any firm documentation – scarcely surprising – the story that Wagner's works had been played in the camps had never been substantiated by research. In accounts of the camp orchestras, specific references to Wagner are difficult to find. Even Moshe Hoch, one of the fiercest opponents of public performances of Wagnerian music in Israel, did not mention Wagner in the bleak description he set down in his book: "The members of the Jewish orchestra played mainly Viennese waltzes, and sometimes we would hear the music in the distance [. . .] They collected the best artists, violinists, pianists, actors, and others, and housed them in a separate building. They would give daily lectures and concerts for the Germans to amuse them."[30]

Fania Fenelon, one such performer, said nothing in her own book about playing music by Wagner, but mentioned music by other composers who were never banned in Israel, such as Franz Liszt and Ludwig van Beethoven. In the first days of the controversy over Wagner and Strauss in Israel at the beginning of the 1950s, former inmates of Auschwitz also testified that the camp orchestra had never played works by Wagner to those marching to their death. Around the same time a story taken from Herzl's diary was circulating, about his writing *The Jewish State* under the inspiration of Wagner's music, particularly *Tanhäuser*.[31] But even this piece of information did not help cleanse Wagner of the stain of Nazification. The possibility that his music had been played in the camps and the dark connotation his name had for Holocaust survivors made any concession unthinkable – certainly at a time when memories of the Holocaust were still fresh and Israeli society included many camp survivors.

In fact, whether or not Wagner's music was actually played in the camps was irrelevant. Feelings about Wagner were dictated by the unique and particularly extreme combination formed by his writings, interpretations of them, and all the anti-Jewish, racist, and murderous reactions to his works. More than a few European artists in different fields had fulminated against Jews; others had been warmly embraced by the Nazi regime; and some of their contemporaries had accepted this happily and felt no revulsion at the creation of a basis for close cooperation between politics and the arts. But rarely were all these characteristics combined in one person. In Wagner's case, the combination was particularly potent, even perfect: Wagner had libeled Jews and called for their destruction (*Untergang*); members of his family and other interpreters had stressed the racist aspects of both his artistic and theoretical writings; and later he was adopted as the Nazi regime's semi-official composer.

Under these circumstances, Palestine and later Israel seemed to have no choice but to ignore his existence as emphatically as possible. A composer whose music was played for leaders of the Nazi regime and Jews who had been sent to their deaths deserved the severe Jewish punishment: ostracism. However, this ostracism soon became a banner of opposition and a symbol of the memory of the Holocaust. Moreover, Israelis took no note of the evolution of the Wagner affair in Germany, and of the fact that the Nazi regime itself denounced some of Wagner's works. Paradoxically, the composer whose works the Nazis had partially removed from the repertoire of the foundering Third Reich – due to ideological reasons –

was also the composer whose works the Israelis removed from the repertoire of the national home of the Jewish people, also the result of ideological reasons. This may be an indication of how comfortably Wagner's works lent themselves to symbolization. The salient messages and the complex plots made Wagner's legacy fertile ground from which different theorists could mold many images with varied meanings.

By another paradox, Wagner was soon linked with Richard Strauss, who was head of the music department of the propaganda ministry headed by Joseph Goebbels. Strauss, who worked in the department for about a year before he was fired for rebelling against the authorities, was also turned into an incarnation of Nazi evil. No one mentioned the bitter war he waged to continue performing the operas he had composed to the lyrics of the Jewish writer Stefan Zweig, nor the agreement he negotiated in order to live quietly in the Bavarian Alps with his Jewish daughter-in-law. Strauss was perhaps a pragmatist rather than a lover of Jews, but his career in the music department of the Third Reich clearly testifies to his disapproval of the Nazi system that compelled the exclusive use of artists untainted by "degeneracy" – that is, who were not Jewish, or members of other "inferior" races, and whose works were not abstract in nature.[32] Even the familiar arguments concerning Strauss's advanced age and his dismissal from his high post because of the blundering of a "senile fool" have never been examined.

Both Strauss and Wagner have been the focus of public controversy in Israel for about 50 years. Additional artists and events were associated with the recurrent debates concerning the public performance of their music. But these two composers, opposed for reasons still in dispute, became particularly conspicuous symbols of the trauma of the Holocaust. The process of symbolization continued for decades, and may still be continuing. However, its early stages in the 1950s and 1960s are crucial to understanding the phenomenon. In the shadow of the Holocaust, and while the State of Israel was developing patterns of commemoration of the worst trauma experienced by Jews, the state's leaders were discussing the possibility of rapprochement with West Germany. Efforts to play works by composers identified with the Nazi regime exposed the nerves frayed by the dozen years of extreme anti-Semitism in the Third Reich.

Notes

1 See A. Z. Ben Yehuda, "Richard Wagner and the Jews [Hebrew]," *Hashkafa* (28 Feb. 1908).

2 It appeared in the form of a small booklet translated by someone identified only as "B.P." The last known copy of the booklet, which was catalogued in the National Library in Jerusalem, disappeared in the early 1990s. The fact that the story was translated at all reflects the general attitude toward the translation of national folk legends from German into Hebrew. One of the

clearest indications of the popularity of this subject was the intensive translation of tales collected by the Brothers Grimm.

3 Kulmus, "The Jews and German Culture [Hebrew]," *Turim* (31 Aug. 1938).

4 More specifically, Mendelssohn wanted Jews to choose between using
German and reviving the Hebrew language – since at the time German had
the status of a lingua franca in large parts of Central and Eastern Europe, and
many Jews were more fluent in it than in the national languages of the countries in which they lived. On Mendelssohn and his counterparts, see S. Feiner,
"Mendelssohn and Mendelssohn's Disciples: A Reexamination," *The
Yearbook of Leo Baeck Institute*, XL, (1995): 133–67. On Mendelssohn, see,
for example, A. Altmann, *Moses Mendelssohn: A Biographical Study*
(Alabama, 1973). On German's special status, see M. G. Clyne, *Language
and Society in the German-Speaking Countries* (London, 1984).

5 On Germany as the center of the Enlightenment, see I. Einstein-Barzilay, "The
Enlightenment and the Jews: A Study in Haskala and Nationalism" (Ph.D.
diss., Columbia University, 1955). On the absorption and transmission of
German culture by young Jewish intellectuals, see J. Doron, "The Impact of
German Ideologies on Central European Zionism, 1885–1914" [Hebrew]
(Ph.D. diss., Tel Aviv University, 1977); and D. Giladi, *Jewish Palestine
during the Fourth Aliyah Period (1924–1929)* [Hebrew] (Tel Aviv, 1973).

6 On the Jews who emigrated from Eastern Europe and their acclimatization
in Germany, see S. E. Aschheim, *Brothers and Strangers: The East European
Jew in Germany and German Jewish Consciousness, 1800–1923* (Madison
and London, 1982). Y. Weiss, *Deutsche und polnische Juden vor dem
Holocaust: jüdische Identität zwischen Staatsbürgerschaft und Ethnizität,
1933–1940*, trans. M. Schmidt (Munich, 2000).

7 Some of the German influences had been brought to the *Yishuv* by the
Templers in the nineteenth century. The most comprehensive work on this
subject is Y. Ben Arzi, *From Germany to the Holy Land: Templer Settlement
in Palestine* [Hebrew] (Jerusalem, 1996). On other models, see Sheffi, *Vom
Deutschen ins Hebräische*, pp. 50–61.

8 On the economic crisis of the mid-1920s and the wave of emigration out of
Palestine that accompanied it, see Giladi, *Jewish Palestine*. On the gradual
development of the *Yishuv* and the establishment of the state, see A. Shapira,
Israel: A History (Lebanon, 2012).

9 On the opera, see *Booklet of the Eretz-Yisrael Opera* (Committee of the
Eretz-Yisrael Opera Circle, Tel Aviv, 1935). On Hebrew theater in Palestine,
see, for example, M. Halevy, *Stagecraft* [Hebrew] (Tel Aviv, 1946); E. Levy,
*The Habima National Theater: History of the Theater in the Years 1917–
1979* [Hebrew] (Tel Aviv, 1981); S. Leshem, "The Palestine Theater"
[Hebrew] (M.A. thesis, Tel Aviv University, 1991); B. Tammuz, ed., *Tenth
Anniversary Book of the Cameri Theater 1944–1954* [Hebrew] (Tel Aviv,
1954). On literary life during this period, see Z. Shavit, "The Formation of
the Literary Center in Eretz-Yisrael in the Institutionalization of *Yishuv*
Society [Hebrew]," *Catedra* 16 (June 1980): 207–33. On the contemporary
Hebrew press, see G. Kressel, *History of the Hebrew Press in Palestine*
[Hebrew] (Jerusalem, 1964).

10 Rabbi Benjamin, "Thomas Mann, Where Did He Come from?" [Hebrew]
Moznaim (20 Dec. 1929). Criticism of Mann increased the longer he stayed

in the Third Reich, as he was perceived as a sort of "official writer" for the Nazis. This did not change until 1936, when he dared to criticize the Nazi regime and the authorities responded by forbidding his publisher, Fischer, to continue publishing his writings.

11 This was a feature in one of Mann's best-known novels, *Buddenbrooks*, which was translated into Hebrew not long after Mann received the Nobel Prize (Stiebel Publishers, Berlin and Tel Aviv, 1930, translated by M. Temkin) and was known throughout the Western world as one of the best novels of the beginning of the twentieth century. It also appeared in the chilling story "The Blood of the Wolsungs," which, less well-known, was not translated into Hebrew until 1997. See T. Mann, *Buddenbrooks* (Frankfurt a.M., 1981), pp. 422–5; and T. Mann, "The Blood of the Walsungs," in *Stories of Three Decades*, tr. H.T. Lowe-Porter (New York, 1948), pp. 297–319. On Mann's attitude to Wagner, Hitler, and the Jews, see H. R. Vaget, "Wieviel 'Hitler' ist in Wagner: Anmerkungen zu Hitler, Wagner und Thomas Mann," in *Wagner und die Juden*, ed. D. Borchmeyer et al. pp. 178–206.

12 "Odds and Ends: Thomas Mann and Richard Wagner [Hebrew]," *Bama 1*, No. 1 (May, 1933): 62. See Mann, "The Sorrows and Grandeur," pp. 96–7.

13 M. Rabinovich, "The Musical Holiday in Bayreuth" [Hebrew], *Moznaim* (20 Oct. 1932): 12.

14 For statistics on immigration and immigrant occupations, see Palestine and Jewish Emigration from Germany (Jerusalem, 1939), pp. 3–4. On the emigration of Central European Jews, see L. Yehil, "The Wanderings of Jews from Germany, Austria and Czechoslovakia (1933–1939): Basic Issues and Main Outlines" [Hebrew], in *History Conference Lectures* [Hebrew] (Jerusalem, 1973), pp. 103–23. On Jewish immigration from Germany, see D. Niederland, *The Jews of Germany – Emigrants or Refugees? An Examination of Emigration Patterns between the Two World Wars* [Hebrew] (Jerusalem, 1996). On the special role played by immigrants from the German-speaking countries in *Yishuv* society, see the comprehensive study by Y. Gelber, *New Homeland: Immigration and Absorption of Cultural European Jews, 1933–1948* [Hebrew] (Jerusalem, 1990).

15 On Huberman see http://www.huberman.info/literature/articles/nazi_germany/

16 On the foundation of the orchestra and its activity up to the establishment of the State of Israel, see the first chapters of U. Toeplitz, *The History of the Israel Philharmonic Orchestra Researched and Remembered* [Hebrew] (Tel Aviv, 1992).

17 On Toscanini, see the biography by H. Sachs, *Toscanini* (New York, 1988), especially pp. 196–269.

18 It is interesting to note, however, that Golinkin claimed that the two strongest influences on him were Herzl's idea of practical Zionism, and Wagner's revolutionary thought. See Y. Hirschberg, "Music in Little Tel Aviv," in *The First Twenty Years: Literature and Art in Tel-Aviv, 1909–1929* [Hebrew], ed. A. B. Yaffeh (Tel Aviv, 1980), p. 104.

19 On the reaction of *Yishuv* leaders to the news of *Kristallnacht*, see D. Porat, *An Entangled Leadership: The Yishuv in the Holocaust, 1942–1945* [Hebrew] (Tel Aviv, 1986), pp. 23–4; and H. Eshkoli (Wagman), *Silence: Mapai and the Holocaust – 1939–1942* [Hebrew] (Jerusalem, 1994), p. 21.

On attitudes to the Holocaust in the *Yishuv*, see the comprehensive study by T. Friling, *Arrow in the Darkness: David Ben-Gurion, the Yishuv Leadership and Rescue Attempts during the Holocaust* [Hebrew] (Jerusalem and Beersheba, 1998). On the conceptualization of the term *Shoah*, see D. Ofer, "Linguistic Conceptualization of the Holocaust in Palestine and Israel, 1942–1953," *Journal of Contemporary History* 31.3 (1996): 567–595. See also: H. Lipsky, "The Term 'SHOAH': Meaning and Modification in the Hebrew Language from its beginning to this day, in the Israeli society" [Hebrew], M.A. Thesis (Tel Aviv University, 1998).

20 On reactions in the local press and comparisons between the Nazi policy and the expulsion of the Jews from Spain, see N. Sheffi, "The Jewish Expulsion from Spain and the Rise of National Socialism on the Hebrew Stage," *Jewish Social Studies* (Fall, 1999): 82–103; and E. Schweid, "The Expulsion from Spain and the Holocaust" [Hebrew], *Alpaim* 3 (1991): 69–88.

21 Controversy regarding the political-ideational belonging of Wagner has continued for decades, see H. R. Vaget, "Anti Semitism, and Mr. Rose Merkwurd'ger Fall!" *The German Quarterly*, 66:2, (Spring 1993): 222–36.

22 See F. Geiger, "Die 'Goebbels-Liste,' Vom. 1 September 1935, Eine Quelle zur Komposistenverfolgung im NS-Staat," *Archiv für Musikwissenschaft*, 59:2 (2002): 104–12.

23 The item appeared in the *Jewish Chronicle* (London, 2 Dec. 1938), in a French paper published in Egypt and Turkey, *Le Journal d'Orient* (18 and 22 Nov. 1938), and in the Italian (6 Dec. 1938) and Yiddish (12 Dec. 1938) press. Clippings of the last two are preserved in the IPO Archives but do not include headlines.

24 On the place of culture as a tool for the creation of nationalism, see Billig, *Banal Nationalism*, especially pp. 37–59.

25 See R. Berg-Pan, *Leni Riefenstahl* (Boston, 1980). Wagner's vision – or at any rate, the vision attributed to him – was also presented in a film by Fritz Hippler, *Der Ewige Jude* (The Eternal Jew), in 1940. The film's narrator quoted this sentence from Wagner's writings: "The Jew is a dark force that destroys man," and explained that the next scenes – of filthy ghettoes and frightening shots of kosher butchering – did indeed document Wagner's diagnosis. On musical effects in *Jud Süss*, see D. Hollstein, *"Jud Süss" und die Deutschen: Antisemitische Vorurteile im nationalsozialistichen Spielfilm* (Munich, 1971), p. 82.

26 On resistance to the German language at that stage, see M. Rinott, *"Hilfsverein der deutschen Juden" – Creation and Struggle* [Hebrew] (Jerusalem, 1971). On the "language war," see Y. Ben-Yoseph, *The Struggle for Hebrew* [Hebrew] (Jerusalem, 1984).

27 On the activity of the Association of German Immigrants, see Gelber, *New Homeland*, pp. 222–316. On the attitude toward German separatism, see Sheffi, *Vom Deutschen ins Hebräische*, pp. 50–61.

28 On the translation of German works into Hebrew in those years, see G. Toury, *Translational Norms and Literary Translation into Hebrew, 1930–1945* [Hebrew] (Tel Aviv, 1977); and Sheffi, *Vom Deutschen ins Hebräische*, pp. 137–216.

29 See, for example, the collection *Knesset, 1930–1940*, ed. Y. Kahan and F.

Lachower, which was dedicated to the memory of the communities annihilated in Europe.

30 M. Hoch, *Return from the Inferno* [Hebrew] (Hadera, 1988), p. 36.

31 See F. Fenelon, *Playing for Time* (New York, 1977). On the facts revealed in the early 1950s, see R. Bondy, *Felix: Pinchas Rosen and His Time* [Hebrew] (Tel Aviv, 1990), p. 489.

32 On Strauss, see B. Gilliam, ed., *Richard Strauss and His World* (Princeton, 1992). On his relations with Zweig, see E. Lowinsky, ed., *The Letters of Richard Strauss and Stefan Zweig, 1931–1935* (Berkeley, 1977).

5

Toward Germany, Away from Germans

Initial reports that the Israel Philharmonic Orchestra was contemplating the performance of works by Richard Wagner and Richard Strauss appeared in the Israeli press toward the end of November 1952. The Hebrew-language daily *Maariv* published a short account of a row that erupted over the issue between orchestra members and the conductor, Igor Markevitch. However, anyone reading to the end of the article discovered that in fact only one of the musicians objected to including the two composers in that season's repertoire, while his colleagues were all unreservedly in favor. The conductor himself explained: "I love Israel, and yet – I am an outsider among you. And the view of an outsider is: Play Wagner and Strauss."[1] A few days later, another short item appeared in the newspaper *Herut* warning the orchestra against playing works by Strauss: "The shameful reparations and reconciliation agreement with Germany apparently constituted a green light for the Israeli orchestra, which is getting ready to play, in one of its upcoming concerts, a work by the Nazi composer [Richard] Strauss, who became known in his day for collaborating with Hitler and for conducting a purge among composers."[2] This item was inaccurate – Strauss's relations with the Nazis had unraveled very quickly. However, it fully explained the fervent opposition voiced by those members of the press identified with the political right.

The connection this journalist made between Israeli-German relations and Israeli readiness to listen to works composed by people suspected of collaborating with the Nazis was in fact the nub of the issue. Members of the IPO faced a difficult dilemma: Should they renounce certain parts of their repertoire out of consideration for public sensibilities and political factors? The general public – which, of course, was far larger than the audiences that actually filled the concert halls – was swept into the debate. The issue of the "Richards" became a hot potato tossed around by politicians. Some sought to manipulate it for political ends; others refused to touch it. Everyone was watching to see what the orchestra would decide to do, and what the political significance of a presumably artistic decision would be. The timing of the debate, too, was particularly sensitive. Only

10 months had passed since the signing of the reparations agreement with Germany, an agreement that had aroused a furor in Israel. Moreover, an important though little-discussed change had taken place in the cultural sphere (a sphere that of course had its political angle): In the summer of 1952 the Bayreuth Festival had reopened, after Winifred Wagner agreed to turn the management of the festival over to her sons, Wolfgang and Wiland Wagner.[3]

Parties and factions of both the right and the left joined in condemning the reparations agreements, but this was not the only political manifestation of opposition to everything related to Germany, as will be seen. The inflexible hostility to Germany and German culture, born in the course of World War II, intensified as concentration camp survivors began arriving in Palestine. The more facts came to light concerning the horrifying dimensions of the European massacre, the tougher the anti-German stance became. Even after the Allies permitted the establishment of two Germanys in 1949 – the Federal Republic of Germany in the West and the German Democratic Republic in the East – hatred of the Nazis remained unchanged. East Germany shut down its borders and closed itself off from all contact with Western countries, including Israel. West Germany, in contrast, invested great efforts in attempting to re-establish a democratic system of government capable of preventing a repetition of past mistakes.

Meanwhile survivors of the concentration camps were doing their best to remake their lives. The State of Israel provided shelter for all Jews who sought it, declaring this an official policy about a year and a half after the establishment of the state. The policy was confirmed by the Law of Return in 1952, which entitled any Jew to Israeli citizenship. In the first three years of its existence, the young state took in nearly 600,000 new immigrants, doubling the Jewish population, and by 1958 the population had tripled.[4] On the practical and political level, the absorption of immigrants was obviously designed to establish a *fait accompli* and justify the existence of the State of Israel. On the moral and emotional level, the immigration policy was proof that Jews looked after one another and exercised their "natural right" to immigrate to Israel. Arab hostility on one hand and the Holocaust on the other were justifications for the right and duty of the Jews to settle in the nascent state. To a great extent, Israel's character in those years was coalesced by the threat of annihilation – the threat that had just ended in Europe and still loomed in the Middle East. However, this willingness to take in every Jew in order to alter the demographic balance and to create at least an illusion of power, severely strained the national budget. Thus, the policy of universal, indiscriminate absorption was another one of the main reasons that Israel embarked on financial talks with West Germany concerning the payment of compensation for damages inflicted by the Holocaust.

The memory of the Holocaust also spurred the enactment of laws against the Nazis and their legacy, laws that permitted justice to be rendered against those who had ordered genocide.[5] In addition, a long series of measures were taken that were designed to create a barrier between Israel and Germany, or at least to put off the establishment of new relations between the countries for as long as possible. One of these measures was an attempt to prevent the import of German products to Israel, although there was no general commercial embargo. The deliberate ambiguity in this sphere was well reflected by the evasive remarks made by Minister of Finance, Eliezer Kaplan: "The government is empowered to confiscate any commodity that is brought into the country without a permit or import license."[6] In other words, it was possible to trade with Germany, but the government was authorized to seize the goods.

Another attempt to reject German heritage was the ban imposed on public performances in the German language. When in November 1950 the singer Kenneth Spencer wanted to sing a selection of Goethe's poems set to Schubert melodies, the Film and Theater Review Board (the state's cultural censor) decided that there should be no performances in German in Israel. Although this ban created a stir, it had no legal power, and consequently in May 1952, when the IPO announced a concert in which the well-known mezzo-soprano Jennie Tourel would sing *Das Lied von der Erde* by Gustav Mahler, with words by Hans Bethge, the Review Board felt compelled to remind the IPO managers of the ban. "It seems proper to remind you of the aforementioned prohibition and to ask you to ensure, when the time comes, that the songs will not be sung in the German language," the Board representative wrote to the IPO.[7] This special request was forwarded to the singer herself, who, far from consenting, talked the young conductor, Leonard Bernstein – who as a Jew would not be suspected of scoffing at Israeli scruples – into persuading the IPO management to allow her to sing in German. Her singing partner, Ernest Garay, obeyed the Israeli behest and sang in Hebrew. Rumors circulated that Tourel had received and rejected a personal appeal from the chairman of the IPO board, Minister of Justice, Pinchas Rosen. Orchestra members denied this report, however, and pointed out that Rosen himself had been in favor of ignoring the Review Board's demand.[8] It merits note that such measures were never taken nor were such long-winded discussions held with regard to any specific composer, including those who were practically banned.

Despite these prohibitions on the German language and restrictions on trade with Germany, the Israeli government was forging ahead with its contacts with West Germany, although from the outset it defined such ties as purely financial, justifying them on moral grounds. The young state's economic problems, compounded by its astronomical construction, security expenses, and unrestricted immigration policy, made the governing party, Mapai (Mifleget Poalei Yisrael – Israel Labor Party), receptive to the idea of reparations from the Bonn government – an idea that had first been discussed by the Zionist leadership back in the second year of World

War II. In early 1951, when Israel's foreign currency reserves were virtually exhausted, Israelis were convinced that they could pressurize the Western powers into helping them obtain reparations from Germany. However, the Cold War prevented the major powers from intervening, and Israel was compelled to embark on independent negotiations with Germany. In September 1951, the West German chancellor, Konrad Adenauer, announced his country's willingness to pay reparations to Israel, without specifying an amount or to whom they would be paid.[9] Given the heightened tension between the two countries, the Israeli government took the precaution of seeking authorization from the Knesset to begin negotiations (albeit such negotiations had in fact been going on throughout 1951), and after a tumultuous debate, achieved its purpose.

Although negotiations with Germany ultimately brought some relief for Israel's depleted treasury, they gave rise to a wave of protest across the country. While the state was still trying to define its relation to the Holocaust, any contact with Germany was perceived as a sin against those who had been murdered in the concentration camps.[10] The protesters were spearheaded by the leader of the Herut movement, Knesset Member (MK) Menachem Begin, a talented and charismatic orator who put his rhetorical skills to good use at mass rallies. Once word got out about the debate scheduled to take place in the Knesset concerning the reparations negotiations, Begin organized a public protest meeting. This came only a few months after Herut's failure in the June 1951 elections, at a time when it was believed that most of the masses of new immigrants would support the ruling party and identify with it as their benefactor. Thus, Begin may have been motivated to a considerable extent by electoral and party considerations, although his dogged dedication to the issue bespoke deep ideological conviction.

In any case, the day the momentous debate began in the Knesset a notice was published in the Herut organ (also named *Herut*) calling on the party faithful and others opposed to ties with Germany to turn out for a demonstration in Zion Square, not far from the then Knesset building on King George Street in Jerusalem. On the same day, Begin entered the Knesset hall for the first time in five months, with the result that the session began with his swearing-in as a member of the second Knesset. Following this ceremony, Prime Minister David Ben-Gurion stepped up to the podium and unhindered reeled off Israel's demands from Germany. At the end of his speech the debate began, and MK Begin left for Zion Square to join the demonstrators. The latter included not only Holocaust survivors and their relatives, but also immigrants recently arrived from Moslem countries who had not been directly affected by the Third Reich.

The demonstration became violent, perhaps a result of Begin's speech; among other things, Begin told the demonstrators that the police officers stationed in the square to maintain law and order were holding German-made gas grenades. All restraint was abandoned and the raging crowd took out its rage on the Knesset by throwing stones through the plenum hall windows. Begin always insisted that he had called upon the demonstrators to surround the building, not to attack it. He himself returned to the hall to deliver his speech, after which the debate was terminated as a result of the bedlam that ensued when the stones came flying in. Two days later, on 9 January 1952, Ben-Gurion announced that negotiations were being conducted with Germany. About a week after that, Begin was barred from Knesset meetings for three months because he had threatened that there would be violence.[11]

In the atmosphere of protest against the nascent relations between Israel and Germany, the possibility of IPO performances of Wagner and Strauss was a spark that reignited the irate arguments concerning Israel's attitude to West Germany and the dark legacy of the Third Reich. The public debate over the reparations agreement appeared to be primarily a conflict between the hegemonic governing party and the opposition. In contrast, the musical controversy revealed the complexity of the Israeli approach to the German problem. Although politically Prime Minister Ben-Gurion could impose his views on his coalition partners and enforce party discipline when an issue was put to the vote, the political echelons could not control public opinion or the views expressed by political personalities in the press. In this case Ben-Gurion did not wave the party whip or brandish the threat of an economic crisis. Everyone followed their dictates of conscience and personal feelings.

The views expressed in the contemporary press reveal the extent to which the debate transcended all the usual sectorial divisions. Once again *Herut* served as the mouthpiece of the main right-wing party in Israel, seconded by the privately owned dailies *Yedioth Ahronoth* and *Maariv*, which employed many journalists from the defunct Revisionist movement. *Haaretz, Davar, Al Hamishmar, Haboker*, and a few foreign-language Israeli dailies all presented the issues involved in the controversy and the spectrum of views held by the left-wing and center. All the newspapers, without exception, felt compelled to take some kind of stand, but their positions were not unequivocal. Some politicians, too, were hesitant to express their views. *Herut* was the first paper to criticize the IPO's plan to play works by Wagner and Strauss, and consistently expressed the most militant opposition. The day after the announcement that compositions by Strauss might be played in Israel, the paper reported warnings by national youth groups that the IPO should not play "works by the Nazi Richard Strauss." *Davar*, the Mapai organ, tried to explain the issue:

> In Leipzig they stopped playing Mendelssohn, in Vienna they would not play Mahler. We continued to play Wagner, until new immigrants arrived who were made anxious by the sounds of Wagner. These immigrants

were not psychologists, and did not spend their time studying the spirit of the music. They were living people who had personally witnessed the horrible effect that Wagner's music exercised on the German beasts of prey. And we stopped playing the melodies of the father of anti-Semitic ideology in music and in art in general.[12]

Davar did not even mention the cancellation of *Die Meistersinger von Nürnberg* in 1938 as a precedent for anti-Wagner sentiment. On the contrary, it portrayed Palestinian Jews as a particularly tolerant people who did not boycott composers because of their ideological views. Consideration for the feelings of Holocaust survivors was the sole motivation for forgoing the pleasures of Wagner.

However, the current issue was the performance of parts of Strauss's *Till Eulenspiegel*. Bluntly rejecting the idea, *Al Hamishmar*, the Mapam party (Mifleget Poalim Meuchedet – United Labor Party) organ, published a detailed article citing specific reasons why Strauss's composition should not be performed. This was consistent with Mapam's traditional rejection of ties with any kind with Germany, which party members had expressed in the Knesset debate on the reparations agreement. The reporter quoted a telegram Strauss had sent to Propaganda Minister Joseph Goebbels (reprinted in the 1944 *Oxford Lexicon*) congratulating him on having "freed Germany from creatures like [the composer and conductor Paul] Hindemith, [the conductor Wilhelm] Furtwängler, and [the conductor Erich] Kleiber," after these men left the country (Furtwängler later returned). Strauss himself, the reporter affirmed, "left Germany before Hitler's regime collapsed, when he saw that his great wealth was in danger and foresaw the end of the whole regime."[13] Thus, since Strauss was a Nazi collaborator, his music was taboo, as in years gone by. The author of this article, like other journalists, reminded his readers at length of the circumstances of the Wagner boycott by first the Jewish *Yishuv* and later the State of Israel.

The same arguments against playing music by Wagner and Strauss came up again and again in the press: the composers' collaboration with the Nazis, their influence on the latter, and their blatant manifestations of anti-Semitism. The various newspapers differed only in their wording. In contrast to the mild explanations proffered by *Al Hamishmar*, *Hatzofeh* headlined one article, "May the Name of Richard Strauss Be Wiped Off Our Orchestra's Program!" The editor of *Yedioth Ahronoth*, Dr. Herzl Rosenblum, wrote an article presenting himself as a champion of cultural liberalism who deplored, for example, the treatment of Wilhelm Furtwängler, a suspected Nazi collaborator, who had been reviled when he tried to perform in the United States in places where the Jewish lobby was particularly strong.[14] Yet the publicist enjoined respect for audience sensibilities: "Let's say that among us there are a few dozen refined souls who are unable to enjoy their lives without Strauss – so what? What is

'Strauss' – bread? It is impossible to live without him; we must besmirch what is left of our image as a people – just so those 'culturally refined' people can listen to that 'music of the gods,' heaven forbid?"[15] Thus, the difference between the various newspapers at that point appeared to be stylistic rather than essential.[16] Rosenblum, however, was already clearly conscious of the image of the Jewish people and the process of national integration, issues that would be prominently featured in his paper at later stages of the controversy. The homogeneous criticism invented part of the national identity, an idea with which many Israelis would associate in later years.[17]

At a time when emotions were running high over the signing of the reparations agreement, antipathy to the idea that the music of a composer identified with the Nazis might be played in Israel led a number of influential people to enter the fray. The head of the Composers' Union sent an urgent letter to the minister of education and culture, history professor Ben-Zion Dinur, warning him against any hasty action by the IPO:

> We do not believe that, after the whole reparations affair, it is wise for the state to embark on a new controversy in this matter [the performance of a work by Richard Strauss]. On the other hand, we are confident that many members of the cultural world will not keep quiet about this, and rightly so, since Strauss, despite his musical importance, was a member of the Nazi party, "perpetuated" the memory of the fallen in his *In Memoriam*, wrote a hymn to [Hans] Frank, arch-executioner of Poland, and frequently panegyrized his leaders in works of praise. We see it as our duty to ask you to prevent this step before we do something about it ourselves.[18]

Copies of the letter were sent to a number of other public figures, and ultimately the IPO agreed to drop that part of its program. The decision was made after the orchestra received a letter from the manager of the music department in the Ministry of Education and Culture, Emanuel Amiran-Pugachov, containing his "*fervent request* to postpone the performance of music of that kind until the minister of education and culture expresses his views on the matter."[19] At the same time, the general secretary of the orchestra, Dr. Kurt Salomon, was called to discuss the issue with Minister of Education Dinur and the IPO chairperson, Pinchas Rosen. Salomon suggested preparing a press release stating that the IPO had accepted the Ministry of Education and Culture's request to postpone the performance of *Till Eulenspiegel*. The fact that the minister of education's position was influenced by his personal views became clear five years later, when he was appointed as one of the two founding editors of the Yad Vashem annuals of Holocaust research. The introduction he wrote for the first collection, in which he stated the editorial board's views and intentions, leaves no doubt about the importance he attached to maintaining a sympathetic and considerate attitude toward Holocaust survivors and commemorating those who had been slaughtered.[20]

Thus the affair ended; the cancellation of the concert was announced in the Israeli press. In consenting to this move, the IPO musicians may have been motivated by a strong sense of solidarity with the citizens of the new state. They may have been cowed by the Ben-Gurion model of authoritarian leadership. Finally, at that stage – and perhaps in the following years as well – the musicians may have failed to grasp the dimensions of the responsibility they bore for the shaping of Israeli culture. It is interesting to note that during this phase of the controversy emphasis was placed on simple consideration for the feelings of Holocaust survivors. The fact that this consideration was also part of the process of commemoration was not discussed, and was most probably not understood as such by policymakers. In retrospect, the strong urge to stigmatize Wagner and Strauss because of their connection with the Nazi regime undoubtedly rendered them classic symbols of the Third Reich and part of the process of Holocaust remembrance in general. In any event, the decision not to play their works calmed the storm of controversy for a short time.

Barely five months passed before the issue flared up again with renewed force. This time the spark was a series of recitals given by the well-known Jewish violinist Jascha Heifetz while he was in Israel performing as a soloist with the IPO. These recitals were to include pieces by Richard Strauss, though this was not specifically announced in advance. The left-wing press instantly abandoned its normally moderate tone, and joined the bitter attacks on Heifetz. On the surface nothing had changed that might explain the blunt denunciation of Heifetz; but anger over the Nazis' deeds in the Holocaust was being channeled into the cultural sphere; the boycotted musicians became a punching bag that absorbed all the emotions that the survivors and those who provided them with a safe haven dared not mention.

The actual events of the Holocaust had not yet been discussed in the early 1950s. Although they evoked different responses, at that point no one was willing to speak publicly about what had actually happened, about the trauma that became the raison d'être for the Israeli policy and for the relentless attitude of Israelis toward Germany. Thus, the Holocaust remained ostentatiously on the public agenda, used constantly by many politicians to bolster their causes – whether it had any connection to them or was a mere demagogic window-dressing. In this context, the periodic outbursts against musicians identified with the Nazis seem perfectly natural. On the personal level, the Holocaust was relegated to the periphery, discussed in private, if at all. Not only was the Holocaust used as a moral–political argument, its survivors were accused of having let themselves be led like sheep to the slaughter. Since those survivors felt a certain measure of guilt in any case, they often preferred to keep private discussion of the Holocaust to a minimum. Long sleeves concealed the numbers tattooed on the forearms of camp survivors, and their stories were censored by their children out of shame. The attacks of rage and despair, the fears, the threats, the comparisons between their present lives and the horrors of the past – all of these were reported only years later, after they had served as a fertile breeding ground for the problems that would henceforth be defined as "second-generation syndrome."[21]

Public expression became traumatic too, at least whenever the subject turned to Germany in general or the Third Reich in particular. The effort to channel national mourning and individual suffering into collective symbols that were gathered and displayed before the general public in the Yad Vashem memorial institute (the various departments of which were inaugurated in the course of 1952–3) did nothing to moderate the altercations that appeared in the press. The mayhem unleashed by Heifetz's recital program broke all barriers as unbridled attacks were launched against anything that smelt of Nazism and anyone who did not denounce it loudly and clearly. At this point of the public debate, Israelis began to see various artists as the most egregious representatives of the Nazi threat – as symbols unequivocally identified with the Holocaust. Anyone who dared to challenge the image given to any of these artists was soon identified as a traitor to the Holocaust legacy or, at the very least, as someone impervious to Israeli emotional needs.

Toward mid-April 1953, around the time of the Memorial Day for the Holocaust and Heroism, Israeli newspapers were filled with articles, editorials, and letters to the editor concerning the performance of one of Richard Strauss's works by the violinist Jascha Heifetz. Some of the articles merely reported the fact, adding simply that "the police, rather than the usual ushers, will maintain order inside and outside the hall."[22] However, most of the articles expressed shock at Heifetz's insolence. The timing of the concerts, so close to Holocaust Memorial Day, compounded public uneasiness. As in the past, *Herut* led the attack. In an article entitled "Degenerate Music Burst Forth on Holocaust Memorial Day," for example, David Yishai interwove graphic descriptions of a Europe "drenched in rivers of Jewish blood," and the industry of soap made from the fat of Jews. Only in the second part of the article did he get around to discussing the music of the "great Nazi composer" – without mentioning Strauss's name – and the degeneracy that was crushing the Israelis and which permitted Heifetz's conduct. "The sounds of spiritual and moral degeneracy arose from the magical violin and entered Jewish ears that remained attached to their heads after 10 years of total annihilation."[23]

This reaction indicates that the fierce opposition to performances of the problematic composers' music was partly attributable to the fear that the memory of the Holocaust would soon be eroded. One must not forget that in the early years of the state, precisely when there were still numerous survivors who were able to describe their personal experiences, Israeli society avoided public discussion of the subject. Consequently, the struggle to preserve the symbolic principle of boycotting "Nazi" musicians may have been intended, at least in part, to institutionalize the process of shaping a collective memory.

The musical critic Menashe Rabina presented a completely different approach. In 1932 he had been sufficiently alert to protest the Nazification of Bayreuth, the site of the Festspielhaus. Rabina recognized the problems involved in performing music by a man who had shared in the dark deeds of the German composers' union during the Third Reich; he took a critical view of the way the subject was treated in Israel. He ridiculed the music critics and others who complained about performances of Strauss although they were incapable of identifying a short piece by the composer unless it was publicly announced. He also stressed the open enthusiasm with which an audience of 1,200 had greeted an excerpt from a Strauss violin sonata performed in the Ohel Shem Auditorium in Tel Aviv. Nonetheless, at the same time he believed that Heifetz was not the person to resolve the cultural maladies of Israeli society.[24]

This was the main issue in most of the features and articles written on the subject. Most of the writers disapproved of Heifetz's attempt to circumvent the requests made by Minister of Education Dinur and Minister of Justice Rosen to refrain from playing works by Strauss in public.[25] The inclusion of the Strauss pieces in the recitals without any advance notice was perceived as an underhanded trick. The Betar movement's governing board asked the IPO to stop "including the works of the Nazi Richard Strauss in the repertoire of a violinist whom you invited to perform in Israel," in order to avoid inflicting "a cruel injury to the memory of the victims of the Holocaust."[26] The soloist himself was called to order as well; Heifetz was described as a guest with poor manners, and the editor of *Maariv*, Dr. Azriel Carlebach, expressed his displeasure in an editorial:

> Minister of Education Professor Dinur requested that no Strauss be played, and Minister of Justice Dr. Rosen seconded the request (despite his different personal views on the identification of an artist with his art). In his capacity as head of the IPO management, he wrote twice to Jascha Heifetz asking him, on his own and on the behalf of the minister of education, not to play the piece. And he sent that request by special messenger, in a special taxi, to Jascha Heifetz in Haifa a short time before the concert.
>
> Yet Jascha Heifetz received the request from two ministers of Israel, shoved it into his pocket, said whatever he said about opposing musical censorship – and refused to comply. He played Strauss in Haifa, and afterwards in Tel Aviv as well.[27]

Rosen's personal letter to Heifetz had indeed been a request not to play Strauss's violin sonata in E flat major, op. 18, but the minister commented that he was not expressing his own feelings, only conveying the wishes of the appropriate authorities.[28] This was an admission of his own predicament: As a private individual and a member of the IPO management, he believed that historical political taboos should not be imposed on composers; but as a public official and minister, he had to obey the governmental dictates of his time.

Rejection of the attitude represented by Heifetz as foreign would be typical of Israel's treatment of performers from abroad for many years to come. Conductor Zubin Mehta would suffer from it the most; his colleague Daniel Barenboim faced bitter criticism for other reasons, primarily his political views regarding the Israeli-Palestinian conflict. At the time, Heifetz's galling behavior provoked some strong reactions, some of which embarrassed the heads of the state and the more senior columnists. Except for right-wing members, who were unyielding in their objection to the performance of Strauss's music, people grappled with various aspects of the issue. The poet Natan Alterman, who was identified with the right wing of the Labor movement and wrote a regular column on current issues ("The Seventh Column"), pointed out the inherent difficulty of the entire situation in "A Poem and Parable" (*Shir u-Mashal*):

[. . .] Because indeed the situation of a crowned Jewish artist is not simple,
Now in the city of the Carmel, before an audience some of which brands snatched from the burning,
He is advised before the concert to abstain from playing a piece
By one of the executioner's helpers. Here one principle collides with another.[29]

Another subject that began to trouble those debating the issue was the affair's international repercussions. Heifetz's name was well known, and news of the conflict between him and members of the Israeli government and society quickly spread overseas. The foreign press was fascinated by the story of the Jew who had met fierce hostility from his fellow Jews when he sought to entertain them. The *Haaretz* correspondent in the US reported that both the thunderous applause that had greeted the performance of Strauss in the concert hall and the government ministers' requests that Strauss's works not be played "received wide coverage."[30] This international interest was only the beginning of a much more significant response.

On Thursday, 16 April 1953, four days after Holocaust Memorial Day, Heifetz gave a recital in Jerusalem. Upon leaving the auditorium, he was attacked with an iron pipe by an unknown assailant. Fortunately, his hard violin case served as a shield, and he suffered only superficial injury. The press reacted with alarm; suddenly it had become clear that the debate waged in the pages of the daily papers and the savage criticism of Heifetz's actions could be interpreted as license to remove the violinist by violent means. The man who had hitherto been a mannerless guest was reinstated as "the world-renowned Jewish violinist," or at least as "the artist."[31] *Haaretz* correspondents sent in more reports from abroad, with the US correspondent writing: "The attack on Jascha Heifetz received huge publicity in America and was bad propaganda for the State of Israel just before Independence Day celebrations," while from London the news came that "the assault on Jascha Heifetz [. . .] made a very bad impression."[32] The unhappy end to the concert series left the question of Wagner and Strauss up in the air. Now it was clear where that question could lead to and the kind of "answers" individuals might seek.

The members of the IPO management called a special meeting. They themselves were accused by some of having encouraged Heifetz to play Strauss pieces, thereby shaping his recital program.[33] Press commentators were apparently aware, in a way that the musicians themselves were not, of the formative influence that the members of the Israeli musical world were supposed to wield, and they examined the issues raised by Heifetz's recitals from several perspectives. First, they showed great sensitivity to the awkward situation of Pinchas Rosen, whose opinions as chairman of the IPO board clashed with his obligations as member of the government. In other words, the critics themselves pinpointed the subtle point of contact between politics and art. At the same time, they also realized that Heifetz's conduct had been perceived as deliberately provocative, and they believed that the violent attack on him must be judged in light of the injury he had inflicted on the feelings of the Israeli public. Most important, since they regarded the performance of Strauss as a vital element in the development of the orchestra, they left the field open to fresh debate in the future.

However, for the time being the country's leaders preferred to remain silent. Their wish to establish formulas for commemorating the Holocaust in Israel and the nature of the formulas they envisioned were given concrete expression in August 1953, about four months after the Heifetz affair, when the Knesset passed the Law of Holocaust Martyrs' and Heroes' Remembrance, the keystone of Yad Vashem activities.

Interestingly, even at that late stage, when Israel was an independent state in which lawmakers were laboring to establish the codes and norms that would have currency in it, the question of freedom of expression – the freedom to play different sorts of music – was never even mentioned. In the initial controversy regarding proposals to perform Strauss and Wagner, tempers had been too heated for any rational debate on the subject of the right to play and to listen, but now both politicians and musicians were able to perceive the growing legal and political loophole. The freedom to listen and the freedom to perform were never discussed, and the politicians could see that their intervention in the repertoire met no real resistance. In 1953 the Supreme Court had already been called upon to rule on the freedom of expression – a right that was not yet codified in any legislation – in an appeal made by the Communist newspaper *Kol Haam* against the minister of the interior. On that occasion, the Supreme Court, headed by Judge Shimon Agranat, ruled that "the right to freedom of expression is not an absolute, unlimited right, but a relative right, subject to restriction and supervision as warranted by important sociopolitical interests that in certain circumstances are considered to take priority over those safeguarded by the principle of freedom of expression."[34]

Insofar as the musical life of the young state was concerned, it was clear that not only did many citizens not object to direct intervention by politicians on the issue, they even welcomed it, and were fully supported in this by all sectors of the press. Moreover, the opposition parties that automatically rejected the idea of publicly performing compositions by the "forbidden musicians" actually encouraged the ruling party to take a hand, totally abandoning the opposition's traditional role of exercising a restraining influence over the central power.

In late November 1956, a few weeks after the Sinai campaign – in which Germany, unlike other European countries, did not intervene – the Strauss issue came back to bedevil the IPO and the government ministries. The conductor Georg Singer wanted to include selections from Strauss's opera *Don Juan* in a concert series, and the IPO consented. An explanatory article was written by flautist Uri Toeplitz (who would find himself in the thick of another controversy over Wagner and Strauss ten years later). As in the past, on this occasion too the response was immediate – not only from the press, but also, and particularly, from the political echelons. The results of the previous skirmish – Jascha Heifetz's injury – may have galvanized the politicians, spurring them to intervene out of fear that the strong current of anti-Nazi sentiment would give rise to new acts of violence; and, indeed, the public furor raised by Israel (Rudolf) Kasztner's trial between September 1954 and June 1955 offered grounds for such fears. In September 1954 Malkiel Grünwald, a freelance journalist, accused Israel Kasztner of collaborating with the Nazis. In the course of the libel suit that Kasztner brought against Grünwald, the climate of public opinion essentially turned Kasztner into the defendant, and subsequently he lost his case. The judge, Benjamin Halevi, proclaimed that Kasztner had "sold his soul to the devil." Kasztner appealed the decision, but was shot in the street before the verdict exonerating him was handed down.

This time the commotion began with a threatening letter sent to conductor Singer, which led the IPO's general manager to tell the chairman of the IPO board, Justice Minister Pinchas Rosen, that the cooperative urgently wanted to discuss the new situation and the Ministry of Education's recommendation not to play Strauss's music. Although the minister of education had asserted that "the decision to play a work by Strauss [is] in the hands of the orchestra,"[35] it was crystal clear that the orchestra would be taking a significant risk in doing so, and would not be able to count on the government's support. At the same time, everyone was waiting to see how the minister of education would answer an interpellation on the issue presented by MK Esther Raziel-Naor (Herut). It is worthy of note that the politicians were mindful of the orchestra's special status as an independent cooperative; but they also considered that it played a special role as "the highest musical institution in Israel," as defined by MK Raziel-Naor in her interpellation.

Because the interpellation was submitted late, Minister of Education Zalman Aranne did not respond until after the controversial concert – which, as it turned out, did not include selections from the Strauss opera. In his response, he asserted that the next time his ministry would issue an opinion, but not a prohibition. During those years, many Israelis saw such opinions not so much as suggestions but rather as a kind of policy dictate; but right-wing politicians still felt that the minister was equivocating. Another question from the same Knesset member provoked an argument in the plenum. The minister asserted that "once sounds are born, they have an independent existence, and I don't think there is any point in forbidding the existence of sounds." This seemed to imply that if his ministry chose to tell the orchestra what to do, he personally would support the orchestra. In response, the head of the Herut movement, MK Menachem Begin, declared that this was a government announcement demanding debate – perhaps thinking he could make political capital out of what seemed to be an assault by a senior government official on the process of Holocaust remembrance in Israel. The Knesset Speaker, Yosef Sprinzak, terminated the discussion.[36] In response, the IPO management published a public statement signed by Chairperson Rosen, declaring the orchestra's intention of fighting for the right to make its own artistic decisions.[37] This was the first time Israeli musicians assumed responsibility for forming public opinions and tastes, while ignoring the measure of support offered them by the minister of education. The explanation of the minister consolidated the attitude toward the freedom of expression in music life for many years to come.

The political debate did not prevent public controversy; at most it moderated the rage that had emanated from the press on previous occasions. On the day of the controversial concert – prior to the Knesset debate – manifestos were published by both the IPO management and those who objected to the performance. The IPO stated: "The performance of works by Richard Wagner and Richard Strauss is, in the opinion of all recognized experts, mandatory in every country that seeks to foster musical culture and the education of the general public, particularly young people – in order to promote an understanding of the development of orchestral music from the end of the classical period to the present day." The orchestra, the manifesto went on to say, gave weight to the feelings of the public and the results of the survey it had carried out, but deplored the publication of the opinion in which the minister of education took exception to the performance of works by these two important composers. That publication had helped create an atmosphere that did not allow the orchestra to act by its own lights, according to its own criteria, which ought to be purely artistic. The manifesto was signed by the chairman of the IPO management, Pinchas Rosen, who, as a member of the Independent Liberal party and senior member of the government, was undoubtedly prey to divided loyalties.[38] On the very same day, Hanoar Haleumi (National Youth), an organization identified with the Herut movement, published a manifesto of its own against the performance of Strauss, ending it with the words: "The Nazi Strauss comes off the program! An end to the abuse of Hebrew public opinion! Do not desecrate our state with Nazi music!"[39]

The next day, the papers reported that the performance of the Strauss work had been canceled, and published a photograph of swastikas that had been spray-painted on the IPO's posters. The Strauss piece was replaced by the opening of *Carnaval*, by Antonin Dvořák.[40] This time, as in the past, all the newspapers published in Israel reported the news, and generally speaking, their views could be classified in the traditional way: *Herut* and the right were ranged against the performance, supported by some of the left wing – mainly *Al Hamishmar* – while *Haaretz* and the center either were neutral or supported the IPO. In addition to the news reports, *Haaretz* also printed a favorable review of the concert. The critic stressed the political involvement – deplorable, in his view – in musical criteria, and the "justified" place of conductor Singer on the orchestra podium.

Again the public seemed willing to forget the issue of the "Nazi composers" for a while, but the IPO and its management continued to discuss it for years. The IPO managing director asked Eliezer (Felix) Shinar, a member of the Israeli delegation to Cologne, to uncover a few facts concerning Strauss's position in the Third Reich and his personal views. Kurt Salomon quoted an extract from *Grove's Dictionary of Music* which seemed to imply that Strauss had not been a collaborator; but he pointed out that Grove's views were not sufficient to convince the Israelis to rehabilitate Strauss.[41] In early 1957, the subject was raised again at a meeting of the IPO board. For the last item on the agenda of the 22 February meeting, the managing director, Kurt Salomon, suggested rediscussing the Wagner issue. "We ought to continue moving toward 'purifying' Wagner's music, and the management ought to declare its consent to include works by Wagner in the orchestra's program – without setting a date for such a performance."[42] In other words: Let's downplay the tendency to see Wagner as a symbol of the Holocaust, and restore him to his rightful place in the pantheon of musicians.

But as always, the matter was far from simple. As evidence, at the end of April 1957, two months after that meeting, Salomon rejected a suggestion by the manager of the press club in Tel Aviv to hold a public symposium on the subject of Wagner and Strauss in Israel. "We do not believe that this is the right time to bring up this subject in a public forum," he explained, and added, "the question as to whether Wagner and Strauss's music should be played in Israel is not a musical issue, but a public one."[43] The public was not yet ready for this, and everyone seemed to realize it. All attention was focused on the latest event connected with the Holocaust and its legacy; only six weeks had passed since the shooting of Israel (Rudolf) Kasztner, who, accused of collaborating with the Nazis, had been exonerated but died of his injuries.[44] The public question remained open for the time being, and for many years to come.

Some Israelis continued to worry that the IPO would try to put one over on its audience by playing works by Wagner without any prior public discussion. In December 1958, one such music lover wrote to the IPO management claiming to have heard, from "reliable sources," about a "secret agreement" that the management had made concerning the performance of works by Wagner. The manager of the orchestra, Abe Cohen, answered: "For the time being, we have no plans to play works by this composer, and we certainly will not do so without first publicizing the fact."[45] The orchestra management remained faithful to this principle, and when it finally decided to include works by Wagner in the repertoire some years later, it announced its decision in the program of the last concert of the season (June 1966). This announcement marked the beginning of the next phase of the Wagner and Strauss controversy, in which the issue became both a symbol identified with the experiences of the Holocaust, and a factor that helped shape at least part of the new Israeli culture.

The public response to the idea of performing Wagner and Strauss in Israel was additional evidence of the process of conceptual construction that the new state was then undergoing, from which it drew on the collective memory of Israeli society. In the 1950s, Israeli society viewed the ideas and policies of National Socialism with anxiety and anger. The concepts of this ideology were deeply imprinted on the Israeli consciousness not only because of the catastrophic experiences of the Holocaust, but also because of the incessant, frequently demagogic references to those experiences – mainly by politicians who saw the acts of the Nazis as the inevitable result of the National Socialist ideology, but also, to a lesser degree, by those survivors willing to speak out.

Just as the debate about establishing ties with Germany had engaged a larger sector of society than merely those individuals directly or indirectly injured by the policies of the Third Reich, so did the debate over what music should be played in Israel. Although at this point the major participants were former Europeans and native-born Israelis, they were gradually joined by immigrants from the Moslem countries as well, who had absorbed the collective memory of the Holocaust. This expansion of the public debate to include additional groups may have been a consequence of the nature of Holocaust remembrance in the first years of the state. During those years, the collective memory of the Holocaust took on a general form, but no attempt was made to define the details of Holocaust commemoration. The musical sphere became an important additional element in the process of translating the Holocaust into symbols and securing its place in the world concept of Israeli society. As increasingly large groups began to identify Wagner and Strauss's actions – and even their works – with the ordeals of the Holocaust, the "forbidden" composers began to infiltrate Israeli consciousness as an integral part of the Nazi horrors that no one was allowed to mention in the State of Israel. This tendency continued to develop in the course of subsequent decades, reaching an apex in the 1980s.[46]

Notes

This chapter was first published as "Cultural Manipulation: Richard Wagner and Richard Strauss in Israel in the 1950s," *Journal of Contemporary History* 34, no. 4 (1999): 619–39.

1   "On Wagner and Strauss [Hebrew]," *Maariv*, 25 Nov. 1952.
2   "Orchestra to Play Works of the Nazi Josef Strauss [Hebrew]?" *Herut*, 30 Nov. 1952.
3   See G. Skelton, *Wagner at Bayreuth: Experiment and Tradition* (London, 1965), pp. 156–7.
4   On the high immigration percentage and the reception of immigrants in the first years of the state, see T. Segev, *1949: The First Israelis* (London, 1986), esp. ch. 2.
5   See "Hok le-Asiat Din be-Nazim u be-Ozreihem [The Law for the Punishment of Nazis and their Collaborators]" (1950). In 1986 a law against Holocaust denial was also enacted. The first law was designed to meet the needs of Israeli citizens who claimed to have identified Nazis who had mistreated them. Initially the Ministry of Justice had been loath to deal with the issue, but in the wake of public complaints that Israel was the only country in the world in which Nazis could not be tried, a law was enacted to permit their prosecution. From the beginning, Minister of Justice Pinchas Rosen expressed concern that the law would be enforced primarily against Jewish collaborators. The law's flexible wording gave the judge broad discretionary powers in deciding cases. See Segev, *The Seventh Million*, pp. 261–2; and R. Bondy, *Felix: Pinchas Rosen and His Time* [Hebrew] (Tel Aviv, 1990), pp. 489–93.
6   *Divrei HaKnesset* [protocols of the Israeli parliament], session 136, 8 May 1950, p. 22. The quotation is taken from I. Gilead, "Public Opinion in Israel on Relations between the State of Israel and West Germany in the Years 1949–1965 [Hebrew]" (PhD diss., Tel Aviv University, 1984), p. 32.
7   The Kenneth Spencer affair is described by I. Gilead, p. 32. On the censor-

ship board's request, see letter from the Film and Theater Review Board to the IPO management, 6 May 1952, IPO Archives, "miscellaneous" file.

8 W. Levy to editor of *HaEmeth*, 8 June 1952, IPO Archives, Wagner and Strauss file.

9 On Adenauer's views in this respect, see Y. A. Jelinek, ed., *Zwischen Moral und Realpolitik: Eine Dokumentensammlung* (Gerlingen, 1997), pp. 55–61.

10 On the economic details of the reparations agreement, see N. Balabkins, *West Germany and the Reparations to Israel* (New Brunswick, 1971). On the difficulties involved in the negotiations and their highly sensitive nature, see R. Vogel, ed., *The German Path to Israel* (Chester Springs, 1969), pp. 42–54. On the controversy in Israel, see Gilead, "Public Opinion in Israel," pp. 37–82, and Segev, *The Seventh Million*, pp. 211–52. On Ben-Gurion's attitude towards Germany during that decade, see Y. Weitz, "Political Dimensions of Holocaust Memory in Israel during the 1950's," *Israel Affairs* 1, No. 3 (1995): 129–45.

11 Segev, *The Seventh Million*, pp. 211–26; Y. Shapiro, *Chosen to Command: The Road to Power of the Herut Party – A Socio-Political Interpretation* [Hebrew] (Tel Aviv, 1989), pp. 90–4. On utilization of the memory of the Holocaust in the political arena in the 1950s, see I. Zertal, *Israel's Holocaust and the Politics of Nationhood* (Cambridge, 2010), pp. 52–90.

12 "With or without the Richards [Hebrew]," *Davar*, 1 Dec. 1952; "The Orchestra Is Urged Not to Play Strauss [Hebrew]," *Herut*, 1 Dec. 1952.

13 A. Zilberman, "Richard Strauss Will Not Be Played by the Philharmonic [Hebrew]," *Al Hamishmar*, 3 Dec. 1952.

14 The purging of Wilhelm Furtwängler is the subject of the play *Taking Sides* (*The Conductor* in Hebrew), performed in Israel to great acclaim; see R. Harwood, *Taking Sides* (London and New York, 1995). The play's success in Israel may be attributed to the musical controversies concerning the "forbidden composers." On Furtwängler's problematic career, see F. K. Prieberg and C. Dolan, *Trial of Strength: Wilhelm Furtwängler in the Third Reich* (Boston, 1994).

15 Dr. H. Rosenblum, "The Orchestra Is Looking for Trouble [Hebrew]," *Yedioth Ahronoth*, 5 Dec. 1952.

16 On the place of journalism in the commemoration of the Holocaust in Israel, see E. Zandberg, "The Right to Tell the (right) Story: Journalism, Authority and Memory," *Media, Culture and Society*, 32 (2010): 5–24.

17 On the creation of national identity, see Hobsbawm, "Introduction: Inventing Traditions," 1–14.

18 Y. Admon to the minister of education and culture, 1 Dec. 1952, IPO Archives, Wagner and Strauss file.

19 E. Amiran-Pugachov to Dr. K. Salomon, 2 Dec. 1952, IPO Archives, Wagner and Strauss file (emphasis in the original).

20 On the termination of the Strauss affair, see K. Salomon, "Report on My Talks with the Minister of Education and Mr. Rosen in Jerusalem, 2 December 1952, in "The Performance of Strauss's Works [Hebrew]," IPO Archives, Wagner and Strauss file. On Dinur's attitude, see B. Dinur, "Yad Vashem's Goals in Researching Holocaust Martyrs and Heroism and the Issues Involved [Hebrew]," *Kovetz Yad Vashem*, 1 (1957): 26–7.

21 For attitudes toward survivors and public and private discussion of the

Holocaust, see H. Yablonka, "The Formation of the Holocaust Consciousness in the State of Israel: The Early Days," in *Breaking Crystal: Writing and Memory after Auschwitz*, ed. E. Sicher (Urbana and Chicago, 1998), pp. 119–36; and A. Shapira, "The *Yishuv* and the Survivors of the Holocaust," *Studies in Zionism* 7 (1986): 277–301.

22 "Jascha Heifetz Will Play Strauss in Israel's Capital, Too [Hebrew]," *Herut*, 15 April 1953.

23 D. Yishai, "Degenerate Music Burst Forth on Holocaust Memorial Day [Hebrew]," *Herut*, 16 April 1953, emphasis in the original.

24 M. Rabina, "Jascha Heifetz Played 'a Work' by R. Strauss [Hebrew]," *Davar*, 14 April 1953.

25 The letters exchange between Heifetz and the government ministers was printed in full in *Herut*, 17 April 1953.

26 Betar Commission in Eretz-Yisrael to the Israel Philharmonic Orchestra, 15 April 1953, IPO Archives, Wagner and Strauss file.

27 Dr. A. Carlebach, "Manners of a Guest [Hebrew]," *Maariv*, 13 April 1953.

28 See Bondy, *Felix*, p. 488.

29 N. Alterman, "The Seventh Column: A Poem and Parable [Hebrew]," *Davar*, 17 April 1953.

30 A. Gelblum, "Reactions to the Performance of Strauss by Heifetz [Hebrew]," *Haaretz*, 12 April 1953.

31 See the changed tone of the press articles, for example, in *Hador* and *Maariv* the day after the incident, 17 April 1953. It is important to note that most of the Hebrew press in Israel had taken part in the debate (*Davar, Haaretz, Herut, Haolam Hazeh, Maariv, Haboker, Hador,* and *Yedioth Ahronoth*), as had the foreign-language press (*Jediot Hadashot, Emeth, Jerusalem Post, Yedioth Hayom*). Reports had also appeared in the foreign press, such as the *New York Post, New York Herald Tribune, Herald Tribune* (Paris), and *Buenos Aires Herald*.

32 A. Gelblum (US) and A. Roth (London), "The Injury to Jascha Heifetz Injured Israel [Hebrew]," *Haaretz*, 19 April 1953.

33 K. Salomon to the Betar Commission, 16 April 1953, IPO Archives, Wagner and Strauss file.

34 See Rubinstein and Medina, *Constitutional Law*, 2: 999–1091. The quotation is from p. 1003, taken from the High Court of Justice Case 73/53 (*Kol Haam* Inc. v. Minister of the Interior). The legal framework was only established with the enactment of Basic Law: Human Dignity and Liberty (1992).

35 Dr. K. Salomon to P. Rosen, 18 Nov. 1956, IPO Archives, Wagner and Strauss file.

36 Interpellation 670, 26 Nov. 1956. A copy of the question and its answer can be found in the IPO Archives, Wagner and Strauss file.

37 Bondy, *Felix*, p. 489.

38 Manifesto of the management of the Israel Philharmonic Orchestra, Tel Aviv, 28 Nov. 1956.

39 Betar Commission in Eretz-Yisrael to IPO management, 15 April 1953, IPO Archives, Wagner and Strauss file.

40 See minutes from IPO board meeting, 28 Nov. 1956, IPO Archives, Wagner and Strauss file.

41 Dr. K. Salomon to Dr. E. F. Shinar, 6 Dec. 1956, IPO Archives, Wagner and Strauss file.
42 Report by Dr. K. Salomon, 22 February 1957, board meeting, IPO Archives, Wagner and Strauss file.
43 Dr. K. Salomon to M. Ben-Gur, 30 April 1957, in response to a letter from M. Ben-Gur to the management of the IPO, 10 April 1957, IPO Archives, local (Israeli) press file.
44 On the Kasztner case, see Y. Weitz, "Changing Conceptions of the Holocaust: The Kasztner Case," *Reshaping the Past: Jewish History and the Historians*, ed. J. Frankel, Studies in Contemporary Jewry, Vol. X (1994), pp. 211–30; Y. Weitz, "The Herut Movement and the Kasztner Trial," *Holocaust and Genocide Studies* 8, No. 3 (1994): 349–71. The Kasztner affair continued to make waves in Israel, and was the subject of a play produced by the Cameri Theater of Tel Aviv in the summer of 1985. See M. Lerner, *Kasztner* [Hebrew] (Tel Aviv, 1988).
45 Y. Cohen to M. Wiesenfeld, 28 Dec. 1958, IPO Archives, Wagner and Strauss file.
46 On this subject, see M. Halbwachs, *On Collective Memory* (Chicago, 1992), especially pp. 46–53.

CHAPTER

6

The 1960s:
An End to Forgetting

At the beginning of 1963, the public board of the Israel Philharmonic Orchestra met to discuss the orchestra's plans, the dilemma of German vocal music, and the dilemma of liturgical music. The last two issues were directly related to the special character of the State of Israel. Since it was a Jewish state, some board members wondered whether such conspicuously Christian music should be performed there. In a country that had taken in many survivors of the Nazi death camps, the very sound of the German language was apparently enough to burn another scar in minds that still vividly recalled the horrors of the Holocaust. This kind of a discussion was typical of the early days of Israeli statehood, which were characterized by a desire to create distinctive patterns and symbols for the new Jewish-secular society. Such attempts began to die out as of the 1970s.[1]

This discussion took place some 13 years after the ban on using German in public performances in Israel, after a decade of near silence on the subject of Wagner and Strauss. It was the first time since the brouhaha of the 1950s that the orchestra's management felt obliged to discuss controversial repertoire issues of this kind. The fact that it held this discussion at all showed once more that efforts to keep politics out of the concert hall were doomed to failure; the managers of the orchestra were again compelled to determine what they could and could not permit themselves in music. This time, too, the discussion addressed the limits the orchestra set for itself, which were dictated largely by audience expectations and the general mood prevailing in Israel concerning national cultural activity.

For all practical purposes, the orchestra management's discussion of the issues of the German language and religious music constituted direct intervention in its artistic decisions. The prominent place played by German vocal works in orchestra repertoires throughout the world and the abundance of musical works based on Christian liturgy gave both these types of music a great deal of weight in the selection that any philharmonic orchestra offered its audience. However, Israel's unique circumstances diverted the focus from the artistic discussion per se to questions concerning the relationship between politics and national identity, an issue that was still in its infancy. Art was only a background to the main problem: national identity.

The debate as to whether the German language should be heard in a place regarded as the national concert hall was held not in the musical, but in the political, sphere. MK Dr. Benjamin Avniel (Herut), a member of the orchestra management, explained that personally he did not oppose to the German language, but in his view "conscience and morality call upon us to preserve a 'memorial' and, at least in our generation, prohibit the use of German in public performances in Israel, even by local soloists and choirs." MK Avniel believed that this was the way to preserve the memory of the "six million" and respect the feelings of the Holocaust survivors living in Israel. For the most part, his position reflected the same line that Herut had always taken with respect to the Holocaust and the sensibilities of survivors: that the commemoration of the Holocaust was of utmost importance, indisputably more important than the rights or wishes of any particular individual. This approach differed from the one taken by Mapam that emphasized the heroic deeds of small groups within the ghettoes and the partisans outside them.[2]

Aryeh Dissenchik, the editor of the daily *Maariv*, reached very different conclusions, somewhat surprising in view of *Maariv*'s opposition to negotiations with Germany: "There is no way to avoid the need for contact with the German people in the period of reparations," he said, "nor is there any opposition to the German culture, including musical works that occasionally, for artistic reasons, can be performed only in the original language."

Like Dissenchik, who was making a case for consistency, MK Yizhar Harari (Liberals) told debaters to take a stand one way or the other: either to prohibit all contact with the Germans, or to maintain normal trade relations and pay reciprocal visits. Since the state had already chosen the second option, "There is no point in being fastidious about German singing in the performance of a work by a 'kosher' German composer."

However, Minister of Transportation Israel Bar-Yehuda (Achdut Haavodah/Labor) totally rejected this view. In his eyes what mattered was the identity of the composer and the piece; and in any case "Hebrew should be used as far as possible, and efforts must be made to ensure good translations." Namely, original compositions and the use of Hebrew were to be encouraged regardless of the German question.[3]

Thus the debate continued, each participant citing different arguments for his or her own view. A successful performance by Marlene Dietrich – in German – was one justification offered for canceling the prohibition on public performances in German, while another disputant maintained the indispensability of Schiller's "Ode to Joy" in the original language – without, of course, mentioning the intensive use the Nazis had made of this particular work. To Israelis, Beethoven remained one of the great composers, and they ignored his own views and his later adoption by a regime that appropriated quite a few artists.

Ultimately, the IPO board decided to give the orchestra free rein to decide the matter; 18 of those present supported this idea, two thought that only guests from abroad should be allowed to use German, and two rejected any use of German. As for playing non-Jewish religious compositions, the management did not bother to discuss it but voted unanimously in favor of such performances.[4] The 1963 debate brought the orchestra to the brink of a normal musical life, albeit to reach that point so much consideration was devoted to political and social factors that at times the musical aspect seemed to play a very minor role. Once again state officials were clearly taking great pains over every decision that would affect the emerging face of society in Israel, refusing to leave anything to chance.

Three years later, in the summer of 1966, the connection between art, society, and politics stirred up another hornet's nest. The concert series that concluded the IPO's 1965–6 season reopened the debate over the performance of Wagner and Strauss in Israel. This time the controversy was fiercer, more vehement, and elicited more diverse responses, pointing up more clearly than before the roles politicians and the press played in whipping up emotions and creating a network of symbols and images that sustained the public.

On this occasion the conflict began with a short article by Uri Toeplitz, first flautist and member of the IPO management, which was printed in the concert programs of the last series of the season. With this article the orchestra was keeping its promise to give the public advance notice of its intention of playing works by banned composers, instead of slipping controversial works in unheralded, as it had been accused of doing in the Heifetz affair. After outlining the circumstances that had led the IPO to stop playing works by Wagner, Toeplitz explained:

> We feel the time has come for a change, not only because of the paramount demands of artistic freedom, but also because opposition to Wagner has become merely a gesture. Why should we go on denying ourselves some of the greatest music by forbidding the playing of Wagner, a loss that cannot be replaced by the works of any other composer, while a mere convenience like the German Volkswagen, with all its associations with the Hitler era, is allowed to crowd our streets? [. . .] Accordingly, this time we must take a rational and courageous stand and allow Wagner's music to be played, thereby reopening the door to works included among the best of the music composed in the nineteenth century.[5]

This was a toned-down version; in the essay appearing the first evening, which had roused subscribers, public figures, and members of the management against him, Toeplitz had explained that "a change has

taken place in the nation's attitude to the exterminators of our people."
However, the heads of the orchestra forced him to alter this section to
make the article more palatable. Toeplitz deleted the controversial
sentence, but otherwise left the article as is, stressing Wagner's great
importance, his place in the pantheon of German musicians, and his
enriching influence on other composers. Such dynamics exemplified the
attitude toward the topic even among those who supported breaking the
ban: openness mixed with a measure of consideration, or even self-restric-
tion the objective of which was the prevention of a scandal as well as a
censorship dictated by the political echelons.

At that time Israeli society was perfectly familiar with the points
Toeplitz's essay made concerning the right time for a change and the widespread use of German products. The absurdity of Israelis consuming
German products as they rioted over the signing of the reparations agreement was mentioned every time an economic or other type of association
was established between Israel and Germany. The simple fact was,
remarked Toeplitz, that long operas were easier to boycott than the highly
coveted cars and electronic household appliances so often pictured in
newspaper caricatures. In any case, he said, the time had come to stop
treating the Federal Republic of Germany as the successor of the Third
Reich; Israelis must rise above their feelings and the harsh memories the
Nazis had branded on the Holocaust survivors.

The timing of the Philharmonic's decision was no fluke. It was
undoubtedly a particularly propitious moment for lifting the ban, owing
to a significant change in the political relations with West Germany; a year
earlier, the State of Israel had established diplomatic relations with the
Federal Republic of Germany. Although this decision had been controversial and subjected to several delays, and initially relations with
Germany were cool, the creation of this first tie was enough to put an end
to five years of turbulent relations between the two countries. The
Eichmann trial, the affair of the German scientists suspected of vital assistance to the Egyptian missile industry, and the establishment of diplomatic
relations all kept Germany in Israeli headlines for at least the first half of
the 1960s.

The IPO's announcement that it would begin to play works by Wagner
in the coming season gave new impetus to the arguments already raging
in the Israeli public sphere in the first half of the 1960s. This time the
controversy reached new heights, and politicians and publicists did not
hesitate to voice their opinions with particularly brutal candor. After all,
on this occasion the issue was not a consequential political problem, but
a cultural one. The different sides in the conflict apparently drew two
conclusions. First, in the cultural sphere Israel could and should do whatever it pleased without considering the international arena as it had been
obliged to do in all previous incidents involving West Germany – the
Eichmann trial, the affair of the scientists, and the establishment of diplo-

matic relations, as well as the signing of the reparations agreement at the beginning of the 1950s, which had halted the deterioration in Israel's balance of payments. I believe that the other conclusion derived from Israelis' concept of themselves as shapers of "Israeliness," as founding fathers of Israel's regenerated culture; as such, they may have seen themselves as committed to preserving the purity of the culture from racist contacts or clear reminders of the injury done to the Jewish people. And indeed, reactions to Toeplitz's article indicate that commentators felt free to use harsh and reckless words to defend their own images of the new Israeli culture.

The publication of Toeplitz's article was preceded by long debates in the IPO concerning the young conductor Zubin Mehta's wish to conduct a performance of Wagner's *Tristan und Isolde*. In those days Mehta was considered a rising star, but had not yet been appointed as music director of the orchestra. The meeting to discuss Mehta's request was attended by only six of the thirteen members of the orchestra board, but those six read out the written opinions of some of the absent members. The Tel Aviv municipal secretary, Zvi Avi-Guy, explained that, musical considerations aside, it was plain that "the timing is not right: This is the last concert of the season, it is impossible to prepare the emotionally opposed minority, and there is bound to be a fuss in the press and the public." Avi-Guy added his own view that Wagner should indeed be played and a clear position should be taken on the matter, but that it should be announced clearly and in advance.[6] In other words, the problem was not whether Wagner should be performed, but whether the Israeli public was ready for such a move – an argument that was already well worn from earlier stages of the controversy.

The next speaker was the former Minister of Justice Pinchas Rosen, who had confronted the issue once before, during the conflict triggered by Jascha Heifetz's 1953 performance of a work by Richard Strauss. As a government minister in the 1950s and the early 1960s, Rosen had been closely involved in the complex relations with Germany and was party to the details of the signing of the reparations agreement and the trial and execution of Adolf Eichmann. Yet although he was well aware of the sensitivity of German–Israeli relations, he continued to uphold the same ideas he had formed on the whole affair back in the early 1950s; he unequivocally supported the view that performances of Wagner should henceforth be subject only to the technical and musical considerations of the orchestra's conductor, stressing that a firm stand must be taken "even if the timing seems unfortunate." However, the most important point he raised was the orchestra's feeling that it was bound by its connection with the state. As a member of the Liberal party, he may not have considered himself committed to the education policy formulated by Mapai – or to the authoritarian patterns set by Ben-Gurion – and he attacked the heads of the system:

As for the government institutions, we have already applied to the Ministry of Education and Culture in the past, and received only evasive answers such as "the Philharmonic Orchestra is autonomous and is entitled to decide the make-up of its programs independently," and "the aforesaid ministry has the right only to give advice," which is: not to play [these works] now.[7]

The reactions of the Ministry of Education, evasive as they were, did not reflect a lack of opinion; the ministry's continuous reluctance to take a stand was a clear statement in itself. It was plainly showing that the ministry did not consider its role to shape and define individual cultural institutions, even where national issues were involved; at most, the ministry was willing to issue general, non-binding guidelines.

One person who did not hesitate to react even before the orchestra's decision was publicized was an orchestra subscriber who appealed to Rosen not only as a private citizen, but also as a public figure: the judge of the Supreme Court, Benjamin Halevi – the man who had ruled that Israel (Rudolf) Kasztner had "sold his soul to the devil" and who had been one of the judges at the Eichmann trial. Halevi fulminated at Rosen: "As a subscriber and a public figure who seeks to identify with his national orchestra, I request a reexamination of the decision to accept the principle of playing Wagner and Strauss, who are associated in public consciousness with the Nazis and all that they inflicted on our people in our generation." Halevi signed the telegram with his full title;[8] his political views were known to all, since the Herut party had defended his decision to head the panel of judges that tried Eichmann – a decision that was revised under pressure from the Ministry of Justice, headed by Rosen. Halevi's protest was one of many: The news of the orchestra's desire to lift the ban prompted an immediate outcry and public figures took clear positions without hesitating to participate in the controversy in their official capacities – perhaps on the assumption that they had a privileged role in shaping the character of the State of Israel.

Halevi's telegram was sent in response to the decision reached at the end of the meeting of the orchestra management concerning Wagner. In the course of the debate those present were informed of the results of a survey the IPO had taken among 400 subscribers: 70 percent had announced that they favored performances of Wagner's works. Encouraged by this decisive statistic, the participants reached the following decision:

We think the orchestra should perform works by Wagner and Strauss. We will inform the orchestra's public board of our decision; to avoid taking the public by surprise, since time is short, we believe that Wagner should not be played at concert number 12 of this season, but should be introduced in the coming season.[9]

Reactions to this rather guarded announcement were not long in coming. Mehta sent a telegram arguing that the IPO management had displayed chickenheartedness and expressed regret that they lacked the courage to take a different position; he urged them to reconsider the whole question.[10] Mehta would not let the matter rest. In a lecture delivered at the orchestra guesthouse in June 1966, when he was conducting a series of IPO concerts, he presented his views on the Wagner issue. He pointed out the permanent connection between art and politics, to which everyone contributed, but brought the problematic nature of the Israeli boycott into sharp relief by citing the example of the Belgian and Dutch citizens, who, despite their suffering under the Nazi occupation, did not nurse their grudges. This way of thinking – comparing between war casualties and racist theories that had led to mass murder – will follow Mehta in later phases of the controversy; he will be presented as foreign to Israeli society and culture. Although Mehta also presented such rational arguments as the Israeli audience's high standards and the importance of playing Wagnerian pieces in order to improve the orchestra's technical ability, in the end nothing could abate the storm that was about to break over the orchestra.[11]

After the decision was announced, reports were published on a Friday in June in the Israeli press and a few British papers: *Birmingham Evening Mail*, *Reading Evening News*, and *Jewish Chronicle*. Two days later, on Sunday, the papers were filled with additional reports. *Lamerhav* announced the decision and discussed it in an editorial. The German-language daily *Jediot Hadashot* reported the decision in a matter-of-fact way, as did *Haaretz*, while *Davar* asserted that "the Government of Israel does not intervene in the policy of art institutions,"[12] apparently going by the statements made by the Ministry of Education back in the 1950s. *Maariv* gave the subject broad coverage, outlining the entire history of the ban and its annulment – beginning with the removal of *Die Meistersinger von Nürnberg* from the first concert of the 1938–1939 season and including the scandal over Heifetz's recital and the reversal, after a storm of public protest, of the decision to play Strauss's *Don Juan*.[13]

The next day the editor of *Maariv* found a letter on his desk from the chairman of the IPO public board, Attorney Haim Korngold. Korngold began by describing the astonishment he had felt at reading the quote from Toeplitz's concert-program article, and then his shock when he realized that the flautist had indeed written those words. Korngold went on to explain the motives for the decision and the reasons that the IPO management wished to postpone the performance of Wagner's works. Toeplitz's statement that "a change has taken place in the nation's attitude to the exterminators of our people" was unacceptable to Korngold, and he added that "although someone mentioned the establishment of diplomatic relations between the two states, this factor was not decisive [author's note: there is no reference to this in the minutes of the meeting].

The grounds for the basic decision were artistic freedom and artistic and educational considerations."[14] Thus, from Korngold's perspective the decision was artistic rather than political, and consequently he saw no reason for Toeplitz's paragraph on political explanation.

Nonetheless, it seems doubtful that the board members were indeed able to separate political events from the creation of the leading Israeli orchestra's musical image, for the decision to lift the ban came almost a year after the establishment of diplomatic relations with the Federal Republic of Germany. In mid-March 1965, the Herut faction in the Knesset had demanded a public referendum on the issue of diplomatic ties with Germany – two days after Prime Minister David Ben-Gurion's political announcement in the Knesset that the nation was ready to institute such ties. Feeling beleaguered, and, above all, loath to be dragged into yet another debate on the issue, the Knesset swiftly authorized the establishment of diplomatic relations with Germany. This step was not finalized until August, when the German ambassador, Rolf Pauls, presented his credentials to the president of the State of Israel, Zalman Shazar.[15] Clearly the government believed the time had come to end diplomatic estrangement; but it made this move despite the objections of a fairly substantial sector of the public.

Moreover, when the IPO made its decision to play pieces by Wagner, the country was still recovering from the commotion of May 1966, stirred by the visit to Israel of former West German Chancellor Konrad Adenauer. Israelis who opposed the establishment of relations with Germany found this visit a convenient opportunity to take to the streets and demonstrate against the guest who was doing everything he could to reconcile the two peoples.[16] These demonstrations were diametrically opposed to the ties the governing party, Mapai, had been developing with the political leadership in Germany. Mapai considered the leaders of the German Social Democratic Party (SPD) acceptable in light of their longstanding anti-Nazi outlook, and greatly admired people such as Adenauer – who had headed the Christian Democrat Party (CDU) for many years – for their resistance to Nazism during World War II. Mapai was also favorably impressed by Adenauer's readiness to overcome the obstacles to relations between the two countries.[17]

Nevertheless, even a year after the establishment of those relations Israelis did not seem to have assimilated the new state of affairs, and still feared that dialog with Germany might obliterate or obscure the gruesome deeds of the Nazis. Contemporary Germany might be a different Germany, but they did not see that as a reason to wipe out the symbols that were a continual reminder of the dark past. The images of Wagner and Strauss that had evolved through the different stages of the musical controversy were two of the most conspicuous of those symbols to date.

Throughout the week of the IPO's announcement about lifting the boycott, the hue and cry in the press continued. The *Jerusalem Post* read-

dressed the subject, but this time, in its report on guest conductors' opposition to the boycott, it began to show signs of taking a stand. This article
elicited a letter from the chairman of the IPO management, Korngold,
seeking to disassociate himself completely from Toeplitz's essay; everything in it was the sole responsibility of the talented flautist, he said.
Hatzofeh, the National Religious Party organ, told its readers that only
three of the nine management members had attended the meeting (as
mentioned earlier, six of the total thirteen had been present, and the views
of some of the absentees had been presented in writing), and that the
orchestra was to re-examine the subject.[18] *Lamerhav*, which had connections with the Labor Party, expressed editorial astonishment over the way
decisions were made in the orchestra: "No laconic announcement, casu-
ally conveyed in a concert program, can end the debate over a problem
that has been the subject of public controversy for some 30 years [. . .]
Even in the name of 'artistic freedom' the Philharmonic Orchestra is not
entitled to erase the memory of those days in this generation."[19] Harshest
of all was an editorial in *Hayom*, the paper that was Herut's political
equivalent. Under the biting headline "Nazification of a Disgraced
Orchestra," the editors wrote:

> Success has come to the orchestra, thanks to the glorious names of
> Huberman and Toscanini which have opened the hearts of the nation
> and the world. It has accumulated financial means and enjoyed grants
> from the public, the state, the city. Generous donors from abroad built
> the Mann Auditorium, which the orchestra had the sense to make its
> home. Then, having established itself, the Philharmonic goes and decides
> – since some 20 years have passed since the Holocaust – to honor that
> Nazi Richard Strauss, and to play his works in Tel Aviv and in its concerts
> abroad.
>
> And just so this bold, degrading step – which insults the memory of
> the six million victims of the regime of which Richard Strauss was a part
> – won't seem too sudden and surprising, the orchestra unearths from the
> dust of its storeroom works by another German – he too a noted anti-
> Semite – whom the Nazis saw as their prophet and pioneer: Wagner.[20]

The article then proceeded to sing the praises of the Herut activists and
partisans who were the only people to rise in protest over this outrage,
and reproached all who had lent their hands to the de-Nazification of Carl
Orff. Orff, it should be noted, was a recognized Nazi collaborator who,
although initially leaving the Third Reich, had returned to it and enjoyed
the unstinting support of the regime. Although the IPO did not play his
compositions, they found their way onto the broadcasting lists of the
Voice of Israel (*Kol Yisrael*) even in the days before the establishment of
the classical music channel, the Voice of Music (*Kol Hamusika*). At that
time, the Israeli Opera also dared to perform *Carmina Burana*, a well-

known work by Orff that had been popular in the Third Reich.[21] As *Hayom* noted, the partisan organizations were indeed trying very hard to prevent the performance of Wagner and Strauss, and urged the IPO management to remove Toeplitz's essay from the concert program.[22]

This time, too, the article in *Hayom* brought a response from the chairman of the IPO management, seeking to clarify that the contents of Toeplitz's article were Toeplitz's sole responsibility.[23] However, this letter did not discuss an additional issue raised by the paper – an issue that was central to the controversy. Underlying all the disputes was the fact that the entity trying to break the taboo was one that was generally viewed as a state body. The importance attributed to this was all the more evident in light of the relative apathy concerning the Israeli Opera's production of *Carmina Burana*. The image of the IPO as a national institution was to determine the pattern of the boycott controversy in the following years – the breakthroughs were ultimately achieved by smaller orchestras that the public did not view as state bodies.

No other Israeli paper took as stern a position as *Hayom* against the orchestra's decision, and some even commended the decision for both musical and ideological reasons. *Haaretz*, a paper known for well-reasoned and moderate reporting, printed a caustic editorial condemning the use of music as an emotional or political symbol. The author – anonymous – feared that art and politics were becoming too closely linked, reflecting in a way "the infiltration of totalitarian thought in our public life" – criticism that may have been directed not only at the opponents of performances of banned music, but also at the centralistic nature of the Israeli government. Moreover, the anonymous writer believed it was "desirable that [the Israeli musical experience] remain unbroken, and in our state we are strong enough to make a distinction between the kingdom of melodies and the kingdom of Satan."[24] However, the article's quotation of Toeplitz's sentence about "a change [. . .] in the nation's attitude to the exterminators of our people" brought the usual clarifying letters from the chairman of the management and the representative of the orchestra members, stressing that Toeplitz had indeed written those words in the original essay that appeared on the first evening of the concert series; but that pressure from the management had resulted in its replacement by the attenuated "we feel the time has come for a change."[25]

The other leading morning paper, *Davar*, the Mapai organ, took a completely different stance. In an editorial, the paper attacked Toeplitz's logic in linking political changes with a readiness for changes in art. "Were the works of Wagner and Strauss banned until now because they were German?" the writer of the editorial asked rhetorically – undoubtedly drawing a parallel with the racism perceived in the composers' views.[26] In short, the official position of the governing party was: We have no problem with the "other" Germany, but we do not forgive those who were actually responsible for the racism and the extermination.

The following day *Davar* published an extensive, informative article on the history of the boycott and on Wagner's personal views. Obviously space did not allow full coverage of every facet of the problem, but the article was fairly comprehensive and opened the door to essential questions. A similar, though more succinct, article was printed the next day in *Haaretz*.[27] In the following days many articles of this kind appeared in other Israeli newspapers. Some of them discussed Wagner and Strauss and their views,[28] others wondered if it was possible to break the link between the Nazis' treatment of certain composers and the Israeli ban on the latter,[29] and a few papers published surveys carried out among intellectuals.[30] These surveys clearly indicated that there was no indisputable correlation between the respondent's occupation or political tendencies and his or her views on the specific issue of the taboo on the banned composers; on this subject responses went to the heart of the matter, regardless of other variables that might seem to have been related.

One of the most important articles published in the first weeks of the controversy was by the musical director of the Voice of Israel, Michal Zmora. In a profound piece Zmora enumerated reasons for playing the music of the banned composers. She argued that the works of Wagner and Strauss had a life of their own; but she was careful to make a distinction between those works and *Carmina Burana* (at the time in production by the Israeli Opera), in light of their different musical significance. Orff's work had been composed as a statement against the system innovated by Arnold Schönberg – who as a Jew and a creator of abstract art had been banned in the Third Reich – and out of a desire to assimilate into the Nazi system. Wagner and Strauss, in contrast, were important to the musical development of the modern age, and therefore should not be put in the same category with him. Zmora continued to uphold these views for many years, and as a result was vilified by opponents of the banned composers in Israel.[31]

A particularly important news item that was published the same first week of the ideological disputes reported the interpellation submitted by MK Esther Raziel-Naor to the minister of education concerning performances of Wagner's music, taking the opportunity to condemn the Israeli Opera for performing Orff's work. Raziel-Naor was well known for her opposition to Germany in both the political and cultural spheres. In 1957 she had already addressed an interpellation to the minister of education on the issue of what the IPO should be allowed to play, and in 1960 she took Prime Minister David Ben-Gurion to task in the Knesset for his supposedly "chance" meeting in New York with West German Chancellor Konrad Adenauer. On the same occasion she also demanded a public referendum on the establishment of diplomatic relations with Germany.[32]

Like the political right's previous attempt (during the reparations talks in early 1952) to directly intervene in the evolving relations with West Germany, this harsh calling to account came at a time when the right wing was in a weak position. Although it was represented by 26 Knesset members, that number represented a decline in the strength of the party that had joined with the Liberal Party in the 1965 elections. Moreover, its members were at odds with each other, and some were even challenging Begin's leadership.[33]

On this occasion, Raziel-Naor demanded an explanation regarding Minister Zalman Aranne's willingness to permit the music of Wagner, Strauss, and Orff to be played in Israeli concert halls. She described Wagner as the Nazis' spiritual father, Strauss as a pro-Nazi, and Orff as the pet of the Nazi regime. Concluding her speech, Raziel-Naor asked the minister of education two questions. First, she wished to know whether he still held by the view he had expressed in replying to her previous inter-pellation, in 1957 – namely, that "for the time being the Ministry of Education and Culture recommends the exclusion of Strauss from [the orchestra's] program." Secondly she asked, "What does the honorable minister intend to do in order to prevent the performance of German–Nazi works by composers like Orff, Strauss, and Wagner on our stages?"

On behalf of the minister, Deputy Minister Aharon Yadlin returned a twofold reply. On the one hand, he stated: "The Government of Israel does not intend to engage in cultural censorship"; on the other hand, he explained that "had [the IPO] asked its advice, the ministry would have recommended excluding the works of Wagner and Strauss from orches-tral repertoires." The deputy minister even attacked Toeplitz's "improper" justification concerning Israelis' changed approach to "the exterminators of our people." The implication here, as *Davar* had already made clear, was that attitudes had not changed toward the exterminators, but toward the "other" Germany; Israel had contracted a diplomatic alliance with that "other" Germany, not with the persecutors of the Jews. In response to another question voiced by Raziel-Naor, Yadlin said that the heads of the Voice of Israel did not consult with the Ministry of Education any more than the orchestra did. In other words, in order to maintain democratic values, the government of Israel did not intervene in the arts, though it was uncomfortable with current developments.[34] This approach paved the way for later official reactions, albeit since the mid-1990s the Knesset Education and Culture Committee pushed for a change of attitude that would be acceptable to both artistic bodies and govern-ment officials.

However, other political figures were less punctilious. Minister of Health Israel Barzilay (Mapam), who was also a member of the IPO's public board, joined another board member, MK Gideon Hausner (Liberals) in calling on the orchestra to revoke its decision. Hausner, it should be recalled, had been the government attorney-general at the time of Adolf Eichmann's trial, and in that capacity had served as chief prose-cutor in the well-publicized trial. Hausner answered Zubin Mehta's arguments by asserting that the issue was a public Jewish one, not a musical one. Hausner's opening speech at the Eichmann trial left no doubt as to his perception of the relationship between Israel and Germany; the prosecutor who had declared "When I stand before you here, judges of Israel, to lead the prosecution of Adolf Eichmann, I am not standing alone. With me are six million accusers,"[35] was now defending Israelis' right not to listen to works that were identified – rightly or wrongly – with the Nazi regime. The mayor of Tel Aviv, Mordechai Namir, also had to address the issue, since the municipality was substantially represented in the management of Mann Auditorium. On 25 June, a week after the initial hullabaloo over the IPO's announcement, the debate was renewed.

The articles and political responses did not offer any real explanation of the great sensitivity shown to the interests and feelings of Holocaust survivors. After all, 20 years had passed since the end of the war, significant political changes had taken place, and a relaxation of musical taboos might have seemed reasonable. Of course, no one was willing to admit openly that the target of anger was due in part to the relative convenience of associating ideological guilt with a sphere that was not very popular in any case. Nevertheless, the intensification of the controversy and the readiness of politicians and public figures to play a part were not solely attributable to the convenience of using musicians as symbols of the Holocaust.

The injection of politics into art in this case is not surprising, for two reasons. First, there had already been political responses to German art during the 1950s, which were strongly and clearly expressed in the sphere of concert music. The other reason was Israelis' special sensitivity concerning West Germany in those years. As mentioned earlier, the first half of the 1960s was characterized by a reawakening of interest in the relationship between West Germany and Israel and between Germans and Israelis. However, more than the establishment of diplomatic relations, the trial of Adolf Eichmann was the event that broke through the barriers of silence and suppression vis-à-vis Holocaust survivors.[36]

In the spring of 1960, Ben-Gurion dropped a bombshell. In a speech at the Knesset plenum, he announced that the Nazi war criminal Adolf Eichmann had been captured and would be brought to trial in Israel. The press pounced on the story, and debates that waged in the pages of the newspapers were so heated that Justice Minister Pinchas Rosen was obliged to intervene and remind editors of the laws of *sub judice*. In the course of the public discussion of the approaching trial – which for the most part continued in the press – arguments were presented concerning the importance of this event to Israelis.

Eliyahu Salpeter, one of *Haaretz*'s leading political commentators, explained that the trial would permit a reconstruction of the horrors of the Holocaust and improve Jews' knowledge of the subject, and that it would be an important learning experience for young people who had not gone through the Holocaust. The testimony would also penetrate the armor of those Germans still unconvinced by the reports about what had happened in the concentration camps; and, finally, those Germans who had lent their hands to the extermination would have to confront their consciences once again.[37]

At least two of Salpeter's hopes were indeed fulfilled. In the courthouse dozens of witnesses recounted details that had never before been heard by the general public, let alone the younger generation. The radio-transmitted voices of the prosecutor, Gideon Hausner, and the witnesses were heard in numerous household in Israel.[38] The testimony of Yehiel Dinur, better known as K. Zetnik, the author of *Salamandra*, one of the most agonizing accounts of the Holocaust, was etched on everyone's mind. While giving evidence, Dinur rose from the witness stand and fell down in a dead faint as cameras frantically clicked; by the next day he had become the hero of the trial, a witness who proved that it was impossible to forget or even to forgive. Reports on the trial played an important role in shaping the memory of the Holocaust in Israeli society.[39]

Journalists from all over the world avidly covered the proceedings, among them the German Jewish intellectual, Hannah Arendt. Her illuminating book – which was translated into Hebrew only in 2000, 37 years after it first appeared in English – on the trial's significance for Israeli society, was published two years after Eichmann was sentenced to death, hanged, cremated, his ashes sprinkled at sea. Arendt claimed that the Israelis were not trying Eichmann, but all the Nazis for all their crimes. She believed that the case was the citizens of Israel versus Nazi war criminals, not the state of Israel versus Adolf Eichmann.[40] Indisputably Eichmann's sentence was determined by the severity of his crimes, but clearly his trial in Israel exposed the magnitude of the pain and the emotional associations evoked by the Holocaust as a whole, rather than just the deeds of one person, no matter how important his role had been.

Thus, in many respects the trial apparently lanced an abscess that had formed in Israeli society over the dozen years of statehood. Israelis who, from ignorance, had not been previously receptive to the testimony of survivors, were shocked by the enormity of the humiliation and torture undergone by Jews in Europe, and for the first time there was a willingness to accept those horrors as suffering rather than weakness. Suddenly there was a great thirst to know more about the hidden past. But this great interest also reawakened a tremendous revulsion toward Germans.

The public clearly saw that not all Germans bore the same measure of responsibility, and was well-aware of Ben-Gurion's view that modern Germany was different from its predecessor. Yet the new compassion for Holocaust survivors carried in its wake a sharpened vigilance against anything that smacked of Germanness.[41] Anger toward Germans was loudly unleashed every time sufficient reason could be found, whether political or cultural. But whereas in the political and legal sphere this anger could not be controlled from above – as when the painful and emotionally wrenching evidence of the Eichmann trial emerged – the cultural sphere allowed sufficient margin for responses that appeared measured and well thought out on the surface. Thus, the battle against performances of the banned composers in Israel was characterized not by emotional outbursts from certain sectors of the public, but by reasoned behavior on the part of public officials.

From this point on, hatred of Germany took on an additional aspect of xenophobia, which was plainly directed against guest conductor Zubin Mehta. Mehta's stubborn demand to perform a Wagner piece with the IPO may have aroused anger, but the way that anger was expressed indicated that the freedom some commentators arrogated to themselves to attack Mehta personally was due to his being a foreigner – and not only a foreigner, but a non-Jew. Mehta was directly attacked at least twice – the first time in a music review printed in *Maariv*, which ridiculed "the interference of the Indian conductor, in preaching mode." This review elicited an immediate response from the chairman of the IPO management, who wrote to the editor of the paper that not only was Mehta a distinguished conductor who "would make many people happy if he consented to accept the role of musical director of the orchestra," but that the article had been discourteous and tasteless. Korngold continued this defense by attacking the radio critic for having ignored a concert broadcast on the Voice of Israel: The program's editors had dared to play a recording of Hector Berlioz's *Benvenuto Cellini* conducted by Ernest Ansermet, who was known for collaborating with the Nazis. He, too, of course, was one of the musicians boycotted in Israel, whom the IPO refrained from inviting.[42]

Only three days later, *Maariv* repeated its offense. This time one of the paper's leading columnists, Shmuel Schnitzer, addressed an open letter to Mehta. The whole article was written as a personal appeal to a foreigner who deserved a great deal of appreciation for his willingness to invest his energy and erudition in enriching Israeli classical music fans. This foreigner was told to learn a chapter from the history of the Jewish people, as well as a lesson in manners and conduct: The foreigner was not to argue – "let us argue by ourselves, among ourselves." Although Schnitzer mentioned Mehta's origins, his comments did not have racist overtones: "You are a native of India and 30 years old. You have, then, all the qualifications required. You were born in a place where there were indeed swastikas, but where Nazis were not very common. And you were nine years old when we began to count our dead." That is to say: You have no idea how profound our problem is; mind your own business and let us mind ours.[43] And "our business," going by the tenor of the article, was an issue not of art but of politics and morality which only those involved were entitled to address.

The 1966 Wagner affair aroused more reactions and controversy than had the attempts to cancel the taboo on the "forbidden composers" in the

1950s. This time the subject was highly charged, perhaps because of the new political and social circumstances, or because Wagner in particular and, to some degree, Strauss, began to assume the symbolic meanings that Israelis assigned to them and were to be associated with those rather than with what they had actually done. They were no longer German composers who were linked to the Nazi movement in one way or another; in many senses they had become the Nazis' representatives on this earth, representatives that Israelis – and not only the Holocaust survivors among them – needed to hate. In 1966, dozens of articles were written about the Wagner affair, and not one newspaper passed up an opportunity to address the topic and update its readers on the public controversy and the decisions taken in the emergency meetings of the orchestra management. Interestingly, all these reports were prominently featured in the press at a time when the main story was actually the economic problems engendered in Israel by the economic recession of the 1960s. At that stage, Wagner provided the only color in a rather gray landscape of news coverage.

The 1966 affair ended with an announcement by the IPO that it had decided not to play Wagner and Strauss pieces after all. At the beginning of August, about six weeks after the latest outbreak of the Wagner controversy, the storm finally petered out. In the last weeks the papers had continued to print readers' letters of for and against, while the orchestra completed its preparations for a long tour to Australia, New Zealand, and Hong Kong. Until the orchestra returned to Israel and the next concert season opened, the unwanted composers were relegated to oblivion.

Only a year after the public brouhaha over the orchestra, Israeli citizens were celebrating in the streets, drunk with pride over the impressive success of the Israel Defence Force (IDF) in the Six-Day War. The sense of power and freedom that permeated all sectors of the public was prime testimony to the degree of existential fear that had afflicted Israelis as they waited for the anticipated outbreak of hostilities; the war that had channeled fears of a second possible Holocaust ended in glorious victory, and relief was intense.[44] Top-level musicians were happy to join the winning side. Three days after the war an outstanding trio landed in Israel: the conductor Leonard Bernstein and the mezzo-soprano, Jenny Tourel, who had been in the center of the 1952 controversy over the language in which Mahler's songs should be sung, and violinist Isaac Stern, who only a year previously had sent the IPO a telegram of encouragement to bolster those trying to eliminate the taboo on public performances of Wagner and Strauss.[45] These three joined the IPO and the Israeli soprano Nethanya Dovrat in performing a particularly symbolic piece: Gustav Mahler's Second Symphony, known as *Resurrection Symphony*. This time no one even raised the question of whether the piece should be performed in the original language or in translation. And of course no one remembered, either, the letter from the partisan organizations in November 1966 demanding that no Mahler piece in the German language be included in an Israeli concert.[46] Apparently the Israelis now had sufficient self-confidence to tolerate the language that only a few years before had been so loathsome.

However, what was acceptable from a Jewish apostate was still taboo if it came from the "forbidden composers." When in the fall of 1969 Zubin Mehta asked to conduct Strauss's *Till Eulenspiegel*, protests were instantly voiced, and before the dispute could gather momentum, the maestro withdrew the suggestion. Once again, those opposing a performance of Strauss included the partisan organizations in Israel, which would not let the subject drop; this time they declared: "We hope that we will not be obliged to take demonstrative measures against your step which constitutes a desecration of the memory of our martyrs and a blow to the Jewish nation's feelings about its murderers."[47] MK Reuven Barkat (Labor) sent a letter to the IPO denouncing "coercion of conscience" and demanded two concert tickets to replace the ones he had – apparently as a subscriber – in order to save him having to leave the concert hall ostentatiously when *Till Eulenspiegel* was played.[48] The Strauss piece was replaced on the program by *Chaconne for Orchestra* by the Israeli Noam Sheriff – who was later to defy the Strauss boycott in 1990 while conducting a concert of the Rishon LeZion Symphony Orchestra.

The discordant notes that had ended the various phases of the musical controversy in the 1960s died down in the silence of the following years. But the undertones reverberating through the public debate of the 1960s prefigured its sequels. In the 1960s Wagner and Strauss were transformed from real people into embodiments of all the Nazis' iniquity and injustice toward Jews. The mention of their names was enough to arouse feelings that were perceived as the norm: opposition, revulsion, and condemnation, all of which were far deeper than the musical issue. In fact, the "forbidden musicians" – particularly these two – had become the most conspicuous symbols of the hatred of Germans. In the controversy of 1966, this opposition was compounded by a measure of xenophobia, although still rarely expressed, against the conductor Zubin Mehta; later on this tendency – to blame the foreign conductor – would become prevalent.

Another phenomenon that began with the 1966 controversy was the total separation of the political echelon's conduct toward its counterpart in the Federal Republic of Germany and the views politicians presented on the "forbidden composers." Their behavior, which distinguished between the advantages inherent in maintaining economic and political ties with Germany on the one hand, and the advantages of building up symbols of the Holocaust and then expressing firm opposition to them, on the other, was also adopted by newspaper columnists and a significant sector of Israeli society. The Eichmann trial, which etched the Holocaust on the consciousness of Israelis of all origins – European, African, or Asian – opened the composer controversy even to people who had no personal or historical bias against the "forbidden composers." From this point on people who did not frequent the concert halls, but who felt that they had a moral right to shape the characteristics of Israeli culture, joined the debate.

This segment of the debate had also shown how big a role the press played in fanning the flames of the controversy. The pressure of newspaper articles and reports in the first week of the uproar, together with the intervention of public figures, led the chairman of the IPO management to make Uri Toeplitz – author of the article that ignited the public conflagration – change the wording of one of the sentences that had aroused such fierce dispute; ultimately the IPO management felt obliged to convene again, only a week after publishing the decision to lift the ban, in order to re-examine the issue. This was the moment that most clearly marks the point at which the subject of the "forbidden composers" left the musical-repertoire sphere and moved to the flagrantly political one. The captains of the government, as Deputy Minister Yadlin had said in the Knesset, did not want to be seen as interfering in art, for fear of being perceived as totalitarian dictators; but when the general upheaval in the Israeli public drove the contentious issue into the political arena, not one of them bothered to defend freedom of the arts and freedom of expression, concepts that had not yet even entered Israeli legislation.

Notes

1 On the place of cultural attributes as identifiers of Israeliness, see B. Kimmerling, *The Invention and Decline of Israeliness: State, Society, and the Military* (Berkeley, 2001), especially pp. 89–111, 173–207.

2 Zertal, *Israel's Holocaust*, pp. 52–90.

3 Minutes of meeting of the public board of the Israeli Philharmonic Orchestra, Jerusalem, 8 Jan. 1963, IPO Archives, internal affairs file.

4 Ibid.

5 U. Toeplitz, "On the Importance of Wagner," *IPO program*, June, 1966.

6 Protocol of the meeting of the orchestra management, 3 June 1966, IPO Archives, internal affairs file.

7 Ibid.

8 B. Halevi to P. Rosen, telegram, 17 June 1966.

9 Minutes of the meeting of 3 June 1966.

10 The contents of this telegram were reported in a letter sent by an orchestra member, W. Levi, to the management chairman, Attorney H. Korngold, 10 June 1966, IPO Archives, Wagner and Strauss file.

11 Z. Mehta, lecture at the IPO guesthouse, June 1966 (exact date not noted), IPO Archives, Wagner and Strauss file.

12 "The Philharmonic Has Decided to Play Works by Wagner and Strauss [Hebrew]," *Davar*, 19 June 1966; "The Orchestra Will Play the Works of Wagner and Strauss [Hebrew]," and "First Column [Hebrew]" (editorial), *Lamerhav*, 19 June 1966; "Wagner und Richard Strauss wieder in IPO-Programm," *Jediot Hadashot*, 19 June 1966; and "The Philharmonic Will

Play Works by Wagner and Strauss Next Season [Hebrew]," *Haaretz*, 19 June 1966.

13 "The Philharmonic Has Decided to Perform Works by Wagner and Richard Strauss [Hebrew]," *Maariv*, 17 June 1966.

14 H. Korngold to editor of *Maariv*, 20 June 1966, IPO Archives, local press file.

15 On the process of forming diplomatic relations, see Vogel, *The German Path*, pp. 159–79.

16 A notable example of the Israelis' continued opposition to Germany was the refusal by a Voice of Israel radio announcer, Yael Ben-Yehuda, to read a commercial for Volkswagen in February 1966. Ben-Yehuda described this incident in the television series *Tkuma* ("Resurrection"), in the episode "In the Shadow of the Holocaust: 1948–1966," which was broadcast on the state television Channel 1 in the winter of 1998.

17 On the relationship established in the mid-1960s between the Social Democratic Party and Israeli politicians, see S. Shafir, *An Outstretched Hand: German Social Democrats, Jews, and Israel 1945–1967* [Hebrew] (Tel Aviv, 1986), esp. pp. 195–6. On the warm relations with Willi Brandt and Helmut Schmidt, the future social democratic chancellor, see also the autobiography of the Israeli ambassador to Germany, Y. Meroz, *In schwieriger Mission* (Berlin, 1986). On Brandt's attitude toward Jews, see W. Brandt, "Germany, Israel, and the Jews," lecture delivered by the mayor of Berlin at the Theodor Herzl Institute in New York City, 19 March [1961], Berlin, 1961.

18 "The Orchestra's Decision to Play Works by Wagner and Strauss to Be Reviewed [Hebrew]," *Hatzofeh*, 20 June 1966; "Visiting Conductors Opposed Ban on Wagner and Strauss," *The Jerusalem Post*, 20 June 1966; and letter in response from H. Korngold to the editor of *The Jerusalem Post*, 22 June 1966, IPO Archives, local press file.

19 "'Musical Education' or Insensitivity [Hebrew]," *Lamerhav*, 20 June 1966.

20 "Nazification of the Orchestra of Shame [Hebrew]," *Hayom*, 20 June 1966.

21 I was told about Orff's being played on the Voice of Israel by the manager of the Voice of Music, Avi Hanani, in a personal interview in Jerusalem (11 Feb. 1996). He claims that the reason had been the personal acquaintance between Orff and one of the senior officials of Voice of Israel, Kar-El Salmon, who had been at school with Orff. A fascinating documentary film was made of Orff's life under the Nazi regime and afterwards: *O Fortuna*, directed by Tony Palmer, Bayerischer Rundfunk, WDR Köln, Ladbroke Productions, LWT Productions, and RM Arts, 1996.

22 Les Organisations des Partisans, des Combattants et des Anciens Déportés, Israel (signed by S. Grayek, Y. Sandman, A. Hess, and H. Faber) to the management of the Israel Philharmonic Orchestra, 22 June 1966, IPO Archives, Wagner and Strauss file. The partisan organizations did not let the matter drop for any length of time, and on 10 July sent another letter to the IPO management, demanding an immediate response to their previous demands concerning the "forbidden composers."

23 H. Korngold to editor of *Hayom*, 22 June 1966, IPO Archives, local press file.

24 "From Day to Day: A Symbol that Was Out of Place [Hebrew]," *Haaretz*, 21 June 1966.

25 W. Levi to the editor of *Haaretz*, 21 June 1966; and H. Korngold to the editor of *Haaretz*, 21 June 1966, IPO Archives, local press file.

26 "Item of the Day – Public Insensitivity [Hebrew]," *Davar*, 21 June 1966.

27 "The Controversy over Wagner and Strauss [Hebrew]," *Davar*, 22 June 1966; and "The Affair of the Wagner and Strauss Boycott [Hebrew]," *Haaretz*, 23 June 1966.

28 See, for example, "Richard Strauss Was Not Toscanini [Hebrew]," *Davar*, 24 June 1966.

29 See, for example, "Wagner, Strauss, and the Dance Around the Hot Porridge [Hebrew]," *Haaretz*, 24 June 1966; "Who Remembers – Who Forgot? [Hebrew]" *Hayom*, 24 June 1966; "Should Performances of Works by Wagner and Strauss Be Allowed [Hebrew]," *Hatzofeh*, 24 June 1966; "Wagner on Jews [Hebrew]," *Davar*, 26 June 1966; "Between Nibelungen and Auschwitz [Hebrew]," *Davar*, 1 July 1966; and "Wagnerian Nightmares [Hebrew]," *Haaretz*, 3 July 1966.

30 See, for example, "Wagner and Strauss – For and Against," *Maariv*, 27 June 1966. In favor: playwright Max Brod; composer Paul Ben-Haim; former musical director of the Voice of Israel, Kar-El Salmon; composer Frank Peleg; and director of the music library at the Hebrew University, Israel Eldar (who advocated permitting only Wagner). Opposed: critic Menashe Rabina, pianist Alexander Tamir, MK Gideon Hausner (Liberals), and Prof. Shmuel Ettinger. In favor of re-examining the issue: pianist Bracha Eden, and Prof. Ephraim Ohrbach. See also "The Voice of Everywhere [radio review column]: Are You a Fan of Strauss?" *Maariv*, 27 June 1966.

31 "Musical Works – A Means or an End? [Hebrew]," *Haaretz*, 24 June, 1966.

32 In March 1960, Ben-Gurion dared to do something he had wanted to do for many years: While on a visit to the state of New York, he held a private meeting with Adenauer. Adenauer had expressed willingness for such a meeting at the time that the reparations were being discussed, but Ben-Gurion had feared possible reaction in Israel. And indeed, when Ben-Gurion returned from New York, he was attacked by the right and the left; the leaders of this opposition were MK Shmuel Mikunis (Maki – Israeli Communist Party) and MK Esther Raziel-Naor (Herut). *Divrei HaKnesset* [minutes of the Israeli parliament], session 72, 16 March 1960, pp. 918–20. On Adenauer's willingness to establish relations, see A. Ben-Natan, "The Path to Diplomatic Relations: The Israeli Perspective [Hebrew]," in *"Normal" Relations: Relations between Israel and Germany*, ed. M. Zimmerman and O. Heilbruner (Jerusalem, 1993), pp. 24–32. It should be remembered that at this stage Israel viewed its historic past and the wrongs done to the Jews for hundreds of years as legitimate argument for international political decisions. Cf. R. Rein, *In the Shadow of the Holocaust and the Inquisition: Israel's Relations with Francoist Spain*, trans. M. Grenzeback (London and Portland, OR, 1997), pp. 59–73.

33 Shapiro, *Chosen to Command*, pp. 142–54.

34 See Interpellation 846, MK Raziel-Naor to Minister of Education and Culture, 28 June 1966.

35 *6,000,000 Accusers: Israel's Case against Eichmann. The Opening Speech and Legal Argument of Mr. Gideon Hausner, Attorney-General*, trans. S. Rosenne (Jerusalem, 1961), pp. 27–43.

36 On the political appeal of the Eichmann trial in Israeli society, see Zertal, *Israel's Holocaust*, pp. 91–127.

37 E. Salpeter, "What May Be Revealed in the Eichmann Trial [Hebrew]," *Haaretz*, 3 June 1960.

38 On the publicity of the trial, see A. Pinchevski and T. Liebes, "Severed Voices: Radio and the Mediation of Trauma in the Eichmann Trial," *Public Culture*, 22.2 (2010): 265–91.

39 Zandberg, "The Right to Tell the (right) Story."

40 See H. Arendt, *Eichmann in Jerusalem*, various editions. For discussion of Arendt herself and her contribution to modern intellectual discourse, see a special issue of the periodical *History & Memory* 8, no. 2 (1996).

41 About a year after the Eichmann trial, in July 1962, Israel unexpectedly discovered that German scientists were aiding Egypt in developing missile systems. The mounting rage that resulted once again posed the question as to the acceptability of Germans and the degree to which they were politically and morally different from their parents. On this episode, see M. Bar-Zohar, *The Hunt for German Scientists* (London, 1967).

42 "The Voice of Everywhere: Are You a Fan of Strauss? [Hebrew]" *Maariv*, 27 June 1966; and H. Korngold to editor of *Maariv*, 28 June 1966, IPO Archives, local press file.

43 "To the Conductor – Do Not Destroy! [Hebrew]," *Maariv*, 1 July 1966.

44 On political and military developments that led to the war and the war itself, see M. Oren, *Six Days of War: June 1967 and the Making of the Modern Middle East* (New York, 2003). On the emotions that were typical of Israeli society at the time, see T. Segev, *1967: Israel, the War, and the Year that Transformed the Middle East* (New York, 2007).

45 I. Stern to management of the Philharmonic Orchestra, 23 July 1966, IPO Archives, foreign protest file. On the involvement of Bernstein and Tourel, see Chapter 5.

46 Les Organisations des Partisans [signed by Dr. M. Dvorzetski] to Management of the Philharmonic Orchestra, 11 November 1966, IPO Archives, Wagner and Strauss file.

47 Organizations of the Partisans, Fighters, and Prisoners of the Nazis in Israel [signed by P. Burstein] to management of the Philharmonic Orchestra, 12 October 1969, IPO Archives, Wagner and Strauss file.

48 MK R. Barkat to management of the Philharmonic Orchestra, 15 October 1969, IPO Archives, Wagner and Strauss file.

7

The 1970s:
Political Furor, Musical Calm

After the turmoil over the IPO management's decision to countenance the performance of works by Wagner and Strauss – a decision it revoked – eight years passed before anyone tried again to lift the ban on the public performance of music by the "forbidden composers." In June 1974 the Israeli press reported a new decision taken by the IPO management to authorize to play Wagner's music for the first time since 1938. As on every occasion that the Wagner taboo had been challenged, outraged responses featured prominently on the opinion pages, together with more neutral views; but this time some journalists expressed outright support of the IPO's decision. Now, too, the conflict was shorter and less polemic than past disputes, when controversy had focused on the question of German composers' "kosherness" and whether some Israelis were capable of coping emotionally with the performance of German music. Yet this round of the controversy exposed more clearly than ever the essence of the dispute between those who wanted Wagner's music performed and those who rejected the very idea.

Once again the IPO waited until the end of the concert season to reveal its intentions to the public. In mid-June 1974, shortly before the conclusion of the season, the orchestra announced that a work by Richard Wagner would be played at the concert scheduled for the 26th of the month. Just as before, the daily press rushed to report the news, and angry letters soon streamed into the IPO administrative office. The first to react were the partisan organizations in Israel, which again clarified the principles they had defended in the 1960s: "It is unnecessary to stress the seriousness of your decision, which deeply offends the feelings of Holocaust survivors in Israel and the Diaspora and desecrates the memory of the nation's martyrs."[1] A week later, the press reported that the partisans intended to disrupt the concert. Other "Wagner resisters" were expected to demonstrate with them, having bought tickets to the controversial concert for the sole purpose of sabotaging it.[2]

Along with other responses of this kind, which had become routine, the IPO management received another, more problematic letter. The workers' committee of the Mann Auditorium had decided to take a stand on the issue, and sent a scathing letter to their superiors. The auditorium's ushers described themselves as a group of people with disabilities that were so employed as a result of their physical condition; the group comprised concentration camp survivors, partisans, resistance fighters, and IDF veterans. All of them were disgusted by the management's decision:

> We learned with deep sorrow and grieving hearts that the management of the Israel Philharmonic Orchestra has agreed to the suggestion of the conductor Zubin Mehta [. . .] Shame!
>   Woe to the Jew in the State of Israel who agrees to play the music that accompanied the six million, the children, women, men, and babies, to the death camps.[3]

On their own initiative, the ushers categorically announced that on the night of the concert the doors to the auditorium would not be opened. A few days later, when the managers of the orchestra changed their minds about the special concert, they attributed their about-face to concern for the audience's safety. The ushers' threat had done its job.[4] Once again, it was not a state decision or a political-oriented verdict, but rather an inner discourse that forced voluntary self-censorship.

As in previous phases of the controversy, the orchestra had also received appeals from public officials who vehemently opposed the idea of Wagner concerts. One of them was an influential figure in Israeli cultural life in general and the city of Tel Aviv in particular: Avraham Schechterman (Herut–Liberal Bloc – Gahal), chairperson of the Knesset Education and Culture Committee and a member of the Tel Aviv City Council. Schechterman asked the IPO management, "Who is behind this renewed plot [playing the music of Wagner, whom he considered one of the spiritual fathers of Nazism]? Who is interested in fanning the flames of hate and controversy in Israel in these difficult days of trial?"[5] Schechterman was thus addressing not only the principle of public performances of Wagner's music, but also the very problematic timing of the IPO announcement.

This announcement, coming again at the end of a concert season – perhaps in the hope of sneaking the change into the program without reawakening the dispute over the issue – was made at a particularly difficult time for the State of Israel. Only eight months had gone by since the Yom Kippur War had shaken the nation to its foundations in October 1973; about six months since hostilities had ceased following the UN resolution imposed on the parties to the conflict; and a little more than two months since the political upheaval occasioned by the publication of the interim conclusions of the state inquiry commission headed by Supreme-Court Judge Shimon Agranat. Prime Minister Golda Meir, Defense

Minister Moshe Dayan, and Chief of Staff David Elazar, all paid for Israel's unreadiness for the war with their jobs.[6]

During this period, when the attention of most Israeli citizens was focused on efforts toward social and spiritual rehabilitation, a single concert by the Israel Philharmonic was obviously unlikely to arouse much interest, even if one of the pieces on the program was by Wagner. This probably accounted for the relative brevity of the controversy this time, and for the national press's evident lack of eagerness for a renewed debate. At the peak of the year that had brought tragedy to thousands of Israeli families, as the nation looked back over the six euphoric years between the Six-Day War and the Yom Kippur War and examined its conscience, publicists apparently did not think they should let themselves be sucked into a public debate of a magnitude similar to that of the 1950s and 1960s. Even the politicians, who normally gained political capital out of affairs of this kind, showed no inclination to touch an issue that seemed quite negligible compared with the burning questions then preoccupying Israeli citizens and their leaders. Moreover, according to sociologist Baruch Kimmerling, the 1970s marked a shift from a secular society to a society that accepted religious belief and embraced the messianic movement, largely by encouraging settlement of the Occupied Territories.[7]

An additional factor was the time that had passed since the original cancellation of the 1938 performance of the *Die Meistersinger von Nürnberg* prelude, and the end of World War II. However, the arguments presented by those opposed to performances of the banned music showed that time had not tempered attitudes – perhaps even the reverse; increasing use was made of the argument that any concession to Wagner fans would further dim the memory of the Holocaust, which had already been eroded by time. By now the youngest survivors were 30 or older, and had lived most of their lives in the State of Israel and put down roots there. Their parents' generation was beginning to retire from active life, and the fear was that once they were gone there would no longer be any sufficiently concrete testimony to the memory of the Holocaust and its meaning for the Jewish world. Later reactions proved that Wagner has become an emblem and an idea, and thus the generational issue became marginal.

A week passed between the IPO management's announcement of the intention to play works by Wagner and its change of heart; three days more and the debate fizzled out completely. It is worthy of note that this relatively short flare-up took place when residents of the north of the country were suffering attacks by terrorist groups. In mid-May 1974, in the town of Ma'alot, 16 schoolchildren from Safed were killed by a gang of terrorists who seized the building where they were spending the night on a school trip. Just around the time that the IPO was announcing its intention of playing Wagner, terrorists infiltrated Kibbutz Shamir and murdered two members and a volunteer worker. The day after the cancellation was announced, another terrorist gang entered an apartment in Nahariah and murdered two children and their mother.

Although these incidents were not mentioned by the people arguing against performances of Wagner, they probably reinforced the siege mentality and sense of isolation that was already strong among some Israelis. The old fears of annihilation, which had seemed to fade after the glorious victory of the Six-Day War, had reemerged during the Yom Kippur War; the terrorist attacks later that year merely intensified those existential anxieties, and revived the possibility that the Holocaust of the Jews might be repeated.

Thus, some of the debates in the new Wagner affair were simply rehashes of the old ones (pre-1967). This was the case with the immediate reaction of the partisan organizations, and with the remarks made by Avraham Schechterman. Similarly, the declaration by Aharon Yadlin (Labor), who had been appointed minister of education, was simply a restatement of the position the Ministry of Education had taken in the past: "The Ministry of Education does not intend to engage in cultural censorship [. . .] Any state intervention in this sphere is apt to set a dangerous precedent," the minister told the press, anticipating the interpellations on the Knesset agenda.[8]

This time, too, the Tel Aviv municipality intervened, since it owned half of the Mann Auditorium, and was similarly represented in the institutions that managed the building. In the municipal council, just as on the national level, discussion of the subject was initiated by a representative of the right, Arye Kramer. During the debate he drew the other right-wing representatives to his side – members of his movement, a splinter faction of the Free Center party, and the representatives of the ultra-Orthodox Agudat Yisrael. In the end, six of the ten participants in the city council meeting voted in favor of asking the IPO management to instruct the orchestra to refrain from public performances of Wagner's music. The mayor, Shlomo Lahat, himself a member of Gahal, opposed making such a request, and in the end compelled the municipal administration not to take advantage of its part-ownership of the auditorium, a position that could have allowed it to veto the IPO management's decision. The municipal council reported the debate and its conclusions, but the deputy mayor explained in interviews to the press that an official appeal from the council would be in bad taste, constituting intervention by elected public officials in matters that were not their concern.[9]

Nonetheless, several senior publicists could not resist the opportunity to take another whack at the punching bag known as the Wagner affair. Zeev Rav-Nof, *Davar*'s broadminded film critic, wrote a caustic personal essay on the subject. To give his firm ideas a ring of authority, he identified himself as someone who had come from "there," whose family had perished in the Holocaust, and who had fought the Nazis himself. He was one of the few people who dared to express their complex feelings and name the controversy for what it was – doubtlessly, in his opinion. He claimed that the actual number of people who were likely to hear a Wagnerian piece on the state radio or in what was perceived as a national concert hall was irrelevant: "The problem is not the music and its significance, but the 'trask' [fuss]."[10] Three days later a news item on the issue by Rav-Nof appeared in *Omer*, a newspaper in simple Hebrew for new immigrants, in which he ostensibly took no stand but which he nevertheless concluded by saying, "It is impossible to continue in this ridiculous fashion."[11]

Rav-Nof did not fear an erosion of the Holocaust heritage and the moral values that had coalesced around it. On the contrary, he felt that those who clung to the notion of "forbidden musicians" were simply missing the original intention of the ban's initiators. This view reflected a broader idea: although it was sensible to develop a means of commemorating the Holocaust and its heritage, that commemoration should not be accomplished with erroneous tools; since at most such an approach would create a fuss over an external – albeit intangible – symbol instead of directly addressing the deeper significance of the Holocaust.

Similar thoughts were expressed by the art critic of *Yedioth Ahronoth*, Immanuel Bar-Kadma, who pointed out what he saw as Israeli society's hypocritical attitude to the subject:

> Only the evening before last the entire nation sat glued to their television sets, watching with excitement and true sporting fervor the obstinate struggle waged on the soccer field between the national teams of the two Germanies [the World Cup match in West Germany]. We did not hear of a single citizen who turned off his set to register a protest; I did not hear of any reaction indicating any emotional undercurrents of any kind in the spectator's attitude toward this game. We all, without exception, were very "good sports" and very "objective" – may the best team win.[12]

This match and those that followed were broadcast on the state channel of Israeli television – the only channel there was at the time. If television viewers wanted to watch something else, their only alternative was the television programs broadcast by the neighboring Arab states. Further on in his article Bar-Kadma dredged up the familiar old arguments from the past, attacking the policy of "Volkswagen, yes, Wagner, no." In this he expressed the disgust that a substantial part of the public felt with respect to the ambivalent approach to Germany and its heritage.

In the current round of the Wagner debate more than a few journalists endorsed this attitude, which dated back to the days of the reparations negotiations with the Federal Republic. Amos Kenan ridiculed the issue in a short poem that proposed "a more suitable repertoire, less repulsive to our wounded national feelings" – a "repertoire" that included "Prelude and Fugue by Adolf Volkswagen," and "Flute Concerto by Johann

Sebastian Grundig."[13] Once again the economic agreements and Israeli fondness for German products were held up as evidence of Israelis' two-faced attitude and the glaring discrepancy between the indulgence shown toward everyday comforts and the inflexible opposition to German culture.

This was also the view expressed by Daniel Bloch, a *Davar* correspondent who condemned what he saw as the IPO management's overhasty reversal of its decision to allow a public performance of Wagner's work. He began by expressing his confidence in the honesty of those members of the Israeli public who claimed that listening to Wagner was very difficult, and surmised that this same public might have been hurt by other matters involving Germany; the establishment of diplomatic relations, trade and import agreements, cultural performances, and the like were all reminders of the days that many people wanted to forget. However, in his very temperately written article, Bloch took his careful analysis of the Wagner issue a step further. He examined the attributes of the public who kept insisting that works by the "banned composers" should not be performed publicly, and claimed that some of that public never visited the concert halls. He cited as an example the complete absence of any reaction to the broadcasting of works by Wagner and Strauss on the Voice of Israel's Radio 1 (the station that preceded the Voice of Music, the classical music station).[14] This disclosure proved that if the boisterous public that protested public performances of Wagner did not learn about performances of banned music from the paper or through news items broadcast by the electronic media, it remained silent. But what was true for the 1970s was not so in later decades: there is no direct connection between interest in classical music and the protest against Wagner. Bloch in fact spotted one of the important features of the controversy at that point in time: it was exploited by politicians and publicists, who turned it into an ideological tool by sequestering it from its natural place – cultural affairs.

Bloch's approach to the issue was to a large extent indicative of the social changes that had occurred in the years since the last big flare-up of the Wagner-related controversy. From 1966 to 1974, the State of Israel had undergone a series of radical social permutations that would not be fully comprehended until after 1977, the year of the first political revolution. These changes had begun with the Six-Day War, which was the first significant national event in which an active part was played by the large population who had arrived in Israel in the mass immigration of the 1950s.

That war ought to have been a golden opportunity to unite the various sectors of the expanding population, which until then had lacked any unifying common denominator. The new national cooperation engendered by the war effort should have undermined the European domination that had prevailed since the first wave of immigration at the end of the nineteenth century, and given other immigrant groups the chance to assume their rightful place in the mosaic of Israeli culture. Instead, the war's unexpected results opened new gaps in society rather than bridging those that already existed.

The problem of finding a political solution after the Six-Day War became a major issue that the parties had to address publicly. Herut had no problem with Israel's new boundaries; it saw itself as the torchbearer of the Revisionists, who had favored a return to the biblical boundaries of the Israeli kingdom – at a minimum, both sides of the Jordan River. The Labor Party, in contrast, had trouble squaring the new reality with its public platform; despite David Ben-Gurion's declaration after the 1956 Sinai Campaign that the "third Kingdom of Israel" had begun, the party had no ambition to recover the domains of its forefathers. Now the party leaders were struggling to decide whether to use the Occupied Territories as a bargaining chip in any future peace negotiations or rather adopt a new ideological line focusing on the advantage of "strategic depth" – a concept that was to become a sacred principle. Ultimately it became clear that only those willing to annex the Territories immediately had any real answer to the new situation; whoever saw the conquered lands as unequivocally "ours" managed to mobilize more and more supporters.

Although the Labor Party had kept its promise to defend the country, after the war it was increasingly perceived as an anti-patriotic party, and as a result, was forced onto the defensive, even though its leaders were in no hurry to announce their willingness to relinquish the Occupied Territories.[15] Moreover, the political concessions it had made before the war, when it had given the defense portfolio to its opponents within – Rafi (Reshimat Poalei Yisrael – Israel Workers' List) – and included its relatively weak rivals from the Herut movement in the national unity government, eroded the Labor Party's ability to maintain the political advantages it had enjoyed since the days of the *Yishuv*. The fact that it was willing to continue cooperating with the right, which had gained no ground in the 1969 elections, clearly demonstrated the difficulty it had in adjusting to new circumstances. Gahal and the Labor Party turned out to hold fairly similar opinions on foreign policy and defense, and the right-wing Gahal, hitherto the Mapai leaders' punching-bag, unexpectedly had the seal of approval from their former rivals. Gahal, for its part, had always emphasized Mapai's neglect of the large voting public known as "the second Israel" (mostly immigrants from Moslem countries). But apparently now all was to be forgiven and forgotten – for the time being.[16]

Increasing support for the political right made patriotism a central issue. Preserving the State of Israel (now once again called by the biblical name "Land of Israel") brought national ideological characteristics into play, entailing a more vigilant fostering of Jewish values and an emphasis on their centrality in the social milieu, as well as a large dose of *Zkifut Komah*, a quality loosely translated as "pride" or "backbone." *Zkifut*

Komah could be achieved only by expanding the boundaries of the state, an act seen as the final stage of the Jews' exodus from the ghetto.

The public that now adopted this way of thinking automatically rejected anything evocative of anti-Semitism or offense to Jews. Accordingly, a substantial proportion of the new nationalists – people who had not been directly affected by the Nazi regime – adopted fierce anti-Nazism as part of their proud, nationalist world view. At the same time, a similar view prevailed among members of the left, most of them European immigrants who had suffered from the Holocaust and wanted to establish a framework for commemorating it.

The link between increasing Israeli nationalism and opposition to enemies of Israel also led the new supporters of the right to embrace the deep-seated rejection of symbols such as German composers, particularly Wagner. The fact that they themselves had no connection to the culture that had produced the Nazis did not stop them from categorically rejecting everything that had ever violated the Jewish sense of nationalism. Thus, the public that hardly ever attended a concert but adamantly opposed public performances of Wagner in Israel – the public that had roused Bloch's ire – may have considered their opposition merely an expression of Jewish patriotic solidarity. For them, rejecting Wagner had nothing to do with origins or personal memories, but was a matter of ideology and collective memory. They regarded the "forbidden composers" as a symbol in Holocaust commemoration: Refusing to hear their music was a way of honoring the memory of the Holocaust; listening to them was a desecration of that memory. In the controversy that would develop at the beginning of the 1980s, this attitude dovetailed with views represented by some of the senior members of the Likud, which had become the ruling party in Israel.

In an article balancing Bloch's on *Davar*'s "For and Against" page, columnist Israel Neumann explained the logic underlying the opposition to Wagner, reviewing the main aspects of Wagner's anti-Jewish views in a way that left the reader no doubt as to the composer's anti-Semitism. There was no longer any need to harp on the use the Nazis had made of Wagner's music; Neumann's explanation clearly showed the venomous nature of the composer's own attitude toward Jews, quite apart from any later interpretations. However, at the same time Neumann presented another aspect of the complex relationship between Wagner and the Jews. He wrote about Wagner's Jewish fans, particularly one who had written a letter to the composer saying that he had no alternative but to commit suicide in order to kill the Jew who lived within himself. And, in fact, after Wagner's death this man had taken his own life on the grave of his idol. "Wagner's fans in Israel will not be asked to go that far," concluded Neumann; they will merely be called upon to show more restraint and to do without IPO performances of Wagner's music.[17]

This was the first time an Israeli journalist had expanded the debate to

include Wagner's anti-Semitic tendencies. He may have done so to reinforce his moral argument, or perhaps because he saw the ignorance of
both parties to the conflict. Some of the disputants now believed that the
entire issue was simply the testimony of Holocaust survivors that
Wagner's music had been played in the camps; the origins of the evil were
growing increasingly obscure.

Yedioth Ahronoth also published two articles – for and against. Those
who wanted the taboo eliminated were represented by law professor
Amos Shapira, who repeated the familiar argument: Let's end the
hypocrisy of using German appliances and visiting Germany while continuing to oppose Wagner so determinedly. "Isn't there just a touch of
exaggeration, and a shade of hypocrisy, in being so anxious to seal the
window of culture and art – that, of all things, and only that! – so that,
heaven forbid, no Wagnerian sounds will penetrate?" he concluded.[18]

The opposing view was presented by Yoela Har-Sheffi, who took a
straightforward view of the dividing line between patriotic zealots and
defenders of the freedom to listen to and play music. Her lucid analysis
of the ban's significance shed light on the battle over symbols that preoccupied both the right and the left: "The whole dispute is about symbols
and is waged around symbols. The art people, who demand in the name
of art that the ban on performing Wagner be lifted – they, of all people,
should understand this very well. For music, like all the arts, speaks in the
language of symbols."[19] At the end of the article, Har-Sheffi urged her
readers not to relinquish the symbol for fear of giving rise to a new, more
searing one.

Maariv returned to the same old approach it had always taken in
regard with Wagner: His music should not be performed under any
circumstances; if his name needed to be mentioned at all, it should be
solely as a symbol of the Holocaust. A piercing article by Yehoshua A.
Gilboa followed the same line the paper had taken in the 1966 controversy. Gilboa began his piece in a sarcastic tone, describing the orchestra's
resolve to "get out of the Diaspora" and the firm decision made by the
IPO's musical director, Zubin Mehta, as a result of which "the people of
Israel would stand erect, the bowed Jewish soul would be straightened."
Once again Mehta was in the center of the public storm, and Jewish pride
was again being used as an argument – albeit very derisively. After a long
series of explanations as to why performances of Wagner's music were
unacceptable in Israel, and why actions like that of Albert Einstein, who
refused the honors offered him in West Germany, were to be admired,
Gilboa concluded by saying, "With all my heart and soul I would like to
be among those enslaved to the 'Diaspora,' who are unable to distinguish
between the wonderful sounds of Richard Wagner and the sounds of
destruction."[20] In short, emphasizing the catastrophe that had stricken the
Jews in the Diaspora would restore the pride of the battered Jew.

The anger of the political right, expressed by Gilboa in *Maariv*, could not conceal a new weariness that emerged in this round of the Wagner controversy: The warring sides did not seem to have the strength to argue. The decision to lift the ban and the reversal of that decision occurred too quickly and too easily. Although the right wing attacked as usual, it never reached its old level of vehemence; the Knesset was not called upon to address the issue, the minister of education stated his position without being urged to do so, the press did not become involved in a commotion over the orchestra.

However, this relatively calm reaction did not mean that the battle had been abandoned or conceded; those who demonstrated against the Wagner performance had complete faith in their actions, and were likely to repeat them to prevent public performances of Wagner. Accordingly, there was considerable truth in the remarks of the editor-in-chief of *Yedioth Ahronoth*, Herzl Rosenblum, who, while recognizing that opinion-makers seemed to have been overtaken by a certain lassitude, pointed out the protesters' profound belief in their actions. After reviewing the reasons for the disturbances in past years, he analyzed the situation in these terms:

> If it is true that the wounds from the days of the great Nazi-Wagnerians pogrom have not yet healed, and that in many Jews they still ooze as much blood as ever, so that the storm that blew up among us this week was not an artificial one at all [. . .] we cannot probe those wounds and cause mental anguish to those who have already suffered enough [. . .] and Mr. Zubin Mehta, a good friend and a tactful person, must also, in future, give up his ambition to press us on a spot so nationally painful.[21]

Judging from the letters sent to the editors of the newspapers (though they were fewer than in earlier stages of the controversy and in those yet to come), Rosenblum was right: Wagner was indeed a sore spot that would not heal. In the eyes of those who supported the ban, Wagner and Strauss were figures against whom the anti-Nazi legislation should be applied. Many shared the opinion of L. Porat from Ramat Gan, whose letter was published in *Maariv*. "Where is the uncompromising law?" Porat inquired. "Does it not apply to the Philharmonic, as it does to other state institutions? They are expressly forbidden to present works by anti-Semites or Nazi collaborators."[22] Although L. Porat had misinterpreted the law against Nazis and their collaborators, his or her explanation was simplicity itself: This culture, though perceived as superior, should not receive superior treatment; it had to be treated as any other inherently base creation.

As usual, some ordinary citizens saw things differently. Dr. Yehuda Diamant, a biochemistry lecturer at Bar-Ilan University, sent letters of protest to the Israel Broadcasting Authority and the IPO, expressing deep shock at the cancellation of the Wagner concert, which he saw as a form of surrender to growing social pressures – one of those pressures being citizens taking the law into their own hands. "No one can stop time, but until 1984 comes round [a reference to George Orwell's apocalyptic vision], I refuse to accept a cultural edict telling me what to read, what to see, and what to listen to, from any cultural commissar, shady politician, local council members, or self-elected pressure group."[23] With respect to the cultural attitude toward Wagner, *1984* landed in Israel three years early, and was in full force in the enormous debate over Wagner in 1981.

However, in the interim the State of Israel underwent a few more essential changes in both its elected political representatives and the lives of wide sectors of the population. It also witnessed another mini-episode in the Wagner saga. In the summer of 1976, the IPO was involved in two incidents associated with the public performance of a work by Wagner. The first occurred at the beginning of July, when the IPO appeared in a concert series entitled "Musica Viva"; this was not documented in the orchestra's concert notes because the performance of Wagner was never on the program – just as on previous occasions, including the 1974 incident. The sole mention of Wagner is found in a reader's letter to *Maariv*, which announced Zubin Mehta's secret intention of playing part of a Wagner piece at the end of the scheduled concert. Since the letter was replete with historical inaccuracies, the statement concerning Mehta's intention may also have been inexact. However, it is interesting to note the connection the writer made between the events that had stirred Israel at the end of June 1976 and the alleged attempt to play Wagner's music:

The fresh attempt by the management of the Philharmonic Orchestra to play Wagner as an addition to a "Musica Viva" concert, conducted by Zubin Mehta, did not come off. This happened on the same Thursday that we found out about the "selection" made by a German terrorist between Israelis and the rest of the hostages at the Entebbe airfield.[24]

Just as the letter was published the hostages from the hijacked Air France plane were released (except for Dora Bloch, murdered in Uganda by Idi Amin's henchmen). Israel was again swept by euphoria: An elite Israeli army unit had liberated the captives in a daring rescue operation. After three years – since the 1973 war – in which Israel had felt rejected by the other world nations, a feeling that reached its peak when the UN made its famous declaration equating Zionism to racism, a real change came in 1976. Europeans were once again on friendly terms with Israelis, proving their good will, in the eyes of many, by the choices made by the judges of two competitions which, although of limited cultural importance, aroused Israelis' nationalist instincts: the Eurovision song contest, won by Izhar Cohen, and the Miss Universe beauty pageant, won by Rina Mor. Between these two competitions the Entebbe rescue added yet another success – albeit of a different nature – to Israel's list of achievements, and the country was able to relax again.

About a month later the IPO made a guest appearance at the Hollywood Bowl alongside the Los Angeles Symphony Orchestra. The hosting orchestra played the prelude to *Die Meistersinger von Nürnberg*, the work whose removal from a concert by the Palestine Symphony Orchestra had signaled the beginning of the ban on Wagner. The Israeli press did not dwell on this occurrence, possibly because it was not the Israeli orchestra that had performed the piece, or because the whole event had taken place far away in another country, or because of the relatively relaxed atmosphere then prevailing in Israel.

In November 1979, for the last time in the decade, the Wagner issue came up for a cursory discussion limited to knowledgeable circles. At the beginning of that month, Natan Dunevich devoted his weekly column in *Haaretz* to the issue of the "forbidden composers." After recounting the permutations of the affair, focusing in particular on what he saw as the IPO's capitulation to threats in the latter part of 1974, he reported a concert broadcast on the Voice of Israel's Radio 1 that had included cantatas from *Carmina Burana* and *Catulli Carmina* by Carl Orff, a composer who had openly collaborated with the Nazis. Dunevich added that the station also broadcast concerts conducted by Karl Böhm, another musician who had made a flourishing career for himself in the Third Reich. For the umpteenth time Dunevich tried – unsuccessfully – to correct the prevailing misconception concerning Wagner's Nazism.[25]

Nonetheless, the low-key character of this round of the debate should not be misinterpreted. Beneath the surface new political and social trends were stirring, some of which had found expression in the months following the Yom Kippur War. However, they did not really erupt until 1977, the year of the elections that transformed the State of Israel. For the first time since the beginning of Jewish settlement in the region, a clear right-wing majority was elected to represent the population. The great victor in the elections was the man who had led first Herut, then Gahal, and now Likud: Menachem Begin, a Knesset member who had good reason to resent the Mapai leadership, was elected to head the government of Israel. His election marked a turning-point in several ways. Not only did it represent the externalization of feelings prevalent in increasingly broad sectors of Israeli society and promise change in the foreign and defense policies – and perhaps in social welfare; his election validated the preferences of numerous citizens who attached great importance to the idea of Jewish pride, and who were interested in both making a public declaration regarding their strength and showing their firm opposition to anti-Semites.

The radical political change was also enormously significant in the cultural sphere. Menachem Begin attacked Israel's relations with Germany more often than any other Knesset member. It was he who had organized the big demonstration in Jerusalem's Zion Square in 1952 to protest the beginning of reparations negotiations with West Germany, a demonstration that ended with protesters throwing stones through the Knesset windows. He persisted in his opposition even after diplomatic relations were established between the two countries. The members of his party, particularly Esther Raziel-Naor, made life difficult for education ministers who did not exert their power – more or less legally – to prevent orchestras and radio networks in Israel from playing works by the "forbidden composers."

Begin frequently emphasized his dedication to the interests of concentration camp survivors and the duty he felt to honor the memory of the dead both publically and privately. Although he himself had not been sent to a camp, he seized every opportunity to recall the bitter fate of others in his family; immediately after his election as prime minister he went to Jerusalem to offer a prayer of thanks at the Western Wall and to recite *Kaddish* (prayer for the dead) in memory of the members of his family who had perished in the Holocaust. This act reflected two prominent aspects of his thinking: a warm appreciation of Jewish culture, and deep emotionalism with respect to the Holocaust. He showed his traditionalist inclinations in the very first days after the 1977 elections, when he invited representatives of the different factions of the Orthodox religious movement to join his government. In doing so he broke the "historical covenant" between the National Religious Party and the Labor party, and strengthened the link he had been developing since 1967 between nationalistic thinking and emphasis on Judaism and religion in Israeli politics.[26] The connection between these two elements also came up in many of Begin's speeches, in which he repeatedly underscored the importance of Jewish *Zkifut Komah* in the State of Israel (which, of course, he preferred to call by the biblically flavored term "Land of Israel"). In twenty-first century Israeli politics the bond between the political right and religion is inseparable, and the presence of nationalism and faith is dominant in public life. In this respect, Begin had accurately foreseen the path the Israeli scene was going to take.

Given this climate, it is easy to understand how West Germany was transformed from a friendly country with which diplomatic, political, defense, and economic relations were maintained and which was once again accepted by the community of nations, to a country that could be kept at a distance, an almost hostile country. The concept of Jewish strength could not be reconciled with the horrors perpetrated by the Germans, and paeans to Germany's rapid rehabilitation and German aid to Israel since the signing of the reparations agreement did not mesh with the constantly repeated allusions to the horrors of the Holocaust. While in the past the resemblance between terrorist attacks and the murder of innocent people in the Holocaust had remained an unspoken feeling, Begin translated that feeling into preachy speeches that both dehumanized the Palestinians and revived the historical wrongs perpetrated in Germany. Once Begin had taken the helm, it was no longer possible to evade the constant evocation of Holocaust anxiety. "Blood revenge" for the pogroms became the prime minister's rallying cry against all murderers, both past and present.

This attitude soon soured personal relations between Begin and the Social Democratic chancellor of West Germany, Helmut Schmidt, which reached their nadir at the beginning of the 1980s. In my view, Begin's attitude also made a definitive contribution to the controversy that developed around the Wagner issue in 1981, and affected the way those who opposed public performances of German music treated both Wagner and the musical director of the IPO, Zubin Mehta. Wagner was German, and Germany once more symbolized evil; Mehta was not Israeli and not Jewish, and this, too, seemed to contradict the idea of *Zkifut Komah* in some way. The next stage of the controversy was undeniably the stormiest that Israel had known so far.

Notes

1 Les Organisations des Partisans to the management of the Israel Philharmonic Orchestra, 17 June 1974, in IPO Archives, Wagner and Strauss file.

2 See, for example, "'Wagner Resisters' Bought Tickets in Order to Demonstrate during the Concert [Hebrew]," *Maariv*, 23 June 1974.

3 The Workers' committee of Mann Auditorium to the management of Mann Auditorium, 20 June 1974, in IPO Archives, Wagner and Strauss file.

4 See, for example, the reports in *Al Hamishmar*, *Davar*, and *Hatzofeh* on 25 June 1974, which noted "This postponement is motivated by a desire to ensure the safety of the visitors to the Mann Auditorium [Hebrew]."

5 A. Schechterman to IPO management, 21 June 1974, IPO Archives, Wagner and Strauss file.

6 On the circumstances of the Yom Kippur War and its aftermath, see U. Ben-Joseph, *The Watchman Fell Asleep: The Surprise of Yom Kippur and its Sources* (Albany, 2005).

7 Kimmerling, *The Invention and Decline of Israeliness*, pp. 1–15.

8 "The Philharmonic Has Postponed the Wagner Concert [Hebrew]," *Haaretz*, 25 June 1974.

9 Y. Artzi, "The Municipality Cannot Decide the Issue of Performing Wagner's Works [Hebrew]," *Haaretz*, 23 June 1974; "Tel Aviv Municipality Officials Will Ask the Philharmonic Not to Play Wagner [Hebrew]," *Haaretz*, 24 June 1974.

10 "Wagner in the Philharmonic [Hebrew]," *Davar*, 21 June 1974.

11 "To Play or Not to Play [Hebrew]," Omer, 25 June 1974.

12 "Unlike Richard – Richard [Hebrew]," *Yedioth Ahronoth*, 24 June 1974.

13 "What to Play? [Hebrew]," *Yedioth Ahronoth*, 26 June 1974.

14 "Hypocrisy Has Won Again [Hebrew]," *Davar*, 25 June 1974.

15 On the political response to the conquests of the Six-Day War, see S. Avineri, "Comments on the Significance of the Elections to the Thirteenth Knesset [Hebrew]," *Alpayim* 6 (1993): 29–31. On the difficulty of quickly changing

political positions, see R. Pedhatzur, *The Triumph of Embarrassment: Israel and the Territories after the Six-Day War* [Hebrew] (Tel Aviv, 1996).

16   Y. Shapiro, *Politicians as a Hegemonic Class: The Case of Israel* [Hebrew] (Tel Aviv, 1996), pp. 113–14. Menachem Begin himself held this view; see A. Naor, *Begin in Power: Personal Testimony* [Hebrew] (Tel Aviv, 1993), p. 22.

17   "A Tempest in a Pot of Tears [Hebrew]," *Davar*, 25 June 1974.

18   "There Is No Point to the Ban Anymore [Hebrew]," *Yedioth Ahronoth*, 23 June 1974.

19   " . . . But the Tune Lingers on [Hebrew]," *Yedioth Ahronoth*, 23 June 1974.

20   "Sounds – and Sounds [Hebrew]," *Maariv*, 23 June 1974.

21   "Better This Way [Hebrew]," *Yedioth Ahronoth*, 24 June 1974.

22   "Playing Wagner – A Disgrace! [Hebrew]," *Maariv*, 23 June 1974.

23   Dr. Y. Diamant to the managing director of the Israel Broadcasting Authority [copy to IPO], 24 June 1974, in IPO Archives, Wagner and Strauss file.

24   "The Attempt to Play Works by Wagner in the Mann Auditorium [Hebrew]," *Maariv*, 13 July 1976.

25   "To Play Wagner [Hebrew]," *Haaretz*, 2 Nov. 1979.

26   On Begin's reaction to his election, see Naor, *Begin in Power*, pp. 13–38. On the coalition negotiations and the inclusion of the Orthodox parties in the government, see ibid., pp. 39–64.

CHAPTER

8

The 1980s:
Xenophobia and Overt
Political Intervention

At the end of 1981, yet another dispute broke out in Israel over the IPO's right to play works by Wagner, triggered this time by an actual perform- ance of a Wagner piece as an encore to a series concert. Despite all the years that had passed, the controversy began to gather momentum again, pulling in many more participants than ever before. The unprecedented magnitude of the public debate this time around was due to a combina- tion of factors. For one thing, it was the first time since 1938 that the orchestra had actually played a piece by Wagner rather than merely talked about it. Secondly, a period of remarkable growth and expansion in the Israeli press since the end of the 1970s had brought the establishment of many local papers as well as an innovation – sectional weeklies directed primarily at the ultra-Orthodox religious public. These all joined the ranks of the existing privately owned papers and party organs.

The religious and nationalist papers played a substantial role in the Wagner controversy. Contrary to the secular public's commonly held image of them, these papers, ephemeral as they seemed, had a wide and significant influence in the ultra-Orthodox and national-religious communities. Moreover, a parallel reading of the religious papers and the Israeli national press indicates that all sectors of the religious press consis- tently responded to the same issues presented to the secular public. Ultimately, increasing competition between the daily papers, compounded by the advent of a variety of weeklies, encouraged increased use of sensa- tionalist headlines and forced journalists to be much more creative in their treatment of most subjects. The Wagner issue well suited the new style of journalism.

In addition to these objective circumstances, the general atmosphere in Israel at the time contributed decisively to the creation of a public storm that recalled the conflicts of the 1950s and 1960s. In October 1981 the political atmosphere in Israel was tense. The previous spring had witnessed a particularly aggressive election campaign, at the end of which the two main political blocs had emerged with virtually equal electoral strength. The political and military threats reverberating through the public speeches and the contemptuous remarks that various figures in Israeli society hurled at one another in the course of the election campaign contributed considerably to the intensifying polarization of Israeli society. At the same time many Israelis were living in fear of the moment when the State of Israel – whichever party ruled it – would be forced to honor the Camp David accords it had signed with Egypt under the aegis of the US, and withdraw from all the territory it held in the Sinai Peninsula.

Significantly, the Holocaust was back as an ideological lodestone in a substantial proportion of the political debates on foreign policy and defense issues; in fact, at times these debates seemed to echo the rhetoric so common at the end of the 1940s and the early 1950s. Occasionally the most traumatic event in the lives of Jews was evoked as a basis for their right to a strong, secure, and independent state. At other times, current traumas – primarily terrorist attacks – were used to stir dark memories of the Holocaust, a device much employed by some politicians. To this seething mixture the IPO added a further bit of pepper, by playing *Liebes Tod* from Wagner's *Tristan und Isolde*.

In mid-October 1981, the Israeli press announced that the IPO musical director, Zubin Mehta, intended to conduct a work by Wagner as an encore at the end of the first concert of the season. However, his plan was postponed for unclear reasons. *Yedioth Ahronoth* thought the explanation was probably related to public mourning for the death of the military leader and statesman MK Moshe Dayan. The reporter added that the fear that Wagner's music would be played had led demonstrators wearing the notorious yellow badges of the Holocaust years to congregate at the entrance to the concert hall; one of them was caught carrying a commando knife. *Davar* correspondents attributed the change of plan to the presence of Minister of Education and Culture Zevulun Hammer (NRP), who was there to inaugurate the new season. *Davar* speculated that Mehta did not want to embarrass the minister and put him to a test that might create problems for the orchestra.[1]

Nevertheless, eventually Mehta did carry out his plan. At the end of one of the concerts of the first series of the season, he turned to the audience and, announcing an encore, suggested that anyone who did not wish to listen to a piece by Wagner should leave the hall; he assured everyone that the musicians would take no offense. Protest was voiced by two members of the orchestra, the violinist Avraham Melamed and the trombonist Zvi Ostrowsky, both of whom retained painful memories of their concentration camp experiences. One of the concert ushers, Ben-Zion Leitner, waited for the first strains of the music before moving to the foot of the stage. There, standing under the conductor's podium, he exposed his scarred belly and cried out his bitterness. His picture – captioned with the information that this Holocaust survivor had also been awarded the highest honors for heroism in Israel's War of Independence – appeared the next day in many papers. The papers also reported that the police had asked the IPO to refrain from playing any more Wagner compositions because of the danger of demonstrations and bomb attacks against the Mann Auditorium. The partisans' organizations also returned to the fray, threatening to take action. The IPO's move had brought the debate back to the same atmosphere of rage and violence that had characterized it 20 and 30 years earlier.

The reporters who had been present in the concert hall described the increasing chaos that had ensued as more people gathered at the foot of the stage. The audience, too, had begun to argue about the legitimacy of the act, and the performance of *Liebes Tod* was accompanied by an unceasing babble of voices. *Maariv* quoted the violinist who had opposed Mehta's decision, Avraham Melamed, as he described his feelings about Wagner's music: "Some time ago I saw the film *Apocalypse Now*, and in one of the scenes helicopters came down and bombed to the sound of music that made my stomach turn. At first I didn't understand what was wrong with me, but afterwards I realized that it was Wagner's music."[2]

Melamed's very convincing, emotional description of this upsetting experience was testimony to the increasing weakness of the musical boycott. In 1981 Israel was no longer the same social and cultural bubble it had once been; economic reforms and technological developments now offered individuals the possibility of exposure – by accident or by design – to the "forbidden composers." The drop in civilian aviation costs, the availability of phonograph records, and even the import of films in which Wagner compositions had not been censored, all facilitated contact with music by the banned composer and others like him. Although in the 1950s the IPO boycott may still have had a compelling influence over all Israeli citizens, this was no longer true in the 1980s – and certainly not with respect to classical-music audiences.

A few days later, on 21 October, *Al Hamishmar* printed a story on the other orchestra member who had objected to playing Wagner, the trombonist Zvi Ostrowsky. The headline was "Orchestra Member Who Did Not Want to Play Wagner Hospitalized in Intensive-Care Unit" – thus implying a connection between the IPO's performance of a short segment from one of Wagner's operas and the health of the dissenting trombonist. Yet in the body of the article the reporter explained: "According to his wife, the musician has been under a great deal of stress in recent days, but she has refused to attribute it to the Wagner performance. One of the musician's friends told our reporter that Ostrowsky has suffered from heart disease for a number of years." The headline, screaming great drama, proved to be deceitful. *Al Hamishmar*, usually a pluralistic paper, kept up its anti-Wagner bias, perhaps as an extension of the anti-German attitude that Mapam had maintained since the 1950s, and at the end of the week following the controversial concert published an instructive article by Yaakov Rabi on anti-Semitic European artists. In Wagner's case, Rabi explained, anti-Semitism was not merely intellectual, but a personality trait. Accordingly, the argument put forward by fans of his music that the composer could and should be classed with a long line of other anti-Semitic creators had to be rejected.[3]

The new phase of the controversy resembled the earlier ones in some respects, but the differences were more significant. Now as before, use was made of the same tired old argument concerning the general apathy about the import of German products to Israel, and the familiar debate was waged as to Wagner's importance in Israel's musical life. Those who favored public performances of Wagner did not trouble to point out, of course, how difficult it was to perform a full-length work by this composer, and those who were opposed apparently did not realize the difficulty. At least those in favor must have realized that in any case the dispute concerned only the performance of segments of the composer's works, since the production of an entire opera would have required huge mobilization of talent from more than one musical institution in Israel.

As always, the Wagner affair was a magnet for politicians, and as usual the journalists piled up arguments for and against – sprinkled with tidbits from the history of the Jewish people and the foundations of anti-Semitism. It all found a place in the many voluminous newspapers of the 1980s. The radio stations added considerable fuel to the fire, whereas the sole Israeli television station – the state channel – chose to play a small part in the affair. The head of the television news department, Dan Shilon, asked permission to invite Mehta to be interviewed on the leading political interview program *Moked* ("Focus"), but the director of Israel Television, Yitzhak Shimoni, turned down his request.[4]

As in the 1970s, the claim was again made that by turning Wagner into a symbol, "we in fact accepted from the Nazis the symbol that they created."[5] However, the counter-argument was that the Israelis' aggressive attitude toward Wagner was not at all unusual. The literary intellectual Moshe Dor told readers of *Maariv* that in 1871 the French had demonstrated in the streets against the plan to mount a production of Wagner's opera *Lohengrin*. The French, who had not yet forgiven the Germans for their humiliating invasion of Paris in 1870, were outraged that culture so distinctly German should invade their concert halls. "Is what was permissible for the French forbidden for us? And can we even equate what the Germans did to them with what the Germans inflicted on us?"[6] In other words, if even estimable Europeans like the French wanted to impose a taboo on Wagner, seeing him as a German symbol par excellence, why should Israelis cavil?

Five days later a longer article by Dor appeared in *Maariv*'s weekend supplement. His opening words left no doubt as to his personal views: "'Anyone who wants to learn something about National Socialist Germany should learn something about Wagner' – Hitler used to say of the composer, the father of great operas and of the introduction to the doctrine of racism."[7] In short, since Hitler himself had defined Wagner as a proto-Nazi, Hitler, Wagner, and racism could and should be equated. Later on someone wrote a letter to the editor quoting selected passages from Wagner's libelous, anti-Semitic essay, "Judaism in Music," which at that point had not yet been translated into Hebrew. These quotations provided additional evidence of Wagner's anti-Semitism.[8]

This round, however, was not to be merely another argument about the "forbidden composers," citing every possible reason for opposing Wagner. Although in the previous phases of the conflict the supposedly issue-oriented arguments had drifted into political and social realms that were not strictly relevant to the Wagner affair, in 1981 the discussion was so heated that politicians and publicists – the first with outright invective, the latter in polished essays – were calling on Zubin Mehta to stop trying to introduce Wagner's music to Israel, and went so far as to ask him to leave the country. These attacks simply continued the abuse that the political parties had been directing at each other in the election campaign four months previously. In the same atmosphere that allowed the division of Israeli citizens into Ashkenazi and Sephardic Jews, secular and religious, Israel and "the second Israel," and Jews and Arabs, shrill voices drew attention to the conductor's Indian origins and faith, and used them against him.[9] The scathing remarks made by politicians and publicists were now reinforced by letters to the press, particularly profuse this time around.

Indeed, one of the notable differences between the polemic of 1981 and those that had preceded it was the amount of attention the affair attracted and the number of newspapers that reported on it in Israel and throughout the Western world. The daily papers that had always covered the Wagner affair each time it came up on the public agenda – such as *Haaretz, Davar, Al Hamishmar, Hatzofeh, The Jerusalem Post, Yedioth Ahronoth*, and *Maariv* – were now joined by smaller papers, such as *Shearim, Hamodia, Mabat, Shaar Lamatchil, Omer, Haolam Hazeh*, Israeli papers in foreign languages (for example, *Nasha Strana, Letzte Neies, Israelski Par, Israel Nachrichten, Viata Nuastra, Novini Kurier, Aurora*, and *Ui Kelet*) and local and sectorial papers, including *Hair, Kol Boker, Hamahaneh Haharedi, Beeretz-Yisrael*, and *Zo Haderech*. In most of these papers, reports on the performance of Wagner's music and related commentary appeared more than once, and did not cease completely until January 1982. The growing interest of journalists in the Wagner debate was an outcome of the expansion of the media, as well as the infiltration of *Shoah* into quotidian discourse. In the summer of 1982 it became clear that the Holocaust was presented as the incentive behind the invasion to Lebanon.[10]

One of the main complaints against the IPO in this round of the controversy concerned the way the special encore had been introduced.

According to some of the papers – it is not clear whether this was also the view of the concert audience – the orchestra had sneaked the forbidden music in through the back door. After all, the audience had been told the piece would be played only minutes before the orchestra actually played it, so anyone who wanted to protest could do so solely by walking out, since the tickets had already been paid for, and in most cases were annual subscription tickets. Accordingly, most of the members of the audience were unable to express their displeasure by means of a consumer boycott.

This grievance was quickly abandoned, and replaced by a personal attack on Mehta. The conductor had indeed fought 15 years for his right to perform Wagner's works in Israel with the IPO, and clearly saw it as a matter of principle. He wanted the IPO to play Wagner in order to gain musical polish, and this was reflected in the repertoire with which he chose to appear throughout the world. When the Wagner affair blew up in Israel once again, someone even asked the maestro whether his insistence on including Wagner in the IPO's repertoire was motivated by a desire to work with music that he conducted well, since at the time some people criticized his interpretation of composers well known in Israel, such as Beethoven and Chopin.

Ultimately, it was not the sneaky stratagem used to introduce the piece or the musical issues involved that put Mehta in the center of the conflict, but his origins and religion. In the past, too, some people had chided the conductor – and not only him – for what they saw as excessive interference in Israel's internal affairs. Before him, reprimands had also been dealt to Sergei Koussovitzky, who had abandoned the entire affair as a result, and Jascha Heifetz, who had been warned to leave matters alone, but refused to comply. Mehta, too, insisted – and was burned for his pains. The editor-in-chief of *Yedioth Ahronoth*, Herzl Rosenblum, who had previously appealed to Mehta to abandon the idea of playing Wagner's works in Israel, once again explained why the conductor should distance himself from this domestic Israeli scandal.

> This whole problem is an internal problem of our own, a problem that must be discussed inside our own house, and no foreigners, even if they are our friends, should enter into it [. . .]. This is also true for our dear friend Zubin Mehta, who loves us with his heart and soul, and we him, but he read about Auschwitz, and we were taken there [. . .]. He must leave us to ourselves, and not try to tell us what to do.[11]

Rosenblum also quoted the leader of the Revisionist movement, Ze'ev Jabotinsky, who had once said that even a mother mourning her son's injury could not ignore the fact that it was his wound bleeding, not hers.

Rosenblum's words went a considerable way toward explaining the process Israelis had undergone with respect to the Wagner affair. For the Israeli public, Wagner had become a figure judged in its own right, quite apart from his international image, his musical importance, and even his ideas. The Israelis had created what seemed to be two Wagners: one of them belonging to them alone, and steeped in controversy; the other (which is beyond the scope of this book) the Wagner of the international arena. Many people saw the "Israeli" Wagner as a figure that only Israelis – or Jews, at any rate – could understand and reflect on; accordingly they sought – politely or aggressively – to prevent any confusion between the two.

Maariv, as it had been doing for some time, took a clear stand against performances of Wagner and those who wanted to lift the ban. Aharon Dolev said venomously of Mehta, "the visitor," that "for years he has been preaching to us all, with surprising zeal, telling us to re-educate ourselves. Meaning, we will make a kind of cultural 'habit' for ourselves, to listen 'only' to Wagner's music, without 'paying attention' to his personality and his ideas."[12] An angry undercurrent also ran through reports on the Wagner affair in *Hatzofeh*, the organ of the National Religious Party. One cynical subheading, for example, read: "Zubin Mehta 'Takes Care of' Democracy," and the one after it, "Fears of 'Giving In'," expressed a certain criticism of the IPO management as well.[13]

An even more caustic stand was taken by the ultra-Orthodox religious paper *Hamodia*, which began one of its reports on the controversial concert with the words: "The 'Israel' Philharmonic Orchestra has a conductor imported from India."[14] At that point the Wagner affair was no longer a struggle over memories of the Holocaust and its victims; it had become outright war against foreigners, especially the "Goy" who wanted to put an end to the ban. This development clearly reflected the connection that had been developing for years between nationalist concepts and the extreme religious trends in Israel. The attitude toward Mehta was an evident result of this connection: The foreigner who tried to interfere in what some of the population considered national concerns was denounced and vilified in the name of loyalty to the Jewish nation and religion.

However, this attitude was also shared by newspapers that did not belong to any part of the religious sector. A veteran reporter for *Yedioth Ahronoth*, Noah Kliger, himself a Holocaust survivor, repeated editor-in-chief Herzl Rosenblum's comments that Mehta could not feel what someone who had been "there" felt. However, Kliger, more than others, addressed Mehta's ethnic sensibilities most unsubtly, offending everything that was sacred to his people. In response to Mehta's suggestion that anyone who could not bear to listen to works by Wagner should leave the concert hall, Kliger wondered "how would Zubin Mehta and his people react if, for example, they were all brought into some place in which there were sacred cows, and someone stood up and said: 'We are about to slaughter the cows. Anyone who doesn't want to see it should leave.' Does that seem all right to Zubin Mehta?"[15] In this affair, nationality, religion, and race were now intertwined to such a degree that they could scarcely be separated. Kliger remained a bitter opponent of the performance of music by Wagner and expressed his harsh opinion for the next 30 years in Israeli and foreign media.

Kliger's article was balanced in the "For and Against" section by a contrasting article in which the music critic Hanoch Ron explained why performance of Wagner's music was indispensable in Israel. This time Ron, known for his sharp, abrasive criticism aimed his darts at the Israelis – both politicians and ordinary citizens – who traded on Jews' feelings about Germany and its heritage. "The reality of 1981 shows a conventional lie: relations between Israel and Germany are close in all spheres of life, except music. It's all right to bash music. That is the soft underbelly of us all."[16] Ron was one of the trailblazers in efforts to perform Wagner's music publicly in Israel. Michael Ohad, who for years had pushed for an end to the ban, noted that only a few months before the current dispute he had listened with pleasure to an entire program of Wagner's works that Hanoch Ron had produced on the army radio station (*Galei Zahal*). He also mentioned a concert outside the walls of the Mann Auditorium – he did not say where – at which the conductor, Frank Peleg, had dared to conduct a work by Wagner.[17]

This time more than ever the press reflected a general attitude that was reinforced by the political echelons. The most moderate view was presented by Minister of Education and Culture Zevulun Hammer (NRP), who followed the same line as his predecessors in office. Like them, he believed that his ministry should not intervene directly in the Wagner affair, but thought it important to show special sensitivity to the issue, and, in particular, to avoid unnecessary conflict among Jews. MK Roni Milo (Likud) forced the minister to take a clear stand on the issue, since, he claimed – like Esther Raziel-Naor years before – that if the IPO insisted on playing banned music, the state funds it received should be cut. Chairperson of the Knesset Education Committee, MK Ora Namir (Labor), presented a more moderate view: She thought that the IPO should give up its efforts to play Wagner, but urged that no sanctions be imposed on it.[18] Another member of her party, MK Shevah Weiss, himself a Holocaust survivor, took a more unbending attitude. Despite his temperate views on other subjects, in this instance he took a stand close to that presented by nationalist and religious circles. In his personal column in *Davar*, Weiss argued that "it is an un-Jewish act by an orchestra that was founded by the survivors of Nazism, by the indirect victims of Wagnerism. It is a narrowness of spirit in Jews, a sort of embracing of the oppressive seigneur. This time the seigneur comes in the form of a German musician."[19]

These Knesset members' views reflected the complexity of the issue and the way it crossed the conventional lines in Israeli politics. The minister, a representative of the NRP who might have been expected to identify with the national-religious sector, took a moderate approach to an issue that was more political and national in character than cultural and musical; a Labor Knesset member took a nationalistic stand on account of his own personal history, while two other Knesset members held more predictable views – Namir issuing distant directives, and Milo showing the militancy that characterized his early days in politics.

Gideon Hausner, the prosecutor in the Eichmann trial who had by then retired from political life (he had been first a representative of the Independent Liberals, then Gahal, and was now head of the board of directors of Yad Vashem), was much in demand at this point as a commentator on the dispute. His article "Insensitivity to the Feelings of Many," which appeared in *Yedioth Ahronoth* – and in *The Jerusalem Post* under the title "The Case against Wagner" – poured oil on the flames. Hausner told his readers about Wagner's reaction to the Ukraine pogroms of 1881, expressed in the pages of *Bayreuther Blätter*. At the time Wagner had recommended the actions of the rioters as an example to emulate; and the Nazis, as every child knows, did exactly that, on an industrial scale.[20] A few years later Hausner wrote a book about the Eichmann trial which included some of his personal memories of the event. In that context he expressed great doubt as to whether the trial had succeeded in awakening public opinion and interesting schoolchildren in the happenings of the Holocaust. Hausner most probably saw the problematic aspect of the process that had turned Wagner into a symbol, but he may also have seen that process as a basis for education.[21]

The chairperson of the Yad Vashem administration, Yitzhak Arad, also tended to focus on Wagner's attitude toward Jews as a barrier to performing his music. In a letter to the IPO management he explained that Yad Vashem could not countenance public performances of works by one of "the anti-Semitic leaders of racism, [a man who was] poisoned and poisonous, whose slanderous writings and music provided inspiration for the Nazis and a major part of their official cultural activity."[22] Performances of Wagner's music in Israel were also condemned in a letter to the IPO from the director of the Institute for Conservation and Research of Jewish Music of the Holocaust (Yad Litzlilei Hashoah), Moshe Hoch, who for years had been studying the music that had been played in the concentration camps. After unfolding the evidence of Wagner's anti-Semitism, Hoch related the story of the camp musicians, and implored the orchestra not to play Wagner's compositions in public.[23]

The daily press was quick to react to the politicians' comments on the Wagner question. *Haaretz* published a fluent editorial in which, in contrast to others, editor Gershom Schocken did not invoke his German origins to settle accounts with the Third Reich. He cast doubt on the "ingenuousness of politicians who rushed to take a stand against the orchestra's decision," and made the now familiar comment about the relative ease of boycotting a musical work, as compared with the unwillingness to ban the import of convenience products from Germany.[24]

Matters came to a head in an interview with the deputy minister in the Prime Minister's Office, Dov Shilansky (Likud), on Radio 1 of the Voice of Israel on 23 October – the first weekend of the controversy. Shilansky, a Holocaust survivor, expressed great anger at Mehta's "hutzpah," and advised him simply to "go back to India." This was the most stinging remark any Israeli politician had ever made on the Wagner issue, and it elicited outrage. A *Davar* correspondent reminded readers of a detail from the deputy minister's past – a detail that had been linked, in a way, with the controversy over "the forbidden composers" back in the 1950s:

> We know who Shilansky is. He is the man who set an explosive device by the foreign ministry building (then in the army headquarters in Tel Aviv) in the early 1950s in order to express his opposition to the reparations agreement between the Israeli government and the government of West Germany.
>
> No one takes Shilansky seriously – not even his friends. For some reason Menachem Begin appointed him deputy minister in the Prime Minister's Office. Everything such a man in such a position says is perceived by the public and the world as an official declaration – expressing the opinion of the government and its head.[25]

About a month later, the deputy minister clarified his real intentions in his own column in the right-wing monthly *Beeretz Yisrael*. He claimed that his words had been taken out of context; he had not meant to send Mehta home, only to explain to him that he should leave the Israelis in peace. He also trotted out the old justification that he himself had lived through the Holocaust.[26]

Surprisingly, Prime Minister Menachem Begin, who was known for both his uncompromising anti-German attitude and his unreserved support for Shilansky, this time refrained from intervening. His spokesman, Uri Porat, stated that Shilansky's remark had expressed a personal view that did not represent the policy of the government – a statement perhaps designed to correct the unpleasant impression made by the deputy minister's remark, or perhaps motivated by the assumption – which proved correct – that Mehta's prestige was such that the affair was bound to elicit reactions from abroad. Begin may also have realized that ethnic arguments against Mehta were hardly an appropriate way to justify opposition to a symbol of racism. Yet Begin sought to exonerate his old friend. In response to a biting letter from the IPO, the prime minister tried to defend Shilansky by appealing to the orchestra members to make allowances for the deputy minister, who "saw our people in the process of annihilation. He himself was in a Nazi concentration camp." Begin went on to explain that it was impossible to forget what kind of symbol Wagner had been to the Nazis.[27]

Begin's partial dissociation from Shilansky is especially interesting in light of his relations with the West German chancellor at that time. Begin, who had never concealed his hostility toward Germans as a group, was caught up in a fierce political conflict with the West German chancellor, Helmut Schmidt. Schmidt, known for his activity in the Wehrmacht but also for his efforts to bring his country closer to the democratic Western states, visited Saudi Arabia in the spring of 1981. There he made a political statement: His country, he said, had a duty to the Arabs, since the refugee problem was a result of the establishment of the State of Israel, and that, in turn, had been one of the results of the Holocaust. Begin, then at the height of his election campaign, took ample advantage of these indiscreet remarks in his speeches in the city squares and, as in the past, transfixed his listeners with outspoken fulminations against the Germans.[28]

Some of the columnists identified with the moderate left did not pass up the opportunity to castigate Shilansky for his rudeness. In an issue of *Davar* that appeared a few days after Shilansky's fateful remark, after all the responses from the right and the left had been heard, Zohar Ben-Asher described the events of the week thus: "This week Deputy Minister Dov Shilansky proved to us how ignorance and hysteria, when combined, create – through lack of political and public insight – a sub-culture based mainly on an inflation of the Holocaust and a distortion of its commemoration."[29] Ben-Asher warned against a phenomenon that was gradually gaining currency during the debates over performances of Wagner in Israel, namely, absolute identification between studying the Holocaust itself and railing against its symbols. Moreover, the ignorance that had characterized the previous stages of the controversy had come to distinguish many of those who led public opinion on the subject.

At the end of that week *Haaretz* published a scholarly article that examined the Wagner conflict from a wider perspective. In the title of his article, jurist Chaim Gans coined the phrase that would become the slogan of the whole controversy: "Who's Afraid of Richard Wagner?" Gans drew a parallel between the general ban on Wagner and the prohibition of public transportation on the Sabbath, and in fact between the theoretical possibility of forbidding an individual to observe Jewish law as he wished in his own home and the prohibition on performing Wagner's music for those who wanted it. This comparison represented the first attempt to examine the issue from the legal standpoint, with an emphasis on civil rights. It also exposed the increasingly close link between opposition to performances of Wagner and the outlook of the national-religious sector. Gans probably assumed that the readers of *Haaretz* – who tended to be of above-average education and pluralistic in their views – would categorically reject efforts to prevent performances of Wagner just as they rejected religious coercion.[30]

On the same day, corroboration of the link between national-religious views and opposition to Wagner appeared: The ultra-Orthodox Jerusalem weekly *Hamahaneh Haharedi* published a short piece saying that Jewish culture had no room for any concert, not only Wagner concerts. This was also the view of the local Bnei Brak paper, *Tmura*, whose reporter, M. H. Sheinfeld, explained: "The problem is not Wagner, and it is not musical education; the problem is prying and rummaging around in foreign cultures."[31] This remark was merely a hint to what was to come; when the controversy resurfaced in 1991, it would be obvious that the national-religious sector saw the dispute as one more element of the general struggle between the religious and the secular over the cultural image of the State of Israel.

The fear of ideological coercion was also the gist of an article by Aharon Bachar in *Yedioth Ahronoth* at the end of that same week. Bachar, who was closely identified with the political left, suspected that the "screechers" and "simpletons," as he called them, would be happy to shut his mouth, too, on another occasion. He presented the two faces of the supposedly pluralistic Israeli, on one hand explaining that Wagner would most probably have rebelled against Adolf Hitler's regime himself, while on the other hand saying:

> But no circumstances could have brought him to it [Nazism], if it were not for the seed of calamity deeply embedded in his heritage. That germ is buried in every human society, in almost every individual. It began to take over the German national fabric many years before anyone had heard the name of Adolf Hitler. Richard Wagner was only one symptom.[32]

His colleague on the paper, Boaz Evron, objected, saying that things were not quite so simple, and that the source of the evil was not a problematic heritage or a unique use of tradition. Evron was a member of "Semitic Action," a group that in the 1950s and 1960s called for a bi-national federation of Israelis and Arabs. His pursuit of the nationalistic endeavor may have been the reason for his interpreting the Wagner affair in a different way. Wagner had indeed employed old folktales to express modern ideas, said Evron, and, to a great extent, his views on political life around him. However, Evron added, he had not deviated from the conventional European norms of the Romantic period, or even from the material used by the Hebrew poets Abraham Mapou, Saul Tchernichowsky, and Jonathan Ratosh in some of their writings, which explored their people's ancient past in order to better understand the present.[33]

The enormous anger Mehta had aroused in certain circles – primarily right wing ones – encouraged members of the IPO to take an unusual step in their professional relationship with the musical director. In reaction to Shilansky's insulting remark, the IPO management stated that the members of the cooperative announced that they had decided to appoint Mehta as their musical director for life. Obviously this decision was based not only on professional considerations, but also – and primarily – on a desire to offset, to some degree, the insult directed at Mehta: "We are wholeheartedly with you, and a slur against you is a slur against our artistic institution and against every one of us," the musicians declared. In addition, they probably wanted to acknowledge Mehta's sense of a shared destiny in his relations with Israel. In an interview with the music critic Yossi Shifman in *Davar*, Mehta explained that "something happens to me every time the plane reaches the shores of Israel. It is something I can't define: I look forward to working with the Israeli orchestra [. . .] I miss them as individuals."[34] Later Shifman became one of the prominent figures behind the attempt to play Wagner in Israel.

Some of those who opposed Mehta's pro-Wagner efforts were aware of his special relationship with Israel. Herzl Rosenblum took care to mention it every time he called the conductor to order, and Yosef Waxman of *Maariv*, remembered in Mehta's favor that he had come to Israel in times of war to share in the national tribulations. Moreover, despite the personal attacks against him, Mehta himself did not despair of musical life in Israel. For example, he helped organize free concerts in the park for the masses, which made him popular with many Israelis who were not part of the usual IPO audience.

As mentioned earlier, the enormous controversy over Wagner in Israel reverberated overseas as well. For the first time since the public uproar over violinist Jascha Heifetz's recitals, the musician at the center of the controversy was enough of a celebrity for the international press to take an interest in the events occurring in Israel. Newspapers reporting the affair included *The London Times*, *The New York Times*, *Newsweek Magazine*, *Frankfurter Allgemeine Zeitung*, *Die Welt*, *International Herald Tribune*, and *The Daily Telegraph*. News of the agitation in Israel also brought the IPO and its musical director letters of support from several Jewish musicians of international renown, including the violinist Yitzhak Perlman, the composer and conductor Leonard Bernstein, and the pianist and conductor Daniel Barenboim, who some years later would himself be fighting for the orchestra's right to play Wagner.[35]

The Israeli conductor Dalia Atlas presented an interesting argument in a public manifesto published in *Yedioth Ahronoth*. She asserted that ideological quarrels should not be allowed to "sabotage the existence of an orchestra and conductor that glorify Israel's name in the world." In short, she used the nationalist argument underlying attacks against the orchestra in the orchestra's defense, simply by shifting emphasis. Another musician who came forward in support of the IPO was the Israeli pianist and conductor Arie Vardi, who was to violate the ban on Richard Strauss in a concert with the Philharmonic in the 1990s.[36]

Ten days after the renewal of public debate over Wagner, the IPO board published a detailed explanation of the situation in some of the daily papers. The board declared its support for the orchestra and for its musical director, expressed displeasure at the intemperate pronouncements made by public figures, announced that it would initiate an educational campaign on Wagner, and undertook to take a survey among IPO subscribers in the near future.[37]

Taken by this idea of a "referendum on Wagner," two local papers also decided to find out how willing classical music enthusiasts were to listen to Wagner's works in the concert halls. In late October 1981, the Tel Aviv local paper *Hair* published the results of a poll it had taken in two musical venues. Reporters had visited the entrance plaza of the Tel Aviv Museum shortly before a medieval music concert was to begin, and asked arriving patrons to fill out a questionnaire about Wagner (rather a strange choice of survey subjects, since these people were fans of medieval music rather than opera). Out of 327 responses, 144 (44%) objected to Wagner performances, while 183 (56%) were in favor. The survey's organizers noted that 70 of those surveyed (about one-fifth of the total) had been born before 1945, apparently assuming that those people would have painful feelings concerning the historical events that had led to the boycott of Wagner in Israel. Another team of reporters polled patrons of a chamber music concert in a well-to-do suburb of Tel Aviv. Here only 34 people were questioned; of those, 14 (41%) opposed Wagner performances and 20 (59%) were in favor. Seven of the respondents (once again about a fifth of the total) had been born before 1945. Obviously the small number of survey participants makes it difficult to judge whether their responses in fact reflected prevailing opinion. The survey was published under the headline: "Tiny Majority Favors Wagner." The poll at the museum had discovered a difference of 12 percent, and the other poll 18 percent; even assuming that an unprofessional survey should involve a significant standard deviation, correcting for this would probably not have changed the survey's conclusion that Israelis once uncompromising views on Wagner had softened. Furthermore, Tel Aviv could not indicate the opinions of other Israelis – less wealthy, and more traditional or religious.

In contrast, the results obtained by the journalist-pollsters of the Haifa local paper *Kolbo* were the complete opposite: The public in the north did not want to let Wagner's music into Israel. *The Jerusalem Post* published a survey carried out by a reputable private company which showed that only 23 percent of the 275 people surveyed favored performances of Wagner's music; more than 65 percent were opposed.[38] The papers also printed the results of polls carried out among artists and intellectuals, who were asked to explain their views on the Wagner issue.[39] The way the

problem was presented in the surveys may have been particularly important in this case. A different wording of the questions may have been
sufficient to produce the significant discrepancies between the various
surveys.

About a month after the IPO concert that had caused all the fuss,
Natan Dunevich, a veteran in the struggle to eliminate the ban on the
"forbidden composers," wrote an in-depth article analyzing the extreme
responses to the event. He began by suggesting that researchers try to
verify whether the whole affair was not a case of clinical hysteria – and if
it was, he asserted, it should be examined as such. According to Dunevich,
the responses and the topics raised – religious–secular relations, relations
between Ashkenazi and Sephardic Jews, and the balance between Likud
and Labor supporters – indicated a hysteria that crowded out any
rational, relevant arguments.[40] And indeed, if there had been any doubt
before, from now on it was eminently clear that the battle was not over
the figure of Wagner as such, but issues related to the Israeli psyche.

Until the end of the 1980s, the "forbidden musicians" dispute occupied only a small place in the lives of Israelis, although they were given a
number of significant opportunities to discuss the issue. One of them was
in November 1982, a year after the uproar over the IPO concert, when
the conductor Igor Markevitch recorded a performance of *Till
Eulenspiegel,* by Richard Strauss, with the Broadcasting Authority
Jerusalem Symphony Orchestra. In previous attempts to play this work
publicly in Israel – in 1953 and 1966 – conductors Georg Singer and
Zubin Mehta had been forced to back down under public pressure. The
recording, which did not require the presence of an audience, took place
undisturbed. A few papers, including some of the foreign press (such as
the *International Herald Tribune, The London Times,* and *Jewish
Chronicle*), reported the event and noted with wonder the calm that
prevailed this time.

In 1982 the Israelis had probably exhausted any reserves of anger that
could be expended on intellectual issues, even if ultimately the supposedly
musical issues always had a political and social aspect. In the first four
months of the year a storm blew up in Israel over withdrawing from the
Yamit region. The last stage of the evacuation, which necessitated military intervention, evoked harsh memories of the separation of parents
from their children, and caused pain throughout the political spectrum;
no one enjoyed the spectacle of soldiers being struck by residents who
refused to obey the government's orders to leave.

Only two months later, in June 1982, Israel called out the army again,
this time in Lebanon. What began as a limited operation became an offensive deep into Lebanon, leading not only to outright war, but also to an
exacerbation of the existing polarization of Israeli society. The conflicts
between left and right, which subsided somewhat after the Sabra and
Shatila massacre, ultimately led to a political assassination: At the begin-

ning of 1983, a demonstrator for the Peace Now movement, Emil Grunzweig, was killed by a hand-grenade thrown into the crowd by a right-wing activist. These events have vastly changed Israeli discourse and directed it to an even more nationalistic path and prompting even deeper differences of opinion.[41]

Another result of the war was an undermining of trust in the government of Israel, leading the prime minister, Menachem Begin, to retire from political life. Begin, known as a man of honor, felt deluded, and perhaps shamed as well by the fact that since he had been misled himself, he had led others astray. He shut himself up in his home, renouncing all involvement in both political and cultural affairs. The man who had led stormy demonstrations against Germany – thus helping in no small measure to establish some Israelis' opposition to German culture – now completely withdrew from controversy.

Before the end of the decade the issue of the "forbidden composers" came up a few more times. An opportunity for a significant revival of the Wagner affair arose in 1983, on the 100th anniversary of the composer's death – an occasion marked around the world by special programs of Wagner's music and publications of new research on his life and work. But no gesture was made in Israeli concert halls – although 1984 saw the publication of the first book in Hebrew on the Wagner controversy. This book, *Who's Afraid of Richard Wagner*, edited by Rina Litvin and Hezi Shelah, comprised a collection of articles written by Wagner himself and his contemporaries, critiques by intellectuals of the early twentieth century, and modern musical and social analyses contributed by Israeli and other intellectuals, elucidating the nature of the controversy over the composer. For the first time Wagner's infamous article "Judaism in Music" appeared in Hebrew. Israelis arguing over how suitable Wagner was for Jewish and Israeli ears could now read themselves what he had actually written. On the whole, the book was well received in intellectual circles. Particularly interesting was a review of the work by the historian Yossi Mali of Tel Aviv University, who examined the ideological connection between Wagner and Hitler. He argued that Hitler had understood that Wagner was an anthropologist and a mythologist, and as such had taken him into the heart of the German culture of the Third Reich. In addition, Mali noted that Israelis were preoccupied by Wagner as though he himself had an anthropological value that over the years had become a kind of cultural fetish.[42] Thus Mali skillfully explained the evolution of the Wagner heritage into conflicting cultural symbols that in fact came from a single source.

In August 1984, the newspaper of the Israeli community of New York, *Yisrael Shelanu* (Our Israel) reported on a new exhibition in the Wagner home in Bayreuth, in honor of the annual festival. Some 10,000 people visited the exhibition in the first five weeks of its run. In Israel it was not reported until 1987, when the author of one of the articles in the anthology *Who's Afraid of Richard Wagner*, Yehuda Cohen, returned from a visit to the Bayreuth Festival with the Israeli composer Ami Maayani. At the end of his article on the subject, Cohen pondered the fact that in Israel even musicians were not always familiar with Wagner's works, although without a doubt he had been an artist of unique stature in his own generation and afterwards. The question of artistic delegit-imization and its significance for Israeli society was raised once more without triggering any dispute, and soon petered out.

At the end of the 1980s the ban on Wagner seemed at times to be crum-bling, as the Voice of Israel broadcasts on the classical Voice of Music channel began to include works written by the "forbidden composers" or performed by boycotted musicians. These became increasingly frequent as no public outcry was made. As long as no one complained, the broad-casts could continue. The fact that the press refrained from taking up the issue again – perhaps because the Voice of Music had a relatively narrow audience sector anyway – probably facilitated the gradual, quiet intro-duction of the "forbidden musicians" in Israel. It is interesting to note that precisely at this time the Voice of Israel decided not to play works by Wagner and Strauss, following a discussion of conductor Igor Markevitch's request to include Strauss's *Till Eulenspiegel* in concerts by the Broadcasting Authority Jerusalem Symphony Orchestra. The members of the music committee of the Voice of Israel's managing board resolved that from now on works by the two significant "forbidden composers" would be played only for didactic purposes, but this policy suffered gradual erosion; short pieces by Strauss and Wagner were included in the music programs, and in time longer works were broadcast as well.

Even when publicists dredged up the Wagner boycott, the controversy remained stubbornly dormant. Such was the case in May 1987, when Michael Ohad wrote a feature including a few tidbits from Wagner's life. The occasion of the article was the festivities marking the IPO's anniver-sary, which were to culminate in three half-staged productions of operas composed by Wolfgang Amadeus Mozart to words by Lorenzo da Ponte. Ohad reminded his readers that 50 years had passed since Toscanini had conducted the preludes to the first and third acts of *Lohengrin*; this anniversary, he noted with sorrow, was not celebrated by the Philharmonic. After mentioning the large number of books written on the composer and the huge success of Wagner's operas, Ohad reported that when asking "the man in the street" what the problem was with Wagner he had met with the response, "Don't you know that Wagner conducted his music in Auschwitz?"[43] Even if not all Israelis displayed such stag-gering ignorance, it was clear that only few regarded Wagner as a man of flesh and blood rather than a symbol.

Just at the time that Ohad was dusting off the Wagner issue Israelis had the horrors of the Holocaust very much in mind, since the man identified as Ivan Demanjuk, the Ukrainian accused of murdering Jews during the Holocaust, was on trial in Jerusalem. However, the trial was overshadowed by other current events and did not revive the same fierce opposition to Germany that Eichmann's trial had in the past. Nonetheless, these years witnessed an impressive renaissance both in the portrayal of the Holocaust in Hebrew theater, poetry, and narrative, and in the audience's response to the subject.[44]

In early 1988, almost 50 years after the first cancellation of the performance of a Wagner piece in Israel, another real effort was made to break the ban. The pianist Gilead Mishory included a piano arrangement by Liszt of *Liebes Tod* from *Tristan und Isolde* in a series of recitals. A *Maariv* item on the upcoming series did not mention the inclusion of a work by Wagner, perhaps in order to avoid conflict. The first two recitals took place peacefully in the Chaim Weizmann House in Rehovot and in the Zionist Federation building in Jerusalem (on 3 and 4 February 1988, respectively). It was the recital that took place in the framework of the "11:11" series of Saturday-morning concerts in the Tzavta Club in Tel Aviv that attracted attention, although not the usual demonstrators. *Davar*'s music critic, Yehuda Cohen, told his readers that this time the performance had gone off without a hitch even though the program had been publicized in advance on the radio and in the print media. *Yedioth Ahronoth* said that Mishory had "made history," in an article accompanied by the de rigueur interview with Dov Shilansky.[45]

In the wake of these recitals, journalist Yosef Lapid wrote down his own ruminations on the subject for his regular spot on the Voice of Israel and his column in *Maariv*. Once again the same tired old material was rehashed: Wagner had been an extreme anti-Semite, but so had other creators, from Shakespeare to Chopin, from Mussorgsky to Hemingway – and only the works of Wagner, whose artistic stature was no less than that of other anti-Semites, were barred from Israel. "The time has come to forgive, if not Richard Wagner the man, then his oeuvre," Lapid concluded.[46] It seemed reasonable to expect that the breakthrough achieved by these recitals on the musical periphery would encourage the major orchestras to try once more to overcome the taboo. But for the time being they continued to wait.

The apparent erosion of the boycott went a step further one Saturday evening in August 1988, when Israeli television screened a feature on the Bayreuth Festival. The occasion was the participation in the Festival of conductor Daniel Barenboim, considered wholly Israeli by many even though he spent most of his time abroad. The feature, which was shown as part of the regular international news program, seemed to be a demonstration of journalism at its best: The Festival opened, and the press reported it. No sign now of the Israeli provincial image – at least not in the eyes of Israelis themselves; there was no longer any separation between the Israeli Wagner and Wagner as perceived throughout the world.

The broadcast was interesting in another way as well: It represented a challenge to the now precarious boycott, and to the hypocrisy of the Israeli attitude to Germany and its heritage. The day after the broadcast, *Yedioth Ahronoth* published an article by Hanoch Ron headed "Last Night Television Broke the Ban on Wagner." At the end of the report he cited the response of the director-general of Israel Television, Haim Yavin, who explained that "television was not broadcasting music by Wagner, but rather a feature on the Bayreuth Festival on account of its topical interest, especially since Daniel Barenboim is conducting Wagner in Germany."[47] Despite the effort to break the Israeli mold of Wagner, the press still felt it had to justify any mention of the man. The director of the sole television station in Israel, a state channel, had been called upon to give his official approval of Wagner in Israel, but refused to do so. Perhaps he reacted out of fear that the public's usual anger would be directed toward Israeli Television, which was already perceived by many as anti-establishment and politically left wing.

A few days later, *Hadashot* – the youngest daily, which had a brash, anti-establishment image – published a weekend feature on the waning boycott. This article on the "non-boycott" focused mainly on the Wagner issue, but also discussed the situation of Hebrew translation of works by Nazi or extreme racist writers. The article claimed that such works were not translated into Hebrew because of their shallow writing.[48] On the subject of the television feature on the Bayreuth Festival, the television foreign news desk editor, David Wiztum, was quoted:

> I received material from Germany on the Bayreuth Festival, I told my superiors, Yair Stern and Haim Yavin, that I was going to do a feature on the Festival, and received their permission. They did not tell me not to broadcast selections from Wagner, nor did we receive any complaints about the broadcast. On the contrary, most of the responses were positive.[49]

The interesting point here is that although the Bayreuth Festival was a cultural event of much lesser importance than the political and international affairs normally covered on the program, the editor had felt it necessary to consult his superiors before running that particular feature. It was obvious to everyone that the cultural aspect was just as important and politically sensitive as international issues, if not more so, and Wiztum's consultation with his superiors was clear indication of this. Further on Wiztum explained that the broadcast was actually a news feature, not a cultural one, since the festival was of significant interest all over the world, Barenboim was Israeli, and the director was an East German who had given a unique interpretation to *Der Ring des Nibelungen*.

Some two years later, in November 1989, Minister of Education and

Culture Yitzhak Navon (Labor) had to address the Wagner issue when he was asked to respond to an agenda proposal submitted by a member of his own faction, Hagai Meirom. Strangely enough, this proposal was submitted 24 hours before the first cracks in the Berlin Wall became visible. That date marked the 51st anniversary of *Kristallnacht*, and in time would become the day that had also changed the relations between Israel and Germany and between Israelis and Germans. As for the proposal itself, this was the first time that a Knesset member identified with the political center-left had raised the Wagner issue for debate. The trigger was the news that the IPO had played two selections from *Tristan und Isolde* and *Götterdämmerung* during rehearsals conducted by Daniel Barenboim. In his proposal Meirom detailed the history of Wagner's anti-Semitism, noting that the composer had "lived in Germany between the years 1813 and 1883. He was born and grew up in the city of Leipzig. One hundred years later in the city of Leipzig my mother was born, and persecuted." Thus, even a young Israeli (born in 1946) brought up in a party committed to renewed cooperation with Germany thought fit to use an argument much like that employed 30 years earlier by Holocaust survivors and his own political rivals. Meirom insisted on the need to continue educating young people in Israel about the danger of anti-Semitism, drawing this analogy: "Richard Wagner and his creed, like others I have mentioned here [Chamberlain and Schermann], provide a basis for the diabolical thought that our people is an inferior race. Can we restrain ourselves under such circumstances?" Meirom asked the minister to "stand in the breach" against people in the big world "who try to take us out of our provincial attitude and to bring into our home the geniuses who lay the foundations for the racist creed." This exhortation matched the approach taken some years later by the critic Ariel Hirschfeld. The minister responded briefly, conceding that the two pieces had been played at rehearsals, but pointing out that this was not the first time that something of the sort had occurred. He also noted that one musician who had asked to be excused from playing those parts of the rehearsal had been allowed to withdraw. Navon then stated on the IPO's behalf that it did not intend to play Wagnerian works in public, and that he supported that position. With that, the issue was dropped from the agenda.[50]

Despite this relatively quiet end to the Wagner affair at the end of the 1980s, the issue was to re-emerge in the last two weeks of the decade, and gather momentum at the beginning of the 1990s. For now it was plain that the attitude toward Wagner was taking an interesting turn. The historical memory of Wagner and his racist heritage had become doubly important. New generations of Israelis who had not directly experienced Germany's destructive side began to hate Wagner as a racist or a Nazi; they had absorbed opposition to Germans as part of the overall Israeli and Jewish experience. These new generations that rejected German culture, took aversion to Wagner and other composers for granted. At this stage there was no longer any need to find rationalizations for abhorring Wagner; everyone understood. It was no wonder, then, that the details of Wagner's biography became increasingly obscure, and many younger people believed that Wagner had been a Nazi himself, alive and active in the Third Reich.

The negative feelings of some Israelis toward Germany now received political reinforcement, since the line taken by the ruling party and some of the opposition was total opposition to German culture, particularly those of its aspects that could be identified with Nazism or racism. Moreover, whereas in the past politicians had addressed the German issue in its immediate political context, now the German issue had become – particularly in the cultural context – another political-partisan ax to grind, further evidence of the general perception that "the whole world is against us."

Nonetheless, at the end of the 1980s, a new trend was visible, one that would change the attitude toward the "forbidden musicians" in the 1990s. The journalistic pluralism that allowed Wiztum to broadcast a feature on the Bayreuth Festival would develop still further. As the concentration camp survivors and the last of the Revisionists disappeared from the journalistic field, the door was opened to change in the attitude toward those who had symbolized the evils of the past. The introduction of Israelis – not just Jews from around the world – to the world of Wagnerian opera (Barenboim being the best known) facilitated the slow but constant infiltration of the "forbidden musicians" into the Israeli cultural scene.

Notes

1   "The Philharmonic Canceled Wagner Performance Owing to Mourning for Moshe Dayan [Hebrew]," *Yedioth Ahronoth*, 18 Oct. 1981; and *Davar*, 15 Oct. 1981. Interestingly, the report appeared in *Davar*'s daily gossip column.

2   "A Matter of Sensitivity [Hebrew]," *Maariv*, 18 Oct. 1981.

3   "Wagner and All the Rest [Hebrew]," *Al Hamishmar*, 21 Oct. 1981.

4   Reports of this appeared in *Davar* and *Haaretz*, 19 Oct. 1981.

5   "Demolishing the Myth [Hebrew]," *Haaretz*, 22 Oct. 1981.

6   "Double Tones [Hebrew]," *Maariv*, 18 Oct. 1981.

7   "Wagner: The Dose for Racism [Hebrew]," *Maariv*, 23 Oct. 1981.

8   "Not a Symbol but a Spiritual Father [Hebrew]," *Maariv*, 3 Nov. 1981.

9   On the various dichotomies in Israeli society, see Kimmerling, *The Invention and Decline of Israeliness*. On the issue of Mizrahi Jews and religion, see Y. Shenhav, *The Arab Jews: A Post Colonial Reading of Nationalism, Religion and Ethnicity* (Palo Alto, 2006). See also: P. Motzafi-Haller, "A Mizrahi Call for a More Democratic Israel," *Postzionism: A Reader*, edited by L. A. Silberstein (New Brunswick, 2008), pp. 275–82.

10   See the extensive explanation regarding the use of the Holocaust as a political and social tool in Israel in: G. Arad-Ne'eman, "Israel and the *Shoah*: A Tale of Multifarious Taboo," *New German Critique* 90 (Autumn, 2003): 5–26, especially pp. 16–17.

11   "To Zubin Mehta, with All Due Respect [Hebrew]," *Yedioth Ahronoth*, 19 Oct. 1981.

12   "Culture Was Not in the Auditorium [Hebrew]," *Maariv*, 18 Oct. 1981.

13   "It is Appropriate Not to Play Wagner's Works in Israel for the Time Being [Hebrew]," *Hatzofeh*, 21 Oct. 1981.

14   "Can't Do Without Wagner [Hebrew]," *Hamodia*, 22 Oct. 1981.

15   "Consideration for Feelings [Hebrew]," *Yedioth Ahronoth*, 21 Oct. 1981.

16   "Alibi for the Boycott [Hebrew]," *Yedioth Ahronoth*, 21 Oct. 1981.

17   "Screeching Sounds [Hebrew]," *Haaretz*, 23 Oct. 1981.

18   "The Orchestra Will Take a Survey on the Wagner Issue [Hebrew]," *Yedioth Ahronoth*, 21 Oct. 1981.

19   "A Musical Ear and an Impervious Heart [Hebrew]," *Davar*, 25 Oct. 1981.

20   "Insensitivity to the Feelings of Many [Hebrew]," *Yedioth Ahronoth*, 26 Oct. 1981; and "The Case against Wagner," *The Jerusalem Post*, 25 Oct. 1981.

21   G. Hausner, *Justice in Jerusalem* (New York, 1968; 1st edn. 1966), pp. 451–2.

22   Dr. Y. Arad to the IPO management, 2 Dec. 1981, in IPO Archives, Wagner and Strauss file.

23   M. Hoch to management and members of the IPO, 3 Nov. 1981, in IPO Archives, Wagner and Strauss file.

24   "Wagner in the Philharmonic: Don't Give in to Violence [Hebrew]," *Haaretz*, 21 Oct. 1981.

25   "And Shilansky Opened His Mouth [Hebrew]," *Davar*, 28 Oct. 1981. Readers' responses to his remark were also published in the papers. One contributor, the clarinet player Eli Eban, suggested that Shilansky go home himself. See "Shilansky Has Gone Too Far [Hebrew]," Letters to the Editor, *Maariv*, 29 Oct. 1981.

26   "I Was 'There' and I Heard . . . [Hebrew]," *Beeretz Yisrael*, Nov. 1981.

27   M. Begin to D. Binyamini, 29 Oct. 1981. The letter from the members of the orchestra and Begin's response were quoted in full in *Maariv*, 3 Nov. 1981.

28   See Naor, *Begin in Power*, pp. 212–13; and Meroz, *In schwieriger Mission*.

29   "Wagner, Shilansky, and the Inflation of the Holocaust [Hebrew]," *Davar*, 30 Oct. 1981.

30   "Who's Afraid of Richard Wagner [Hebrew]," *Haaretz*, 30 Oct. 1981. Gans related to the subject from an academic perspective, dealing with the attitude of the State of Israel to liberalism. See Ch. Gans, "The Israeli Ban on the Performance of Wagner: Moral Perspectives [Hebrew]," *Zmanim* 79 (2002): 22–32.

31   "Screeching Sounds [Hebrew]," *Tmura*, 30 Oct. 1981.

32   "Richard Wagner: The Seed of Calamity [Hebrew]," *Yedioth Ahronoth*, 30 Oct. 1981.

33   "*Meistersinger* [Hebrew]," Yediot Ahronot, 30 Oct. 1981. On Evron's attitude to Israeli nationalism, see B. Evron, *Jewish State or Israeli Nation*, (Bloomington, 1995).

34   "My Heart Breaks Too in Such Circumstances [Hebrew]," *Davar*, 23 Oct. 1981.

35   Telegram from Y. Perlman to members of the IPO, 27 Oct. 1981; letter from A. Vardi to Z. Mehta, 22 Oct. 1981; and telegram from L. Bernstein to the IPO, 17 Oct. 1981, in IPO Archives, Wagner and Strauss file.

36 For Dalia Atlas's comments, see "Where Is the Criterion [Hebrew]," *Yedioth Ahronoth*, 26 Oct. 1981, and also her telegram to the IPO, 1 Nov. 1981. It should be noted that the IPO was not recognized as a national orchestra until the fall of 1997. See "The Philharmonic – The National Orchestra [Hebrew], *Haaretz*, 8 Oct. 1997.

37 Layout for the announcement of 28 Oct. 1981, in IPO Archives, Wagner and Strauss file.

38 "Tiny Majority Favors Wagner [Hebrew]," *Hair*, 30 Oct. 1981; "Survey: Wagner in Haifa – No Way! [Hebrew]" Kolbo, 23 Oct. 1981; and "Most Israelis against Wagner," *The Jerusalem Post*, 20 Dec. 1981.

39 See, for example, "Orchestras in Israel: The Current Situation [Hebrew]," *Davar*, 19 Oct. 1981; and "The Reader's Domain: Wagner – Yes or No? [Hebrew]," *Al Hamishmar*, 5 Nov. 1981.

40 "Anatomy of Hysteria [Hebrew]," *Haaretz*, 13 Nov. 1981.

41 See Y. Yadgar, "From the particularistic to the universalistic: national narratives in Israel's mainstream press, 1967–97," *Nations and Nationalism* 8.1 (Jan., 2002): 55–72.

42 See Y. Mali, "Who's Afraid of Richard Wagner? [Hebrew]," *Zmanim* 20 (Winter, 1986): 93–6.

43 "An Ignoble Genius [Hebrew]," *Haaretz*, 22 May 1987.

44 See B. Feingold, *The Theme of the Holocaust in Hebrew Drama* [Hebrew] (Tel Aviv, 1990), especially pp. 13, 23–32; C. Shoham, *The Drama of the "Native Born" Generation in Israel (Challenge and Reality in Israeli Drama)* [Hebrew] (Tel Aviv, 1989), pp. 255–62. There was also an upsurge in the portrayals of the Holocaust in Hebrew literature. See A. Holtzman, "Trends in Israeli Fiction of the Holocaust in the 1980s," *Modern Hebrew Literature* (new series) 8/9 (Spring-Fall 1992): 23–8.

45 "Three Times Gilead [Hebrew]," *Maariv*, 29 Jan. 1988; "Not Only Wagner [Hebrew]," *Davar*, 15 Feb. 1988; and "For the First Time: A Work by Wagner Was Played in Israel [Hebrew]," *Yedioth Ahronoth*, 6 Feb. 1988.

46 "Tommy's Column: Wagner Nevertheless [Hebrew]," *Maariv*, 12 Feb. 1988.

47 "Last Night Television Broke the Ban on Wagner [Hebrew]," *Yedioth Ahronoth*, 21 Aug. 1988.

48 This argument is strange; suffice to recall the dispute that had arisen in Israel a few years earlier when the Am Oved publishing house chose to publish a translation by I. Hammerman of Louis-Ferdinand Céline's *Voyage au bout de la nuit* (original French edition, 1932), considered a superb book.

49 "Actually There Is No Boycott [Hebrew]," *Hadashot*, 22 Aug. 1988.

50 Agenda proposal 1699, submitted by M.K. Hagai Meirom (8 Oct. 1989). *Divrei HaKnesset*, session 110, Twelfth Knesset, 1990, I: 334–6.

CHAPTER

9

The 1990s: A Breakthrough and Stagnation

The low-key reactions to the rehearsal of Wagner's music in Israel in 1989 seemed to indicate that sensitivity concerning the "forbidden composers" was declining. The 1990s marked the beginning of a more moderate public attitude to the subject, due to diverse reasons. As it moved toward a new, brief, status quo, Israeli society underwent one more storm over the Wagner issue, triggered by an attempt by Daniel Barenboim to conduct a special concert of Wagner's works in December 1991.

This particular Wagner crisis showed many of the characteristics familiar from previous stages of the controversy over musicians identified with Nazism, and on this occasion the circumstances seemed to lend themselves to full exploitation of all the usual arguments against public performances of Wagner's music in Israel. Attitudes toward Germany were highly charged; the idea that Israel's national orchestra should lift the ban was strongly resisted; and circumventing the effects of that ban was easier than ever, as cable television gradually infiltrated the restricted circle of the Israeli media and broadcasts of Wagner's music by the Voice of Music continued.

A new factor at this stage was the Gulf War trauma, which had left Israelis with indelible memories of their terrible fear that Iraq would employ chemical warfare against them – using gas bought from Germany. This reactivation of the old dread of poisoning by gas – and German gas at that – was a spur to Israelis' collective memory, and few managed to eschew the obvious analogies with past horrors in Nazi Germany. Similarly, the fear of the current enemy evoked images of the enemy of the recent past, and even the more level-headed columnists rushed to symmetrize Saddam Hussein and Hitler; the gas theme was just another manifestation of the growing complex of anxieties.[1] Attitudes toward Germany were tense for another reason, too: Only two years before the last effort to play Wagner in Tel Aviv's Mann Auditorium, the Berlin Wall was torn down and the process of German reunification began. In Israel, as in other Western countries, there was concern that Germany, growing stronger, would become once more a dangerous power.[2] Oddly, the

Wagner issue seemed to interest Israelis more than the question of reunification and the new path German commemoration of National Socialism was taking.[3]

These prejudices against Wagner concerts were reinforced by the usual anger at the IPO's behavior as a national orchestra. The Public Committee of the Heritage of the Holocaust and Heroism took a particularly strict view; the IPO's plan to play works by Wagner led it to send the IPO board a letter in February 1992 demanding the removal of the word 'Israel' from the orchestra's name.[4] Thus, a sector of the population continued to see an absolute contradiction between Israeli identity and performing music by Wagner.

Another aspect of Israeli identity that surfaced at this point was the widening gap between religious and secular Israelis; in the musical context the struggle between these two groups revolved not only around Wagner performances, but also the place of Western culture in general in the State of Israel. In this respect, the Wagner affair was only the tip of the iceberg in an ideological conflict that would continue to deepen throughout the 1990s. This specific composer was a tool in the hands of ideologues from the national-Orthodox camp, chosen because the controversy associated with him provided a relatively easy way of rallying the wider public. In the past, too, when Holocaust survivors and the political right had used him to substantiate their arguments, Wagner's critical instrumental role had at times overshadowed what the man himself had said. One issue that did not find full expression in the current conflict was the social and institutional recognition that Israelis could not be isolated from the foreign cultural influences that were permeating the country with increasing persistence.[5]

Notable during this installment of the conflict were significant indications of "battle fatigue" over the constantly recurring disputes over Wagner. As mentioned earlier, the major opponents of relations with Germany in general and the import of German culture to Israel in particular, were gradually growing old and retiring from both the political arena and the media. Those taking their places had been children during the Holocaust, or were born afterwards. Strangely enough, those most adamantly opposed to performances of Wagner often turned out to have no personal stake in the heavily charged relationship between Jews and Germans; their opposition was apparently based on anti-German ideas that had been internalized as part of a certain Israeli world view, part of the collective memory. Many of these young protesters were armed with ideological arguments, but had no knowledge of the actual facts of the case. They saw Wagner as an emblem of the Holocaust, which should be maintained as such for the sake of the survivors and as part of future commemoration of the Holocaust in Israel.

A similar changing of the guards and mellowing of attitudes were also evident in the other camp, among the proponents of Wagner performances. Since the end of the 1980s Israel had been enjoying economic prosperity it had never known before, and anyone who wanted to listen to works by the "forbidden composers" could easily do so by listening to compact discs or in concert halls throughout Europe. Thus, the dispute now was really about public endorsement of music by composers associated with the Nazis versus the possible musical development that the boycott denied to the members of Israeli orchestras, particularly the Philharmonic. The right of Israelis to listen to the music of their choice came under discussion, but certainly did not take center stage. One reason may have been a certain lack of public alertness to the issue of civil rights, a concept that was still rather loosely anchored in the law; it was not until some months after this stage of the controversy that a formal piece of legislation – albeit an extremely flexible one – was enacted to protect certain civil rights in Israel.[6]

The feeble arguments of both camps and their huge difficulty in reconciling their views with contemporary Israeli reality exposed the cracks throughout the controversy. It was becoming increasingly clear that there was nothing new to be said on the subject, and arguments that had been strong and persuasive in the 1950s and 1960s had little impact in the 1990s. During these years a clear distinction was also made between Wagner and the other "forbidden musicians." Wagner was now the only composer who still engendered fierce opposition, since the Voice of Music had in effect discontinued the boycott of performers identified with the Nazis, and relaxed the ban on Nazi-associated composers. Israeli orchestras, too – including the IPO – broke through the barriers and began to play works by composers who had collaborated with the Nazis, including Richard Strauss, Franz Lehar, and Carl Orff.

The first taboo to go was the prohibition on Richard Strauss. The trailblazer in this respect was the Israeli musician Noam Sheriff, who dared to conduct the Israel Rishon LeZion Symphony Orchestra playing a work by Strauss for the first time in public. The work chosen for this concert, which took place on 18 March 1990, was *Metamorphosis*.[7] Surprisingly, the performance made no stir.

Hanoch Ron, who reported – in his eyes – the happy event in *Yedioth Ahronoth*, wondered whether there was a legal prohibition against playing Strauss publicly in Israel. His modest investigation disclosed the fact that Israel had no such law or regulation, the idea had never been discussed, and no enforceable resolution had ever been passed. On the contrary, requests to refrain from playing the works of specific composers appeared only later, in 1994, 2000, 2001 and 2012. Yet for decades the IPO had been laboring under the impression that the ban had some kind of formal basis – at the very least a binding resolution – since the orchestra's founder, Bronisław Huberman, had wanted to ban all musicians who had not resisted Hitler. Ron explained to his readers that the Nazis had appointed Richard Strauss as head of the music department of the Third Reich because they wanted a well-known musician in the post. Strauss, 70 years old at the time, was indeed a noted composer and conductor, but retained the new post for only a year; his efforts to assert his right to maintain ties with the Jewish writer Stefan Zweig proved his undoing. Ron went on to point out that the fact that Strauss's daughter-in-law was Jewish made him the grandfather of two Jewish children – according to Jewish law.[8]

The Strauss affair in effect ended here. From this point on his works would be played on the radio, on television, and in the concert halls without arousing any untoward reactions. The radio began to broadcast his works in increasingly large doses: Strauss was no longer one of the "forbidden musicians." In the summer of 1994, Channel 8, the culture and science channel whose programs were included in the standard packages offered by all the cable-television companies in Israel, screened a series of full-length operas by Strauss, including *Der Rosenkavalier* and *Intermezzo* with words by an "anonymous" librettist – Stefan Zweig.

Following suit, the IPO also began to include works by Strauss in its programs. Like the Voice of Music, which had tested the waters by playing short pieces before progressing to complete works, the Philharmonic, too, needed a trial run. Toward the end of the 1993–1994 concert season, the Israeli pianist and conductor Arie Vardi included short pieces by Strauss in special narrated concerts, including one for children and youth. Only after this experiment passed without incident did the orchestra begin to play Strauss's works in its regular series as well. The 1994–1995 season opened with a series of special concerts of *Lieder* by Strauss, and subsequent concerts from the regular series included his *Das Heldenleben*, which was also played during the IPO's tours in November 1994 and February 1995. The following concert season opened with selections from Strauss's famous works *Salome* and *Don Quixote*. In the ensuing years more Strauss operas were screened on Channel 8, as well as a documentary film that shed light on the composer's controversial life and the opportunistic tendency that had, to some extent, shaped his career.[9]

The gradual lifting of the ban on composers and performers identified with National Socialism gave birth to the most profound statement against playing the music of these artists. In January 1994, after several sessions of Knesset debates on the performance of works by anti-Semitic composers identified with the National Socialism, its Education and Culture Committee came up with a status quo document. Its statement that freedom of expression is a supreme value in Israel was accompanied by an appeal "from the heart," requesting the cultural institutions to refrain from performing the works of the anti-Semitic composers, should these hurt the feelings of the public.[10] The public in question was specific – Holocaust survivors who identified the music of the anti-Semitic composers with their lives in the labor, concentration, and death camps. This was the first time the Knesset had ever formulated such a clear-cut request-instruction.

Wagner's case was and remained more complex. First, the Israeli public's old problems with him were evoked in October 1990, when the northern local paper *Kol Hakrayot* revealed that music by Wagner was being played in the passenger cars of Israeli trains. The train company's spokesperson asserted that the complaint would be investigated, and the matter was indeed settled.[11]

A year later the Wagner controversy made a more significant comeback. In mid-December 1991, the media published a report stating that the members of the IPO had decided to play a special concert of works by Richard Wagner, conducted by Daniel Barenboim, who had taken over the cause of fighting the ban from Zubin Mehta. At the time Barenboim was a welcome and regular guest in Bayreuth, and he used every occasion to explain the great benefit each player and the orchestra as a whole would derive from a working acquaintance with Wagner. The members of the IPO made their decision at a meeting attended by some 60 of the 85 people entitled to vote; 39 musicians supported the idea of a special concert of works by Wagner, while only a dozen were opposed. The concert was to include the overture to *Der fliegende Holländer* and the prelude *Liebes Tod* from *Tristan und Isolde*,[12] two of Wagner's best-known and most popular works.

The day after this decision was made the public disputes over Wagner began again. Some claimed that the orchestra was once again trying to sneak Wagner in through the back door, since it had not formally announced its decision to the press but leaked the information through the musicians, and, contrary to the usual custom for special concerts, this concert was limited to an audience selected in advance, with no tickets available for purchase by the general public.[13] Other publicists saw similar craftiness in the musicians' decision to play works by Wagner in a special concert rather than as part of the subscription series, thereby avoiding confrontation with some of their usual audience.[14] But apart from a few accusations of this kind, the polemic that was incited this time bore all the earmarks of the previous rounds in the controversy. The usual disputants were familiar, and the press returned to them or applied to commentators whose views were crystal clear from the start. For once there were few surprises; the press coverage was mostly a summary of ready-prepared scripts.

This was the case, for example, with the many interviews with the IPO violinist Avraham Melamed who had taken such a firm stand against playing Wagner back in 1981, in the previous round of the controversy. This time Melamed spoke to a number of media representatives, repeating what he had said before: Wagner aroused in him disgust and physical revulsion, and consequently he could not play his music or forgive what

Wagner represented to him. Nevertheless, even Melamed was aware that the strength of his feelings was beginning to be uncommon. In an interview on the army radio station's morning news program broadcast, he explained: "I do not suppose there will be the same public reaction there once was, because to use a phrase, the arms with the numbers tattooed on them, well, the skin has shrunk a lot."[15] Melamed felt that among the Holocaust survivors who were sworn opponents of Wagner, no one was left to fight; the following decade attests to the fact that the survivors' opposition was vivid more than ever. Melamed did not take into account all those people who had internalized an opposition to Wagner even though they had no personal experience of the Holocaust, and were ready to fight against any slackening in attitudes toward the composer. He also overlooked an entire sector of the population who for the most part did not attend classical music concerts but who saw Wagner as a symbol of anti-Semitism and pernicious imitation of the Gentiles: The Orthodox and national-religious public proved to be resolute fighters in the cause of Hebrew culture, and perceived Wagner as an agent of desecration. However, in another interview Melamed said frankly that, to his sorrow, the Knesset had never discussed the subject seriously, and all the official deliberations had been simply efforts by various Knesset members "to hitch a ride on the wave of publicity the affair received"[16] – in short, to make political capital out of it. Melamed himself made further headlines by playing *Kaddish* (the Jewish prayer for the dead) outside the Mann Auditorium while his colleagues were giving the special Wagner concert inside.[17]

In the same interview on the Army Radio, Melamed also pointed out the weakness of the opponents of public performances of Wagner: They clung to Wagner as a symbol as they clung to other symbols that had nothing to do with any racist or destructive elements: "First of all the Nazis took Wagner's music as a symbol. They also took a symbol like the swastika, which is actually an ancient Indian symbol. They took these symbols and turned them into a symbol. Today, if I draw a swastika somewhere outside, the police will come and arrest me."[18] Thus, according to Melamed, the adoption of Wagner by the Nazis may have turned the performance of his music into a crime.

It appeared that Melamed himself realized that the battle was about a symbol, while the underlying reality had already dimmed – at least to some extent. However, in another interview Melamed said that "Hitler copied Wagner's teachings virtually word for word," an idea that was not supported by the facts. If any link existed between Wagner's thoughts and the Nazi *Weltanschauung* it was limited to Wagner's *Gesamtkunstwerk* which the Nazis interpreted as strict totality. Just as Wagner perceived art as an entirety in which all parts serve all other parts, thus the Nazis considered all parts of the state as serving one another. Melamed may have been referring to the perverted descriptions of Jews in Fritz Hippler's film *The*

Eternal Jew or Veit Harlans's *Jew Süss* – descriptions that were reminiscent of those found in "Judaism in Music."[19] In short, at this stage at least some of the disputants realized that the battle was actually about symbols, the real significance of which was none too clear.

The numerous comments in or about the electronic media underscored the new status of these media. The early decades of the debate were conducted exclusively in the print media. The last two decades of the twentieth century saw a significant change. The radio – that had played an important role in the consolidation of the commemoration of the Holocaust in Israel since the Eichmann trial – became a powerful tool of nation-building through its broadcasts on the Day of Remembrance of Holocaust and Heroism.[20] Moreover, since the mid-1990s a growing number of newspapers closed down due to the declining number of readers, most of them newspapers affiliated with political organs and foreign language readership. Most readers shifted to the larger newspapers, thus accelerating the centralization of the Israeli print media.

Other musicians interviewed by the press presented more complex and varied positions than Melamed's. The newspaper *Hadashot* interviewed the cellist Paul Blassberger in tandem with the clarinetist Yaacov Barnea. Barnea explained that the problem lay in Wagner's music, which was imbued with megalomania and nationalism, while Blassberger strongly objected to this idea, arguing that Wagner's perverted views and unbearable personality could not be heard in his compositions. Blassberger also challenged Ben-Zion Leitner, the Mann Auditorium usher who had caused a stir a decade earlier at the momentous concert conducted by Zubin Mehta. Blassberger, who had done forced labor in a camp on the Austro-Hungarian border and was later transferred to the Mauthausen camp, insisted that Wagner's music had not been played to the Jews, for ideological reasons; since the Germans had perceived Jews as subhuman, playing the music of their national idol, Wagner, would have been truly a desecration. Leitner, who had also been a prisoner at a forced labor camp in the Ukraine, said angrily that the Germans had played "all sorts of operettas by Wagner," and with one bitter cry of anguish wiped out the arguments of historians who rejected the possibility that Wagner's music had been played in the camps.[21] This time Leitner's anger was expressed only through press interviews, since he had promised not to disrupt the concert scheduled for late December 1991. He attributed his conduct in 1981 to the fact that on that occasion the orchestra had slipped a Wagner composition in the program without any prior warning; the advance notice given this time relieved him of the need to protest inside the concert hall.[22]

A popular interviewee this time around was MK Dov Shilansky (Likud), the deputy minister who had lashed out at Zubin Mehta in 1981 and suggested he return to his homeland. Shilansky was now the Knesset speaker, a position of state, with not merely partisan significance. His predecessor in this office, Menachem Savidor, had supported the IPO's actions in 1981. However, Shilansky's official status did not prevent him from loudly denouncing the decision, or from explaining his feelings. One of his arguments was that "they [the musicians who wanted to lift the ban] want to do this for the sake of pleasure. But there are people to whom this causes pain. Pleasure can be forgone by choice; no one can choose to forgo pain. Pleasure versus pain is a completely disproportionate contest." Even when told that Barenboim was Jewish, Shilansky was unmoved; his response to this argument was "but he is young,"[23] implying that Barenboim's age prevented him from sharing the collective memory of Israeli society. In another interview, Shilansky extended the significance of advocacy for and resistance to Wagner's music, equating them with identification with or opposition to the Jewish people: "I cannot comprehend people in whom the obsession with playing Wagner is stronger than their love for the Jewish people," he explained, and perhaps he was implying that different sectors had different collective memories.[24]

The importance of Barenboim's Judaism was emphasized in a number of articles. After all, in this case the conductor could not be sent back to his homeland, since Israel was the home of all Jews. Barenboim's Judaism was also a central issue to Zubin Mehta; he himself had been subjected to stinging insults 10 years earlier as someone who, owing to his own background, would never understand the hearts of Israelis or Jews. In an interview with *Haaretz* at his residence in Los Angeles, the day after the news of the IPO's decision was published, Mehta said:

> After I tried to conduct Wagner in October 1981, we reached the conclusion that only an Israeli conductor would be able to do so. After that attempt and the scandal, we decided to let it rest for a few years, and we thought that the person who could do it would be either Lenny Bernstein or Daniel Barenboim. We've been talking to Barenboim about it for five years.[25]

The IPO management believed that only a Jew whom Israelis considered as "one of ours" could slip Wagner into the orchestra's repertoire. One of the musicians' representatives in the IPO management, Yaacov Mishori, presented a similar view, although he stressed his empathy with the suffering of those who opposed performances of Wagner. In contrast, violinist Itzhak Perlman, who frequently appeared with the orchestra as a soloist, said that he thought the IPO should continue to respect the feelings of the Holocaust survivors who were sensitive to the issue.

Following the special Wagner concert, another view was added to the assortment expressed on the issue, when *Haaretz* printed a translated excerpt from a script that the conductor Leonard Bernstein – deceased by then – had written for a television program about Wagner's music recorded at the Vienna Opera House. Bernstein, who had a strong Jewish consciousness and often expressed his opinions on various issues of Israeli policy, ended with the familiar refrain: If great works of music are available to us, why shouldn't we sample them? Wagner and the politicians who adopted him as a symbol of the Third Reich had in any case been dead for many years.[26]

As the violinist Avraham Melamed had anticipated, a rather large number of Knesset members took stands on the issue. Besides Shilansky, who was now considered the standard-bearer for those who opposed performances of Wagner, several Knesset members with predictable views were interviewed by the various media. They consisted mainly of those who had expressed their opinion in a debate held on the subject in the Knesset on 17 December 1991, following the presentation of three agenda proposals by two opponents of Wagner concerts – MK Elyakim Haetzni (Tehiya) and MK Avraham Burg (Labor) – and one supporter, MK Mordechai Virshubski (Shinui) respectively. However, the Knesset members did not resolve the question, and the Ministry of Education issued the standard statement concerning the ministry's policy of non-intervention in the orchestra's professional decisions.[27] Shilansky's deputy, MK Shevah Weiss (Labor), who had also rejected public performances of Wagner during the 1981 controversy, now declared he was tired of the whole business and thought that in any case the dispute was being waged in the emotional, rather than the rational, sphere.[28]

Musicians who had no close ties with the IPO, once again called to address the Wagner issue, expressing almost unanimous support of the performances of Wagner's music. The composer Zvi Avni, who showed heightened awareness of the issue, also sought to distinguish between the man and his work. But more important was his general attitude to the entire dispute. After noting his feeling that the conflict was losing its sting and becoming obscure over the years, he reminded his readers that "the boycott is not of the composer but of the cultural medium and what it represents."[29] In short, the point was not Wagner, but his image in the eyes of both Nazis and Israelis.

A frontal attack was launched on the opponents of Wagner concerts by Michal Zmora, who had once headed the music division of the Voice of Israel and was known for her liberal views and unreserved support for performances of Wagner's music. Zmora believed that the Israeli attitude to Wagner showed a great deal of hypocrisy; after all, Israelis were perfectly happy to use every other German product. But her strongest argument, like Avni's, concerned the Israelis' unheeding adoption of the faulty German approach. Telling the story of the delegitimization of Jewish composers in the Third Reich and the burning of their musical scores in the town squares, Zmora pointed out that the Nazis' conduct had been classically fascist and anti-cultural, and concluded with a rhetorical question: "Will we share that with them?"[30]

Her words did not go unnoticed. The religious weekend paper *Yom*

Hashishi attacked Zmora directly and ended by sketching the boundaries of the Israeli cultural war: "They [the "bleeding hearts"] will remember only one thing, that Orthodox Jews do not stop for a meaningless, empty moment of standing at attention [a custom on Holocaust Day to commemorate the victims]. Only then do they recall that the Holocaust is being 'forgotten,' but in the meantime they go to the concert halls to enjoy the pleasant sounds of Wagner."[31]

The dispute, then, was not merely about Wagner; it was about lifestyle in general. Wagner was being used as a weapon in a general attack on the hypocritical culture of secular Jews. Indeed, by the end of the decade it was clear that an outright cultural war was being waged between those who clung to religion as a cultural and political foundation, and those who aspired to a universalist culture. Both sides employed their ideas for glaring political purposes.

Yom Hashishi's attack echoed a similar diatribe presented by the religious right-wing paper *Yated Neeman* a week earlier; the paper had rejected out of hand the "secular" approach that endorsed foreign culture in general and Wagner in particular. The similarity of the two papers' views only strengthens the supposition that Wagner was a tool rather than the target of serious criticism as an artist or an individual. To explain the interest the paper itself seemed to be taking in the defective foreign culture, the editors explained at the beginning of the article that "it is not by banning Wagner that we preserve the memory of the Holocaust. Thus, we must ban all 'humanistic' Western culture, which is the root from which grow putrid fruits like Wagner. The whole culture is essentially negative." Just to make his meaning patently clear, the article's author, N. Katzin, went on to explain the difference in mentality between the religious and the secular: "We, who commemorate the Holocaust in the true way of the Torah, are told to stand at attention during the [memorial] sirens [sounded on Holocaust Day to mark a moment of solidarity], in order not to hurt anyone's feelings [. . .] They continue to sit there calmly listening to sounds from the camps."[32] Thus, the war was being fought not just over current affairs, but also – and perhaps mainly – over the shaping of the national identity and the constitution of the collective memory.

To judge from the nationalist and religious press, the Wagner controversy was – at least to the more extreme right wing sectors of Israeli society – not only a symbol of the evils the Nazis had inflicted on the Jews, but a symbol, which they themselves had formed, of the widening gap between the different groups of Israeli society. In their eyes, the dispute over the Wagner issue was not merely a question of preserving the memory of the Holocaust and respecting the feelings of others; it was also one of the opening shots in a wider cultural war between religious and secular Jews. The different ways that the two sides sought to shape collective memory revealed the chasm between the secular and the religious. It is interesting to note that the battle over the collective memory was identified by the political right wing five years before it actually found expression at the polls in the elections of 1996, as well as afterwards in the political conflicts over educational values, budgets, and the form that ceremonial state occasions should take.

In the strongly right-wing press, the correlation between a paper's general tendency and its position on the specific issue of the Wagner controversy was readily apparent. However, in the disputes of 1991 the traditional alignments were not always observed. Although some of the standard rules held true, this time certain changes could be detected which derived from the personal views of the reporters covering the affair.

One of the papers still politically dominant in the affair was *Maariv*, which continued to feature highly opinionated articles by its former editor, Shmuel Schnitzer. In addition to painful descriptions of the Nazis' horrifying actions and his familiar arguments that Israel must not count the years since the war but continue to honor the memory of the Holocaust and its victims, Schnitzer threatened: "And if the Philharmonic orchestra includes his [Wagner's] music in its subscription concerts too, I will part from it with sorrow, grateful for the magical experiences it has given me in the past, but without hesitation."[33] This sentence, appearing in the first paragraph of the article, seems to indicate that Schnitzer had ceased to argue the principles involved. His objection had become personal: If the orchestra took this action, his response would be to boycott it. This position also says something about the general weariness with this rearguard battle; even the bitterest opponents of public performances of Wagner had been worn down by the exhausting necessity of repeating and reinforcing their arguments over and over.

In contrast to Schnitzer, Michael Handelzalts, the cultural editor of *Haaretz*, took an unequivocal stand in favor of eliminating the taboo, notable in one of the articles he wrote during the first days of the dispute. This article ended with the statement that liberation from forced symbols was a sign of maturity in a nation, and that the time had come for the State of Israel to rid itself of the yoke of such symbols and restore Wagner to the purely musical realm whence he had come.[34]

A few days before the controversial concert Handelzalts wrote another article advocating immediate lift of the ban. This time he discussed two points that most publicists, either by oversight or design, had not mentioned. First, he noted that after the prelude to *Die Meistersinger* had been removed from the program of the concert held three days after *Kristallnacht*, the orchestra had played works by Wagner during its tour at the beginning of 1939 in Cairo and Alexandria. Clearly, there had initially been no thought of imposing a general ban on performances of Wagner – only of avoiding a concert that at the time might have grated unpleasantly on the ears of some of the audience. Then Handelzalts returned to what really bothered him about the boycott:

But perhaps we need precisely a subject that is so remote from the experience of our immediate lives – from the political decisions that determine our fate, or the treatment of an Arab population in the [occupied] territories, for example – to free us from the adherence to symbols that provide nothing but adherence itself. That is why it is important that Wagner be played, as music and not as a symbol, by the Philharmonic in particular. When we stop clinging to the symbol, perhaps we will be able to come to grips with the deeper historical significance of this recent, terrible historical experience.[35]

The symbol cast a giant shadow over the real thing, and thereby impeded the process of shaping the nation's image, goals, and guiding ethics. Handelzalts's opinion accorded with the ideas expressed in an editorial published the next day in the same paper; the time had come for Israelis to shake off their old sense of frailty, and give rein to the spirit that had permitted the nation's renaissance as an independent state. Similar ideas linking Jewish history with the Israeli-Palestinian conflict were later proclaimed by Daniel Barenboim, who was fiercely attacked for expressing his opinions.[36]

Haaretz balanced these articles with a different orientation provided by the critic Ariel Hirschfeld, whose arguments seemed to have nothing to do with the dispute that had been going on for years over the Wagner affair. Hirschfeld completely rejected the validity of ridiculing buyers of Volkswagens who refused to listen to Wagner's works; he insisted that attitudes to material goods and attitudes to spiritual goods could not be compared. Accordingly, he praised the instinct that made Israelis reject Wagner out of hand, saying that the State of Israel was, among other things, the home of the Holocaust survivors of Europe, and consequently rejecting Wagner was the same as protecting the survivors. Although Hirschfeld explained at the outset that he was not relying on historical or sociological conceptions, he was clearly presenting the Wagner debate as a kind of test case for theories concerning collective memory and the essential elements that shaped the lives of individuals or groups in society. The article's conclusion was a complete departure from the usual intellectual condemnation of the boycott as provincial: "Abstaining from Wagner is one of the few truly cosmopolitan acts carried out here in the musical field, an act that does not resemble the provincial, imitative sycophancy typical of musical life here and of the Philharmonic in particular."[37] Nonetheless, Hirschfeld's views, albeit interesting to Israeli intellectuals, did not offer a solution to the musical needs cited by the conductors who worked with the orchestra. Hirschfeld ignored conventional musical criteria in Israel and abroad, and simply raised a general problem with respect to the IPO's activity, discussed in articles by other musical critics as well; but unlike them, he took no interest in the musical aspect of the affair.

Ever faithful to the view defended by Mapam since the 1950s, that Holocaust survivors' feelings should be respected, *Al Hamishmar* published an interesting confession by its cultural affairs correspondent, Yossi Shifman:

> I must admit that I, too, when I was younger and more energetic, was one of those who battled for performances of Wagner's music in Israel, and thought that "whoever doesn't want to listen, doesn't have to." But in the last decade I have felt a growing conviction that the Israel Philharmonic does need to respect the wishes of the victims of the Holocaust by not playing Wagner. It is not a question of pure logic, for after all, I myself can lecture and write about how important it is for every orchestra to play Wagner. It is a question of feelings, and that's all. Just as I am incapable of listening to the shouts of the traffic wardens in the train stations in Germany, because they give me the chills.[38]

It may well be that Shifman identified with the objection to Wagner since he acknowledged the power of sounds. Yet, Shifman reduced the whole affair to the worn-out argument against Germany and the possibility of the creation of "another Germany." In fact, he was the opposite of protesters such as Shevah Weiss, who, weary of the role they had assumed as soapbox orators, were ready to drop the subject. Shifman had crossed the lines in the opposite direction; once an enlightened liberal willing to fight for the right to listen to and play music, he now evinced a closed outlook that sought to perpetuate a picture of the world as it was during the years of the Third Reich.

This change may have been brought on by fear that the younger generation, who had not lived through the Holocaust, was ignorant of its heritage and indifferent to its significance. Yet these were the years in which the Ministry of Education and Culture began to encourage activities to promote Holocaust awareness in the schools. Besides expanding the educational activity of institutions that specialized in the subject, such as Yad Vashem, Masua, and Kibbutz Lochamei Hagetaot, the ministry supported programs that organized school tours to the death camps in Poland.[39]

An interesting innovation in the press's approach to Wagner appeared in *Davar Aher*, *Davar*'s satirical supplement. There journalists dared to express directly what they had hitherto hesitated to say, or had concealed with a mask of discretion. *Davar Aher* addressed the Wagner affair on the actual day of the special concert, making fun of everyone involved in it.[40] On the front page it announced a "discovery": Wagner had resurrected a Jew – Menachem Begin, who had shut himself up in his home since withdrawing from public life in despair over the Lebanon war, but who had consented to tell the reporter of *Davar Aher* that he opposed performances of Wagner. Thus, the satirical paper presented this Israeli politician, so strongly associated with opposition to all ties with Germany, as someone who agreed to break his determined, self-imposed silence solely for the sake of the Wagner affair; only that subject, perceived by most as irrelevant to the lives of Israelis struggling with immediate existential problems, could draw a response from Begin.

Another item in *Davar Aher* recounted that an IPO subscriber "whose gas mask had once been sold to Germany for 65 cents, and was bought back just before the war for 17 dollars," had sighed with relief when he heard that Wagner would not be played. On the inside pages was a report about a survey revealing that most IPO subscribers were deaf, to which a joke was added: "How do you fit all the subscribers to the Philharmonic in one Volkswagen? – You play Wagner."[41] The worn-down arguments of the opposing sides in the conflict were presented here in a grotesque way that robbed them of their sting – at least in the eyes of some of the public.

Davar Aher was only one channel through which the younger generation interpreted the Holocaust. This tendency was also felt in the electronic media, which pushed for relaxation regarding the Holocaust by adding a humoristic tone. The Holocaust, once a sacred idea in Israeli society, was now dealt with in various ways, none of which aimed to hurt the feelings of survivors and their families.[42]

At this point the Wagner controversy essentially came to an end in Israel. The IPO took a poll which showed overwhelming support for performances of Wagner. Yet the management announced that out of respect for those who were disturbed by public performances of Wagner, the orchestra would not include his works in its repertoire. Since then no new effort has been made to play music by Wagner in public concert halls, albeit it is performed in music academies and on radio and television, where Wagner programs have been well received. Once Strauss had opened the way to a thawing in attitudes toward the "forbidden composers," the producers of the Voice of Music began to include excerpts from works by Wagner. Gradually longer and longer pieces were played, culminating, at the beginning of January 1995, with an eight-part series on the life of Richard Wagner, edited by Michael Ohad. In the summer of that year, Wagner's *Der fliegende Holländer* was played on the radio network's weekly opera program. The broadcast was mentioned briefly in the weekly musical recommendations in the *Haaretz* supplement. Beyond that, there was no press response to the event.

On television, the breakthrough was more gradual. In 1994 Channel 8 screened *Der fliegende Holländer*; but until the summer of 1997 – when the status of the Israeli cable-television channels was regulated – the editors, taking no risk, refrained from including Wagner's music in their programs. In the summer of 1997, however, an abundance of Wagnerian operas filled the screen: *Tannhäuser*, *Der fliegende Holländer*, *Der Ring des Nibelungen* – in installments – and even *Die Meistersinger von Nürnberg*. Some of them were screened in honor of the opening of the Bayreuth Festival, while the others were not motivated by any special occasion. The festival was celebrated the same way in the following years (1998 and 1999). In addition, Israelis could now watch on cable television – to which most households subscribed – a plethora of programs about Wagner or other composers who had been banned in Israel for years. The channels broadcasting in German that were included in most of the Israeli cable packages – notably the German cultural channel 3-SAT and the European channel ARTE – were an inexhaustible source of concerts and operas that had undergone no Israeli-style filtering. The advent of satellite broadcasts expanded the possibilities still further.

By the summer of 1997, other "forbidden" composers were part of the Israeli repertoire. In addition to Strauss, whose music could be found on the concert programs of all the orchestras, the IPO decided to lift the ban of many years standing from another two composers who had worked in the Third Reich, Franz Lehar and Carl Orff. Orff's well-known works had already been on the airwaves for some time, and had even been performed by the national opera company back in the 1960s. The Philharmonic added his music to its repertoire in October 1994, when it played his most famous work, *Carmina Burana*. A year and a half later it played for the first time a work by another banned composer, *Die lustige Witwe* ("The Merry Widow") by Franz Lehar, whose works were familiar to all music fans who had lived in the Weimar Republic and the Third Reich. The New Israeli Opera began to explore the possibility of performing some of Wagner's works in public. However, a public debate on the subject that took place in a Tel Aviv performance center in the spring of 1998 revealed how difficult it was going to be to change public attitudes toward this composer. An attempt by the event's organizers to play a recorded excerpt of one of Wagner's works was met with angry cries from the audience.

All these changes in orchestra repertoires and radio and television programming took place in an atmosphere of nearly total calm – certainly without arousing any controversy. There may have been several reasons for this, two of which have already been mentioned. The simplest explanation, of course, is the long period that had elapsed since the end of World War II, during which many survivors of the Holocaust had passed away. Similarly, many of the politicians and columnists who had most fervently rejected the musicians identified with Nazism were no longer active in public life. Still another possible factor was the pluralism that characterized the Israeli media since the early 1980s, when the national written press had expanded to include local papers, and particularly since the 1990s. The inauguration of a second television channel in November 1993, aggressive marketing of cable-television packages throughout the country, and the opening of the airwaves to local radio stations all made the Israeli media more pluralistic. The possibility of restricting Israelis to local or state-provided information was gone forever.

Another reason for the new acceptance – more or less – of the "forbidden composers" may have been the changes Israeli society itself was undergoing. In the five years before Channel 8's "Wagnerian summer," the State of Israel had been shaken by a series of cataclysms that completely changed the face of society. The outward sign was two political upheavals that revealed rifts much deeper than could be expressed at the polls. The second of these, in 1992, moved to a new peace initiative – which led, in turn, to the murder of Prime Minister Yizhak Rabin. That was followed by a third political shake-up in 1996, which revealed how divided and disintegrated Israeli society was and how diverse the self-definitions of the groups composing it.

The maelstrom of Israeli everyday life over the past several years seemed to have ended the need to keep attacking the annulment of the boycott against the "forbidden composers." Moreover, during the 1990s Israel has been compared to Nazi Germany more than once by Palestinian demonstrators and the anger of Israelis themselves is being channeled into other directions, a comparison that may have left any room in daily life for the collective anti-German memory. On the other hand, these very comparisons may give rise to more years of perpetuating anti-German symbols in Israel. At this point perhaps Israelis would rather develop an alternative national memory than rely on the well-assimilated abhorrence of Germans and their culture. But it may well be a little too late to neutralize the classic symbol of German evil, Wagner – as witness, for example, the murderer in Batia Gur's thriller, *Orchestrated Murder: A Musical Case*: an eccentric Israeli conductor working abroad who insists on playing works by Wagner despite disapproval in Israel.[43]

Notes

1   See an interesting analysis by M. Zuckermann, *Shoah in the Sealed Room: The "Holocaust" in the Israeli Press during the Gulf War* [Hebrew] (Tel Aviv, 1993), especially pp. 62–91 and 111–25.

2   See M. Wolffsohn, *Keine Angst vor Deutschland!* (Erlangen, 1990). On European attitudes to reunified Germany, see A. S. Markovits and S. Reich, "Should Europe Fear the Germans," *German Politics and Society* 23 (Summer, 1990): 1–20; and R. J. Evans, *Rereading German History, 1800–1996: From Unification to Reunification* (London and New York, 1997), pp. 213–20.

3   On the different ways the memory of National Socialism was interpreted in the two former German states, see J. Herf, *Divided Memory: The Nazi Past in the Two Germanys* (Cambridge, Mass., 1997).

4   Jerusalem Public Committee of the Heritage of the Holocaust and Heroism to the board of the Israel Philharmonic Orchestra, 16 Feb. 1992, in IPO Archives, Wagner and Strauss file.

5   The Central Bureau of Statistics in Israel does not reveal the number of religious and secular Israelis. Yet, it is known that the number is growing and

since 1995 the Bureau has been examining the level of homogeneity in ultra-Orthodox areas, which are gradually expanding. See more on this subject in chapter 10.

6 Basic Law: Human Dignity and Liberty, 1992. On the Israeli attitude to civil rights, see Ch. Gans, *From Richard Wagner to the Palestinian Right of Return: Philosophical Analysis of Israeli Public Affairs* [Hebrew] (Tel Aviv, 2006).

7 Back in 1966 the musical director of the Voice of Israel, Kar-El Salmon, testified that he had conducted the Voice of Israel orchestra in a performance of this piece, and that the recording had been broadcast. See "Wagner and Strauss, For and Against [Hebrew]," *Lamerhav*, 24 June 1966.

8 "For the First Time in Israel – a Public Concert of Music by Strauss," *Yedioth Ahronoth*, March 16, 1990.

9 See the film *Richard Strauss between Romanticism and Resignation*, written by Pit Rietmüller and Roland Zal, and produced by Medias Res for Bayerischer Rundfunk & RM Arts, 1989.

10 D. Lahav, "Background document [Hebrew]," p. 3.

11 "Against Wagner on the Train [Hebrew]," *Yedioth Ahronoth*, 2 Oct. 1990.

12 See, for example, "The Philharmonic Orchestra Will Hold a Special Concert of Works by Wagner [Hebrew]," *Haaretz*, 15 Dec. 1991.

13 On the dissemination of information through press leaks, see "We Can Do without Wagner [Hebrew]," *Al Hamishmar*, 24 Dec. 1991. On the complaints about audience screening, see "Wagner in the Underground [Hebrew]," *Al Hamishmar*, 29 Dec. 1991.

14 "Wagner at the Back Door [Hebrew]," *Hatzofeh*, 30 Dec. 1991.

15 A. Melamed in an interview on *Good Morning Israel* [Hebrew], Army Radio (*Galei Tzahal*), 15 Dec. 1991, 8:43 a.m.

16 "For Me Wagner Does Not Exist [Hebrew]," *Haaretz*, 16 Dec. 1991.

17 See, for example, "*Kaddish* in Front of Mann Auditorium [Hebrew]," *Globes*, 27 Dec. 1991.

18 Interview on *Good Morning Israel*, 15 Dec. 1991.

19 "For Me Wagner Does Not Exist [Hebrew]," *Haaretz*, 16 Dec. 1991.

20 On the role of the radio and cinema in the commemoration process, see O. Meyers and E. Zandberg, "The Sound-Track of Memory: *Ashes and Dust* and the Commemoration of the Holocaust in Israeli Popular Culture," *Media, Culture & Society* 24.3 (2002): 389–408. On the Holocaust Memorial Day broadcasts, see O. Meyers, E. Zandberg, M. Neiger, "Prime Time Commemoration: An Analysis of Television Broadcasts on Israel's Memorial Day for the Holocaust and the Heroism," *Journal of Communication* 59 (2009) 456–80.

21 "Yes, He Was an Anti-Semite [Hebrew]," *Hadashot*, 20 Dec. 1991.

22 "Wagner Comes to Mann Auditorium [Hebrew]," *Maariv*, 16 Dec. 1991.

23 "The Time Has Come for Wagner to Be Just Music Again [Hebrew]," *Haaretz*, 16 Dec. 1991.

24 "Wagner Comes to Mann Auditorium [Hebrew]," *Maariv*, 16 Dec. 1991.

25 "Only an Israeli Can Conduct Wagner [Hebrew]," *Haaretz*, 16 Dec. 1991.

26 "There Is No Racist Music [Hebrew]," *Haaretz*, 29 Dec. 1991.

27 On the position of the Ministry of Education, see "Report on the Position of

Deputy Education Minister P. Goldstein [Hebrew]," broadcast on *Evening Broadcast*, the Voice of Israel, 17 Dec. 1991, 19:30.

28   "Not Only Wagner [Hebrew]," *Hadashot*, 25 Dec. 1991.

29   "Not a Boycott of a Composer, a Boycott of a Symbol [Hebrew]," *Al Hamishmar* (weekend supplement), 20 Dec. 1991.

30   "Without Wagner We Are Musically Handicapped [Hebrew]," *Maariv*, 17 Dec. 1991.

31   "Life without Wagner . . . [Hebrew]," *Yom Hashishi*, 27 Dec. 1991.

32   "Now the Feelings of Secular Jews Are Being Hurt, Too [Hebrew]," *Yated Neeman*, 20 Dec. 1991.

33   "The Last Barrier [Hebrew]," *Maariv*, 20 Dec. 1991.

34   "The Time Has Come for Wagner to Be Just Music Again [Hebrew]," *Haaretz*, 16 Dec. 1991.

35   "Another Round of Wagner Is Over [Hebrew]," *Haaretz*, 25 Dec. 1991.

36   See D. Barenboim, "German Jews and Music," *Parallels and Paradoxes: Explorations in Music and Society*, by D. Barenboim and E. Said (New York, 2002), pp. 169–74. See also E. Said, "Barenboim and the Wagner Taboo," *Parallels and Paradoxes*, pp. 174–84.

37   "The Overt Simplicity of that Honor [Hebrew]," *Haaretz*, 27 Dec. 1991.

38   "We Can Do without Wagner [Hebrew]," *Al Hamishmar*, 24 Dec. 1991.

39   The ministry also published a guide for participants in these missions. See N. Keren and M. Gil (eds.), *"I Seek My Brother": Along the Way, Youth Tours in Poland* [Hebrew] (Jerusalem, n.d.). See also N. Keren, "Preserving Memory within Oblivion: The Struggle over Teaching the Holocaust in Israel [Hebrew]," *Zmanim* 64 (Summer, 1998): 56–65. On the educational tours to Poland, see J. Feldman, *Above the Death Pits, Beneath the Flag: Young Voyages to Poland and the Performance of Israeli National Identity* (New York, 2008), especially pp. 56–228.

40   *"Davar Aher," Davar*, 20 Dec. 1991.

41   *"Davar Aher," Davar*, 27 Dec. 1991.

42   E. Zandberg, "Critical Laughter: Humor, Popular Culture and Israeli Holocaust Commemoration," *Media, Culture & Society* 28.4 (2006): 561–79.

43   B. Gur, *Murder Duet: A Musical Case* (New York, 1999).

10

The Early 2000s:
A Mounting Wall

One need not go into the minutiae. There is no question that in the sensibility of the people Wagner has become the absolute symbol of anti-Semitism and the spiritual forefather of Nazism. This cannot be disputed and one can offer a thousand proofs, but even if we dispute it, this is what has transpired, becoming one of the inalienable assets of the culture of the State of Israel. The first ban on Wagner was imposed by the art people themselves, by the State of Israel's Philharmonic Orchestra, when after *Kristallnacht* it removed Wagner from the concert program. In other words, the artists themselves felt they could not play his music.[1]

This is how MK Shaul Yahalom explained the Wagner debate in a kind of interim summary of the long-drawn-out controversy. The connection between Yahalom's approach and his partisan commitment to the National-Religious party (Mafdal), and the timing of the special meeting held by the Knesset's Education and Culture Committee in which he spoke (8 May 2001, the 56th anniversary of the fall of the Third Reich), accorded his words an additional dimension and fine-tuned the roots of the disagreement: it was based on an emotional struggle regarding the process of building an Israeli memory that related to the common past of Jews and Germans. Yahalom expressed what was and had been present throughout the entire Wagner controversy: opposition to Wagner was primarily emotional; arguments for and against playing his music, arguments that had been chewed over ad nauseum, were blurring the simple truth that while using rational tools, the debate was, in fact, emotional.

At the dawn of the twenty-first century, the Wagner controversy reemerged, the lion's share in the 2000–2001 concert season and a small part in the spring of 2012. In the 2000–2001 season the musical dispute was divided in two: the first time with the performance of *Siegfried Idyll* by The Israel Symphony Orchestra Rishon LeZion in the municipal culture hall, and the second, before the performance of the Staatskapelle Berlin in the Israel Festival in Jerusalem. In both cases a discussion was held prior to the event in the higher political and judicial instances. The overt public discussion in the first case, following which the Israeli courts of law were required to pass a decision – but avoided doing so – quickly died down despite its importance. The second case, which entailed the political involvement of the Knesset's Education and Culture Committee in cultural and artistic life, stirred up a tidal wave of relentless reactions for and against playing Wagner in Israel. The Wagner debate was raised again in late 2001, with the one-day symposium "Wagner in context – art, ideology, and politics" held at Tel Aviv University. Over 300 people came to listen to a comprehensive discussion of Wagner's work and its meaning – for the first time in Hebrew and in Israel.

Exactly one year earlier, in October 2000, the Rishon LeZion orchestra subscribers attested to the fact that there were people in Israel who wanted to listen to his works publicly. The announcement of including *Siegfried Idyll* in the repertoire was stressed in the spring of 2000 and was received without any stir. At this stage it seemed that the concert would go by amicably, and that the orchestra would continue in its role as trailblazer, as it had been in the past when it was the first Israeli orchestra to perform Richard Strauss' *Metamorphosis* in 1990. However, several weeks before the concert the tables turned.

From the outset the orchestra and the municipality under whose auspices it performed, sought to avoid irritating those who might be offended by Wagner's music. Some two weeks after the 2000–2001 concert season was announced, Meir Nitzan, the Rishon Lezion mayor, approached Ehud Gross, the orchestra's CEO, and asked him "to play down the issue of the Holocaust survivors – and say that they could leave [. . .]. I, as mayor give **full artistic** freedom to the conductor, to the orchestra's CEO, and to the orchestra itself: anyone who does not want to listen to Wagner can leave and no harm will be done."[2]

This sensitivity did not prevent the struggle around playing the music. Several weeks before the public discussion, the Wagner issue was brought before the Supreme Court. Advocate Jacob Westschneider, who habitually represented the Holocaust survivors and their umbrella organization, submitted a petition on behalf of Arie (Louis) Garb against the Broadcasting Authority and its intention to broadcast a work by Wagner. In its reply, the Broadcasting Authority published its decision according to which "The governing council, together with the CEO, has decided this morning that the Broadcasting Authority will not change its long-lasting policy against broadcasting Wagner's music, to the sounds of which millions of Jews were led to their death. The Broadcasting Authority has received numerous requests from Holocaust survivors who were shocked that Wagner's concert would be played on Saturday, and thus it came to a decision this morning to cancel the planned broadcast." As a result, the petition was removed.[3] In this context it merits note that in the 1990s Wagner's works were often played on The Voice of Music. In the first decade of the twenty-first century the number of broadcasts of Wagner's music significantly diminished.

In September 2000, Westschneider sent a long letter to the mayor of Rishon LeZion, the symphonic orchestra's CEO, and music director, and listed the reasons for not playing Wagner's works in Israel. After presenting his arguments with regard to Wagner's anti-Semitism and spelling out Wagner's connection to the Nazis and the undeniable offence the Holocaust survivors might feel, he concluded with the following words: "Should my request [to refrain from playing works by Wagner and Strauss] not be acceded within 7 days of the date of this letter, the Holocaust survivors will be left with no alternative but to appeal to the Knesset's Education and Culture Committee and to judicial instances for full implementation of their rights in accordance with the law."[4] The detailed reply of the orchestra's CEO, who tackled each of Westschneider's arguments, concluded with a moral statement:

> Removing Wagner's music from the depths of darkness in the State of Israel means illuminating it in an artistic light and severing it from polit-ical, ideological and other contexts. This would be a kind of spiritual victory for the Nazis, defying their appropriation of the composer's works, which they carried out arbitrarily after his death. So far, taking this music out of context weakens the force of the symbol and restores Wagner's works to their natural place – the concert hall.[5]

The Yad Vashem chairperson also appealed to the mayor and the orchestra's CEO, joining the arguments against the orchestra's intention of playing *Siegfried Idyll*. He maintained that the musical work should not be removed from its historical context. Once again Gross laid out his counter arguments. Yaakov Zilberstein, a Rishon LeZion honorary citizen and a Holocaust survivor also approached the orchestra, seeking to raise the issue for discussion with the orchestra's management in order to remove the piece from the program; he added:

> For us, playing Wagner is like returning to the inferno. It gives legit-imization to the Holocaust deniers. Playing Wagner by Jews, in a city which awarded me the title of honorary citizen is for me one more night-mare. A nightmare that will be detrimental to my health and the health of other Holocaust survivors. One unnecessary nightmare which you have the power to prevent.[6]

The orchestra's management reviewed the program that had already been confirmed and listened to miscellaneous arguments. Eventually the concert was approved by a vote of seven in favor and four against, while two abstained.[7] At the same time Advocate Westschneider appealed to the Tel Aviv District Court on behalf of two Holocaust survivors, residents of

Rishon LeZion, requesting to issue an injunction ex parte against holding the concert.[8] In his decision Judge Yehooda Zaft related to the way in which Wagner had been received in Israel over decades, but rejected the request due to two main issues: the long delay in submitting the request – some seven months after the orchestra's announcement of the program and nine days before the scheduled performance – and his view that opposed the court's intervention in the matter:

> The controversy over playing Wagner and Strauss's music in Israel is fundamentally an ethical controversy and a question of worldview [. . .] in a pluralistic democratic society like Israel, a variety of opinions and beliefs, which compete in their methods of persuasion and public debate, should be allowed, and the court of law should not use its power to tip the scales to one side or the other.[9]

The petitioners contested this decision before the Supreme Court, which rejected their appeal.

Finally, on Friday noon, October 27, 2000, a handful of protestors stood in front of the Rishon LeZion concert hall – Holocaust survivors and youngsters, members of the Beitar youth movement. They were surrounded by a crowd of journalists from Israel and abroad who sought to document reactions to the playing of *Siegfried Idyll* at the last part of the subscription concert in the "Friday noon chamber music" series. Before playing the piece, which spurred emotions, a group of some 20 members of the audience left the hall; several minutes later a member of the audience, an elderly gentleman later introduced as a Holocaust survivor, disturbed the peaceful music by wielding a rattle. Other members of the audience began to argue, the ushers tried to calm things down, and the argument became animated. Toward the end of the short piece one of the ushers took hold of the rattle, and Shlomo Luxemburg left the hall followed by a host of journalists. Short reports of the event were broadcast that evening on both the state and commercial Israeli news channels. On Sunday the event was briefly mentioned in the papers. Noam Ben Zeev of *Haaretz* summarized by saying: "And then, a few seconds later – a rattle, like in the synagogue on Purim when the cantor calls out the name 'Haman.' But that night the Jews' bitter enemy Wagner was not banished."[10]

The Rishon LeZion orchestra's management was involved in the affair long after the concert. Letters of support and opposition sent to the orchestra's CEO were answered in detail, explaining the worldview leading to the decision to play Wagner's music. Two of them outlined the boundaries of the debate. One was sent by residents of the city, the couple Shoshana and Daniel Halfin:

In view of the fact that works by the composer Wagner were played in the Rishon LeZion concert hall, a hall which we so love and which gives us a boundless sense of pride, something in our hearts was broken, which we must, in line with our belief, protest against, to remember and not to forget, our relatives who were led to the gas chambers and the crematoriums to the music of this Jew-hater composer.

Our family, that to this day never buys anything made in Germany or in Austria, has been offended to the depths of its soul by this event and we hereby request to cancel our subscription without delay [. . .][11]

The orchestra's CEO added to his succinct and emphatic reply a photocopy of the letter written by Shmuel Santo, a Holocaust survivor and resident of the city, who said, inter alia: "I am looking at the pictures of these people who have made a profession of being Holocaust survivors. They use every incidental event in order to shout and whine [. . .] I am also a Holocaust survivor, and an invalid as a result of Nazi oppression. Some of my family members were murdered by the Nazis. But I still manage to preserve my sanity, to differentiate between the past and the present, to differentiate between emotion and rationality, and between politics and art."[12]

This letter introduced an issue that will be dealt with later during the concert season: regarding Holocaust survivors as one homogenous group, whose members seemingly have a well-consolidated opinion regarding the way the Holocaust should be commemorated in Israel. For the first time the survivors declared in public and not in the silence that until then had typified some of them, that they held numerous views. The main part of the discussion of the subject was postponed until the spring and summer of 2001, in the context of the performance of the Staatskapelle Berlin in the Israel Festival.

In early 2001 the Rishon LeZion municipal council decided to postpone playing Wagner and Strauss until the issue was settled in a public debate. In early March the orchestra's management once again dealt with this issue when Holocaust survivors and their central organization appealed to the Tel Aviv regional court requesting to issue a temporary injunction which would implement the decision reached by the municipal council. The presiding judge, Amnon Straschnov, decided at the conclusion of the deliberation that he saw no room for modifying the decision reached by the judges who had dealt with the issue before him, and refused to issue the requested injunction. However, he recommended continuing the public debate in the way decided upon in the meeting of the Rishon LeZion municipal council, and stated that it was proper that the orchestra announce its decision on the subject in a timely fashion in order to accord the petitioners room to maneuver, and asked both parties to reach an agreement and remove the request.[13] The Wagner and Strauss issue remained pending, and any future intention of the Rishon LeZion orchestra to play their works would be bound up in opening the subject to public debate. From 2001 until the 2012–2013 season the orchestra refrained from playing Wagner; on the other hand, Strauss, who is played on a regular basis, is included, for example, in the 2012–2013 season.

The Rishon LeZion concert is a watershed in the Wagner controversy in Israel. Despite the fact that appeals to the legal systems were fruitless, the very fact of appealing to a court of law as a source of authority which would decide on the boundaries of cultural life is significant in itself. Until then appeals of this sort were limited to issues related to the tension between the religious and the secular, for example, about opening businesses and cinemas on Friday night. In the context of Wagner, those against made do with forming a political lobby and participating in the public debate in the press. Now the legislative arm, the Knesset, was no longer enough; until then the Knesset had displayed patience and left the decisions to the artists themselves. Now those against playing Wagner sought to substantiate their arguments on the decisions of the judiciary. The fact that the courts refrained from deciding on the matter cannot diminish the importance of the appeal. In my view, this appeal was a turning point in the process of consolidating the Israeli memory of the Holocaust.

The debate on playing Wagner in Israel was rekindled in the spring of 2001, before a concert of the Staatskapelle Berlin hosted by the Israel Festival in Jerusalem. About six weeks before the opening of the festival and three months before the concerts, the festival's management announced three concerts by the Staatskapelle Berlin, conducted by its director, Daniel Barenboim, who had conducted a concert that included Wagner for invitees only in 1991. In one of the concerts the prelude to *Walküre* was included, the second part in *Der Ring des Nibelungen*.

Two discussions held by the public management of the festival, initiated by its two professional managers – CEO Yossi Tal-Gan and artistic director, Micha Levinson – preceded the decision to include this work. This type of discussion was unusual; as a rule the festival's management refrained from intervening in artistic considerations. Barenboim's proposal to play the prelude to *Walküre* was discussed in September 2000, based on the acknowledgment of the public's sensitivity to the issue and with the intention that the public management – and not the professional managers who could not vote in this framework – would decide on the matter. Despite the positive atmosphere in the discussion, one of the participants, who adamantly objected to the idea, requested another discussion. One of the participants believed that performing a work by Wagner might create antagonism toward the entire festival, while another member of the management, a Holocaust survivor himself, who was absent from the discussion, said that if a vote on the matter was held, he would abstain, but would not vote against it. At this point no vote was taken, and decision was postponed for the next discussion which would be held in November 2000, some two weeks after *Siegfried Idyll* was to be played by the orchestra. The management's chairperson opened the meeting, emphasizing that it was about Barenboim's proposal, not the festival's management, and asked to discuss the Wagner issue once again due to its public importance. Most of the arguments raised in the debate related to refraining from any form of censorship, and the problem of turning Wagner into a symbol and using the boycott as a weapon against him. In the vote in which all those present could participate, six supported playing Wagner, three were against, and two abstained. One of them, a Holocaust survivor, explained his deliberations that stemmed from his opposition to the connection made between Wagner, the Staatskapelle Berlin, and holding the Jerusalem Festival, versus supporting the freedom of expression.[14]

Only in April 2001, after the sale of tickets to the concerts to be held in early July had begun, did the subject reemerge in the Knesset, and was passed on to the Knesset's Education and Culture Committee, initiated by MK Shaul Yahalom, who was a member of the committee. Thirty-nine guests, conversant with the subject, were invited to the debate: heads of the Israel Festival, politicians who were involved in the issue in the past, representatives of the Ministry of Culture, Science and Sports, representatives of organizations of Holocaust survivors, experts in history and music, people of the media, a university and a high school student who were requested to voice their opinions; only six Knesset members participated. For two hours the participants raised familiar arguments for and against. From time to time the argument reached a high pitch, mainly on the part of those who opposed playing the music. At times there was a feeling that the committee's chairperson, MK Zevulun Orlev (Mafdal) showed partiality toward the participants when he urged those supporting the music to quickly conclude their arguments and allowed those who opposed playing the music to take their time.

At the end of the discussion the education committee laid out its request before the management of the Israel Festival to cancel the Wagner piece planned for the concert to which tickets had been quickly sold out – 900 tickets were sold in the course of two weeks despite the fact that they were the most expensive tickets in the entire festival. Following an agreement, those who had bought tickets could use them for an alternative concert or they have their money refunded; a large number preferred the latter alternative.

The financial question regarding the concert had two implications. The sale of tickets to this specific concert was designed to fund two other concerts performed by the Staatskapelle Berlin. In an interview, Tal-Gan emphasized that as an unusual step the German government decided not to offer financial support for the Staatskapelle Berlin's concerts, apparently due to heightened sensitivity around the Wagner issue. Another financial problem was Israel's budgeting of the festival. Tal-Gan explained to those who demanded stopping the government's support of the festival as response to the controversial concert that "anyone who uses the argument that we stop financial aid and anything similar [. . .] will obtain the reverse outcome, because they will raise the question of censorship and it will mean an entirely different ballgame [. . .] I do not recommend a style of threats or dismissals or stopping payment because if we do so we will be shooting ourselves in the foot as a democratic state."[15]

During the weekend after the discussion of the Knesset's committee the festival's management dealt once more with the subject. The Ministry of Culture, Science and Sports' CEO, Arie Shumer, who was present at the meeting, made it clear that the minister in charge did not want to intervene or threaten, but asked to take the emotions of the public into consideration. Professor Menachem Zur, the chairperson of the composers' league, pointed out that he was representing himself and repeated what he had said a few days earlier at the Knesset's Education and Culture Committee: the critical point in Wagner's work was the artistic abstract, which had nothing to do with ideological preaching. In the course of the meeting someone quoted the argument voiced by the public according to which the festival's management had initiated the concert that included Wagner. A member of the board, Advocate Yeheskell Beinisch replied that the initiative was Barenboim's, who was not Wagner's missionary, but he believed that playing his music was important for Israeli democracy.

During the meeting several discussants changed their minds. Of particular interest was the reaction of the member of the management board, Michal Zmora, former head of The Voice of Israel's classical music department, who had fought for years for lifting the ban on Wagner; now she believed that despite all her reservations about leaving Wagner the only musician banned in view of the political and economic relations with Germany, she felt that it would be impossible to ignore public reaction. The other members who now changed their minds pointed out that they were doing so due to their consideration for the feelings of those offended, despite the fact that it was apparent that the survivors were not one monolithic group. At the conclusion of the meeting the management decided that it did not regard itself as censor and emphasized that all requests to its members were made without a trace of threat. According to Tal-Gan, some 30 letters reached the festival's management, for and against playing Wagner. He and his colleague Levinson had to negotiate with Barenboim about the change in the program. At first Barenboim considered cancelling the entire concert, but eventually responded to the request to change the program.

In May 2001, two petitions were submitted to the High Court of Justice against the festival, one on behalf of Professor Dov Levin and the Simon Wiesenthal Center, and the other on behalf of Dov Shilansky and coordinator of the Holocaust survivors' organizations in Israel. These were cancelled with the decision to change the controversial concert program.[16] On the day the Knesset held the discussion, an article by mathematics professor Yuda Molk appeared in the opinion section of *Haaretz*. He sought to refute the arguments of those who were opposed to playing Wagner's music in the Israel Festival. The way in which he contradicted his opponents was familiar from the past, but at the end of the article Molk shifted the discussion to the political field: "It may be inferred, for example, that the government should not invest in the settlements only because the investment is made possible by the taxes paid by those who are against the settlements [. . .] from the appointment of the management of the [Israel] festival, this management has the authority, and not the government, to decide who will participate."[17] This political link, which Barenboim often employed, was one of the reasons for the animated spirits at this point in the controversy. Soon afterwards more articles were published for and against playing Wagner; all of them repeated, in one way of another, familiar arguments, and all chose to relate to the Holocaust survivors as the pivot around which the decision for or against Wagner should be taken.

Despite agreement to refrain from playing Wagner in the Israel Festival concert, at the end of the alternative concert that took place in early July 2001, and after playing the encore, composer Daniel Barenboim turned to the audience and announced that he wished to play another encore – *Liebes Tod* from *Tristan und Isolde*. Barenboim stressed the fact that this was his own personal addition that was not part of the festival, and had nothing to do with the decision of the Staatskapelle Berlin. The fear of the Israel Festival managers of such an event prompted them to convey several messages to Barenboim prior to the concert. The professional managers and his friend MK Dan Meridor (Merkaz – center party) and member of the festival's management, Yeheskell Beinisch, spoke to him in this spirit. Barenboim kept his final decision to himself. A film shot secretly in the concert hall documented a small group in the audience that defied Barenboim's proposal; the majority left the hall quietly, among them Supreme Court President Aharon Barak, and the minority argued with other members of the audience in the hall. Barenboim asked those who opposed his proposal to come up on stage, join him, and argue openly, but they refused, and finally the conductor turned to the orchestra and the piece was played.

At that moment the argument about playing Wagner in Israel was renewed and reached the most strident tones ever. Some people demanded to reprimand that heads of Israel's judicial system, Dorit Beinisch, a Supreme Court judge, and State Attorney Edna Arbel, who remained in the hall and listened to the music, perhaps based on their assumption that the obligation of statism applied to them even during an event that has nothing to do with their work, but was part and parcel of a deep public controversy. Dorit Beinisch was the wife of the member of the festival's management who had asked Barenboim to refrain from playing Wagner in the festival.

The papers were inundated with articles on the subject. Professor Israel Nebenzahl, a member of Professors for a Strong Israel, a body identified with the Israeli right, opened his opinion piece with general criticism of holding the Israel Festival during The Three Weeks, the three weeks that separate the 17th day of Tammuz, the date of the breach of the walls of Jerusalem, and the 9th day of Ave, the date of the destruction of the First and Second Temple. At the end of his article Nebenzahl returned to the argument that linked the Jewish calendar to universal culture:

> How symbolic it is that on the 17th day of Tammuz, the day declared as a day of fast because on that day the walls of Jerusalem were breached and the golden idol was placed in the temple, the representatives of German culture managed to ruin the walls of culture and Jewish honor, and by playing Wagner placed a German cultural idol in the Israeli cultural temple. With audacity and gall the German musicians joined Barenboim, the Jewish Israeli who chose to annex himself to their estate, and together created a precedent here.[18]

Nebenzahl also argued that "there is no doubt that Germany, and all its institutions, is seeking to absolve itself of the sins of the Holocaust, and there is no place better than Israel to do so. Refraining from playing Wagner's music in public in Israel is, from their point of view, an emblem of the transgressions which they want to erase." It is important to remember that the government of Germany refrained from assisting in the funding of these concerts.

The Knesset's Education and Culture Committee adopted a firm approach. Playing Wagner at the end of the festival was perceived by many as breach of promise or disrespect of the request made by the Knesset's Education and Culture Committee. The committee convened for a renewed discussion under the initiative of MK Eliezer Cohen of Yisrael Beiteinu – Haichud Haleumi (National Union), who argued that Barenboim was mistaken when he assumed that this was a musical issue; the subject was sensitivity vis-à-vis the commemoration of the Holocaust and the survivors. In conclusion the committee decided that Barenboim had taken advantage of the opportunity, which was "deceitful." The committee admonished the heads of the festival and called upon them to reach personal conclusions, expressed surprise that "senior people in the legal world chose to remain in the hall while the Wagner encore was played, behavior that might be interpreted as justification of the foolish decision of Daniel Barenboim," and called the cultural institutions in Israel to see in Barenboim "a cultural persona non grata" until he apologized for his actions.[19]

This was the first time the state chose to overtly intervene in the controversy and propose an unequivocal standpoint. Taking this stance was the outcome of several factors. One may have been the expectation that Wagner would be accepted in the concert halls; unlike the precedent of the Philharmonic Orchestra playing Wagner in 1981, which was accompanied by a vociferous argument in the concert hall, the performance in 2001 was received peacefully. It may well be that the members of the Knesset's Education and Culture Committee felt that Wagner's instrumentalization in Israel was fragile, and they sought to reinforce the emotional attitude toward the composer. Another reason may be the attitude toward the survivors. Since early twenty-first century the State of Israel has been chastised by its citizens who claim that the Holocaust survivors have been neglected, elderly people, some of whom are sick and cannot afford to pay for treatment and a way of life that suits their needs; the critics demand that the state respect the survivors by providing them with the financial and physical means it has at its disposal.[20] It may well be that the education committee's bear hug of the survivors was also a way of atoning for the problematic treatment on the part of the establishment. But more than anything it seems that the education committee's change in stance reflects the changes that took place in Israel's social, cultural and political fabric. The signs of intensifying nationalism and messianic awakening – both religious and ideational – that began to emerge after the 1967 Six Day War, appeared after over three decades as a rise in the percentage of Jewish citizens who defined themselves as traditional and religious (on varying levels) and a clear-cut tipping of the political scales to the national right. This change was also expressed in deep identification with the vulnerability of the Jewish people throughout history. The case of Wagner and Israeli society became part of this vulnerability.[21]

Response to the decision of the Knesset's Education and Culture Committee was no less stormy. Knesset members Dan Meridor and Amnon Rubinstein (Meretz) approached the committee chairperson, Orlev, and requested that the committee reconsider its decision. They argued that Barenboim's longtime musical endeavor in Israel should be their first consideration. Orlev replied that he would agree to renew discussion of the issue only if Barenboim would participate in a meeting together with representatives of the survivors. This time it was apparent that parts of the public realized that the Holocaust survivors were a heterogeneous group, some of whom opposed the instrumental use of their suffering. Several days after the education committee published its decision, the liberal paper *Haaretz* published a proclamation entitled "A very grata personality," signed by over 200 intellectuals, artists and journalists. They expressed their disgust at the Knesset's Education and Culture Committee's decision that brought shame to Israeli democracy, and asked to remember the great contribution of Barenboim to musical life in Israel; "The decision to impose this stupid boycott has been consigned to the garbage can of history just like similar decisions in the past."[22] Strong opposition to playing Wagner in the next decade shows otherwise. In an opinion piece, Professor Dina Porat, head of The Stephen Roth Institute for the Study of Contemporary Anti-Semitism and Racism at Tel Aviv University, explained the source of her opposition to playing Wagner in Israel: "Wagner is the last symbol of the attitude to Germany after the Holocaust, and playing his music will clip the remaining thin strings."[23] For the same reason those who supported playing Wagner demanded to put an end to this prolonged boycott.

About a year and a half later, in December 2003, Barenboim's issue was raised again for discussion, after the announcement of his winning the Wolf Prize. Minister of Education and Culture Limor Livnat (Likud) announced that she refused to award the prize to the conductor until he apologized for playing Wagner at the Israel Festival. Barenboim refused, but expressed his regret if anyone had been offended by the public playing. The Knesset's Education and Culture Committee discussed the matter in March 2004 and decided to award Barenboim the prize. At the ceremony that took place in May the same year Barenboim attacked the Israeli occupation and announced that he would contribute the prize money, 50,000 dollars, for the encouragement of music among Jewish children in Israel and Palestinian children in Ramallah.[24] The Wagner affair, which was increasingly presented as emotional, now took on a political dimension.

The duality of emotion and politics was also manifested in the fall of 2001 following a seminar initiated by the Tel Aviv University's Institute for German History. Three meetings were adjoined to the seminar: chamber music adaptations of Wagner's musical works at the Tel Aviv University's music academy; an open discussion between the conference's speakers and the audience at the Felicja Blumental Music Center in Tel Aviv; and the screening of the film *Villa Wahnfried*, Wagner's home in Bayreuth, at the Goethe Institute in Tel Aviv.[25] All these events were extremely successful from the point of view of public interest, and only one of them was interrupted by those who opposed playing the music. At the opening of the concert at the music academy Shlomo Luxemburg once again wielded his rattle that had served him a year before at the Rishon LeZion concert hall. On the night news broadcast of the state Channel 1, the reporter explained that Luxemburg had gone through the security "selection," problematic wording in itself, charged tenfold in the context of a Holocaust survivor, and managed to draw attention to his perception. The following day Luxemburg was interviewed on the current affairs program on the commercial Channel 2, where he declared that the supreme goal of his life was to prevent playing Wagner in Israel.

Other reservations were expressed behind the scenes. Several days prior to the seminar MK Yahalom approached the president of Tel Aviv University, Professor Itamar Rabinovich, and asked him to cancel the event. The Knesset Member conducted a radio debate with the head of the German history institute, Professor Moshe Zuckermann, who explained that it was a question of realizing academic freedom. All the events took place as planned, but none of the heads of the university came to greet the seminar's participants, as customary. In an open discussion between the lecturers and the audience, emotional arguments were voiced alongside rational reasoning. The lion's share of the discussion dealt with preserving and consolidating the memory of the Holocaust in Israel, the degree to which Israelis identify with European culture in general, and German culture in particular, the myth that Wagner created and his mytholization, the charged relations between Hitler and Wagner, and the different implications of the controversy on social and political perceptions in Israel.

The first speaker pointed out that those who left the hall before *Tristan und Isolde* was played at the Israel Festival belonged mainly to the 30–40 age-group, a fact that invalidated the argument about the vulnerability of the Holocaust survivors as the main reason for removing the piece from the program. A woman turned to the audience, introducing herself as a Holocaust survivor, and asked why not wait another decade for the sake of people like herself who had listened to Wagner in Auschwitz; someone burst out and shouted that he would not tolerate dictatorship and the woman left the hall to the audience's protest and rebuke of the person who shouted out. The statement of a young person in the audience who claimed that the Wagner affair was the mystification of ideology according to which the very thought about something was harmful – an argument which he wanted to prove in the context of the attitude of Israelis to the Palestinians – was received with overall resentment.[26]

The difficulty involved in accepting emotional arguments and the political use of Wagner are apparently the reason for the continued involvement in Wagner in Israel. In early October 2010 a news item appeared in the Israeli press about the cancellation of Katharina Wagner's (Wagner's great-granddaughter) visit to Israel. During the planned visit, a public invitation was to be given to the Israel Chamber Orchestra to open the July 2011 Bayreuth Festival. The press conference was supposed to open with greetings from the German Chancellor Angela Merkel. The orchestra's visit was meant to reflect the conciliation between the Wagner family and the State of Israel, and the concert comprised a piece written by an Israeli composer, works by Mahler and Mendelssohn – a Jew and a son of apostates whom the Germans banned – and the *Siegfried Idyll* by Wagner himself. Leaking out news of the event aroused Wagner's fear of a heated reaction.[27] Even the non-event prompted a flood of reactions in the international press. *ABC News* quoted *Reuters* about the invitation before the cancellation of Wagner's visit, and the following day the *New York Times* and *Sky News* published the item; Noah Kliger, a veteran Israeli journalist, was interviewed on the German international state radio, *Deutsche Welle*; he declared that the State of Israel did not need any conciliation with Wagner.[28]

The concert took place as planned, but Katharina Wagner was absent. The orchestra opened with the Israeli national anthem, *Hatikva*, a piece written by the Israeli composer Zvi Avni, and a piece by Wagner. The orchestra's music director, Roberto Paternostro, conducted. Paternostro was the son of a Jewish mother whose parents were sent to Terezin; he regarded the event as an opportunity to declare a distancing from nationalism and racism of any kind, an idea that was also quoted in the national-religious media network, *Arutz 7*. The conductor's views met with strong criticism in an Israeli blog that linked Wagner's ideas and National Socialism, and stressed the relationship between the Nazis and the Wagner family.[29] Conflicting criticism was voiced by Martin Kettle of the British *Guardian*, who claimed that: "Of all the things that are important about Wagner's musical works, anti-Semitism is not, by and large, one of them. Wagner was one of the most free-ranging artistic geniuses in European history."[30]

One could hear a few of Wagner's tones in Israel in March 2011. In a talk, accompanied by examples, the Israeli conductor Asher Fisch explained his feelings toward Wagner: "You need to understand that when I came to Germany I had never heard and was unfamiliar with Wagner's music [because in the academy in Israel he was hardly taught any Wagner, author's comment]. My attraction to Wagner's music is a physical feeling. When I conduct or play Wagner, something happens inside me that does not happen to me with any other composer." The event that took place in the auditorium, owned by the Tel Aviv municipality, attracted an audience of several hundred and passed without incident.[31]

Another initiative of Fisch came up against a brick wall. In late May 2012 the Israeli Wagner Society planned to hold a special concert of Wagner's works during a seminar titled "An academic musical encounter: Herzl – Toscanini – Wagner." The day opened with academic lectures and in the evening Wagner pieces, including songs, were to be played. One hundred musicians were hired privately to participate in the concert, and Asher Fisch undertook to conduct the concert. The Smolarz Auditorium, owned by Tel Aviv University, was hired for the occasion. Within a few days the deputy chairperson of the Holocaust Survivors Organization Center approached the president of the university, Professor Joseph Klafter, asking him to cancel the event. "His [Wagner] music, which was played in the camps as part of the deception plan, should not be played by a handful of protestors at Tel Aviv University. It will offend the feelings of the Holocaust survivors and a great many people in the State of Israel." At first, the university's administration responded, saying that it had no knowledge of the events that took place in the rented hall to different organizations, but the following day, the heads of the administration announced that "To our amazement it has recently come to our knowledge that musical works of the German composer Richard Wagner are planned for the concert. This piece of information was hidden from us intentionally, as well as the topic of the event and the exact name of the organization planning it." The Israeli Wagner Society did not give up and tried to hire another hall, but to no avail. Hilton Tel Aviv also refused their request.[32]

Two issues merit special attention: the first was the date of the planned concert in mid-June, which was close to the date of the assembly of the university's board of governors, that doubtlessly made things more difficult for the university's administration; however, only a month earlier the administration demonstrated its willingness to encourage cultural pluralism when it allowed a rally in memory of the *Nakba* Day, celebrated on May 14th by the Israeli-Palestinian population.[33] The second issue was the arena of discussion. This time arguments for and against playing Wagner took place not only in the press but also over the Internet. Despite restrictive legislation which demands preventing offensive content in the responses of readers on active websites with numerous surfers, many of the Israeli respondents did not refrain from using scathing language. In this case, the proximity of dates between the *Nakba* Day ceremony and the hiring the Smolarz hall determined the particularly vitriolic reactions. Nonetheless, some of the letters to the editor dealt with the gulf that exists between anti-Semitism and taking concrete action against Jews, as well as Arturo Toscanini's view of the connection made between art and politics.

On the eve of the Wagner Year, when the Western world will mark 200 years to Wagner's birth, large parts of Israeli society are still strongly opposed to playing Wagner. Today it is clear that the reaction to Wagner is emotional and is relevant to a larger public than merely the Holocaust survivors and their families. Opposition to playing Wagner seems particularly strong in view of the overall positive standpoint of Israelis vis-à-vis Germany and its culture. Since the 1990s Wagner is the only cultural symbol boycotted in Israel. At the same time an ever-growing number of Israelis have visited Germany, particularly Berlin, to the extent of their becoming a real social phenomenon.[34] It may well be that the softening of the attitude of many Israelis toward Germany and its culture is what renders opposition to Wagner more decisive. If all other symbols disintegrate, Wagner will always remain a mark for all time.

Notes

1 Minutes No. 268 from the meeting of the Education, Culture and Sports Committee, 8 May 2001.

2 M. Nitzan to E. Gross, 10 April 2000, emphasis in the original. I would like to thank the Israel Symphony Orchestra Rishon LeZion's CEO, Ehud Gross, and members of the orchestra's administration for the help they offered me.

3 Decision of the governing council of the Broadcasting Authority of 1 Sep.

2000; High Court of Justice, 6032/00, A. Garb vs. the Broadcasting Authority, 24 Aug. 2000.

4 Advocate Westschneider to M. Nitzan, E. Gross, G. Bertini, 13 September, 2000. Westschneider appended to his letter letters written in the past by political figures about earlier debates on the orchestra's playing works by Strauss.

5 E. Gross to Y. Westschneider, 24 Sep. 2000.

6 Y. Zilberstein to members of the committee of the orchestra management, undated.

7 Minutes from the meeting of the committee of the orchestra management at the Rishon LeZion concert hall, 19 October, 2000.

8 Miscellaneous civil requests, 27053/00, 18 Oct. 2000.

9 Miscellaneous civil requests 27228/00, Oct. 2000.

10 "A Holocaust Survivor Produced a Rattle, and the Orchestra Continued Playing Wagner [Hebrew]," *Haaretz*, 29 Oct. 2000.

11 S. and D. Halfin to Y. Bitan, 14 Nov. 2000.

12 S. Santo to the Israel Symphony Orchestra Rishon LeZion, undated.

13 Miscellaneous civil requests 6280/01, 4 March 2001. In July 2001 the *Bulletin of the Central Organization of Holocaust Survivors in Israel* published an item about the success of the struggle against playing Wagner in Israel, and gave an extensive report on the verdict of Judge Straschnov.

14 Information on the meetings was given to me by the Israel Festival CEO, Yossi Tal-Gan (personal interview, 2 Jan. 2002). Tal-Gan refused to hand me the minutes of the meetings. I would like to thank Micha Levinson for the issues he raised (personal interview, 26 Dec. 2001).

15 Minutes No. 268 from the meetings of the Culture, Science and Sports Committee, 8 May 2001. That year the festival's budget was NIS 15 million that were divided between a NIS 3 million allocation by different government ministries, NIS one million allocated by the Jerusalem Municipality, and the rest from foundations, sponsorships, foreign embassies in Israel, support from foreign governments and ticket sales.

16 Supreme Court 3/83 before Judge Dalia Dorner.

17 "Independent Tones [Hebrew]," *Haaretz*, 8 May 2001.

18 "A German Idol in the Temple [Hebrew]," *Haaretz*, 15 July 2001.

19 Minutes No. 316 from the meeting of the education and culture committee, 24 July 2001.

20 "The Dorner Committee: The Governments of Israel Neglected the Survivors [Hebrew]," *nrg* (online), June 22 2008.

21 On the Connection between Religion and Politics in Israel, see A. Cohen and B. Susser, *Israel and the Politics of Jewish Identity: The Secular-Religious Impasse* (Baltimore, 2000).

22 "A Very Grata Personality [Hebrew]," proclamation, *Haaretz*, 3 Aug. 2001.

23 "Hitler on Wagner: His Music is My Religion," [Hebrew] *Haaretz*, 17 August, 2001.

24 "A Compromise: Barenboim to Receive the Wolf Prize [Hebrew]," *ynet* (online), 16 Dec. 2003. M. Caspi, "A Background Document on the Subject: Awarding the Wolf Prize to Daniel Barenboim. Submitted to the Knesset's Education Committee [Hebrew]", 29 Feb. 2004. "The Education Committee Confirmed: Barenboim to be Awarded the Wolf Prize [Hebrew]," *ynet* (online), 1 March 2004. "Barenboim Received the Wolf Prize and Attacked

the 'Continued Occupation,' [Hebrew]", *ynet* (online), 9 May 2004.

25 Some of these lectures have been published, see G. Kaynar, "Das Gesamtkunstwerk ind sein Widerhall bei Hanoch Levin und anderen," *Tel Aviver Jahrbuch für deutsche Geschichte* XXXI (2003): 372–84. Ch. Gans, "Moralische Aspecte des israelischen Wagner-Boykotts," *Tel Aviver Jahrbuch für deutsche Geschichte* XXXI (2003): 385–400. B. Brock, "Der Ring schließt sich – Wahnhaftes Wähnen über Musik und Geschichte," *Tel Aviver Jahrbuch für deutsche Geschichte* XXXI (2003): 401–8.

26 A summary originated in a recording of the debate that took place on 14 Nov. 2001 in Tel Aviv.

27 "Wagner's Great-Granddaughter Cancelled her Visit to Israel due to Fear of Criticism [Hebrew]," *Haaretz*, 6 Oct. 2010. "The Orchestra Will Play Wagner, But Not in Israel [Hebrew]," *Haaretz*, 7 Oct. 2010. In response to reports, the journalist Mati Golan wondered why Wagner's great-granddaughter was unacceptable while the Dumont family – whose paper, *Kölnische Zeitung* supported Hitler in the 1930s – purchased part of the *Haaretz* group in Israel. See "Why Only Wagner? [Hebrew]", *Globes*, 6 Oct. 2010.

28 "Israeli Orchestra Set to Play at Wagner Festival," *ABC News Online*, 5 Oct. 2010; "Israel Doesn't Need Reconciliation with Wagner, Says Holocaust Survivor," *Deutsche Welle Online*, 6 Oct. 2010; "Israeli Group Set to Play in Bayreuth," *New York Times Online*, 6 Oct. 2010; "Wagner Row: Israeli Orchestra Vows to Play On," *Sky News (UK) Online*, 7 Oct. 2010.

29 "The Swastikas are Returning to Bayreuth at the Wagner Festival [Hebrew]," *Haaretz*, 1 Aug. 2011; "They're Playing *Hatikva* in Wagner's City [Hebrew]," *ynet* (online), 25 July 2011; "The Chamber Orchestra Play Wagner – in Germany [Hebrew]," *Arutz 7 – News* (online), 25 July 2011; "Shameful: Israelis Playing Wagner in Germany [Hebrew]," *Isi Leibler from Jerusalem*, 28 July 2011.

30 "Richard Wagner was no Ranter," *Guardian online*, 25 July 2011.

31 "The Boycott of Wagner in Israel – Absurd [Hebrew]," *ynet* (online), 16 March 2011.

32 "For the First Time a Full Concert of Wagner will be Played in Israel [Hebrew]," *Haaretz*, 30 May 2012; "Holocaust Survivors to Tel Aviv University: Do Not Play Wagner [Hebrew]," *ynet* (online), 3 June 2012; "Tel Aviv University Prevented a Wagner Concert: 'Crossing a Red Line' [Hebrew]," *Mako* (online), Channel 2 News, 4 June 2012; "After Tel Aviv University: Hilton Hotel Cancels a Wagner Concert [Hebrew]," *Haaretz*, 11 June 2012.

33 "The *Nakba* Day Ceremony at Tel Aviv University Despite Criticism [Hebrew]," *Haaretz*, 14 May 2012.

34 See F. Oz-Salzberger, *Israelis in Berlin* (Frankfurt: 2001).

Epilogue: Wagner and the Israelis – A Multifaceted Commemoration

When Bronisław Huberman sought to remove *Die Meistersinger von Nürnberg* from the season's opening concert, he could not have foreseen that this would be the beginning of a never-ending boycott. On the eve of the Wagner Year, which marks the 200th anniversary of the composer's birth, Richard Wagner is known in Israel largely as a symbol of the Holocaust. Moreover, the violent storms that attend any attempt to play his music in public are the last visible sign of the charged attitude of Israelis toward post-Holocaust Germany. In general terms, the two countries maintain full and correct diplomatic relations, which include commercial ties and lively tourism.

In all aspects of the cultural field, the relationship is even stronger. Some 500 Israelis devote their summers to studying German at the Goethe Institute. According to a survey conducted by the institute, 43% study due to an interest in the German language and culture; 55% of all students are between the ages of 16 and 34, people who perceive Germany as one entity, and not as two entities torn apart by the war.[1] The concert repertoire of orchestras and chamber music ensembles is still based on the German classics. Theaters produce plays translated from German such as Friedrich Dürrenmatt's *The Visit of the Old Lady* and Georg Büchner's *Woyzeck* and the Israeli opera has produced Mozart's *The Magic Flute* and Richard Strauss' *Salome*. German literature – its classics, contemporary literature, and children's literature, are regularly translated into Hebrew. At the 2010 World Cup about a third of Israeli men hoped the German team would win.[2]

Today Israelis feel comfortable in their country and within their culture. They can relate to Germany because their agenda includes a structured commemoration of the Holocaust, commemoration that has been shaped by the state institutions to which everyone is exposed. The state allocates large resources to nurturing the memory of the Holocaust. Under its auspices, institutions act to immortalize the Holocaust; the leading among them is Yad Vashem, the largest body documenting the Holocaust worldwide. Every year the Holocaust and Heroism Remembrance Day is marked in state ceremonies and events at schools and workplaces. Alongside the distinct symbols of the Holocaust – the concentration and death camps, the deportations stations, the trains, and the testimonies themselves – Israelis chose another symbol, Wagner.

The Wagner affair emerged in Israel when the state was still struggling for its existence and its society shaped its character. The political leadership made an effort to help the Jews of Europe, but this was not always enough and was not always successful.[3] Saving the culture created by Jews in the German-speaking region and an ambivalent attitude toward the German culture of non-Jews were the only possible reaction at the time. After the war, after the establishment of the State of Israel, and furthermore – after the signing of the reparations agreement with Germany (1952) and the establishment of diplomatic ties between Israel and West Germany (1965) – it seemed that Israeli society needed a token that would preserve the schism between the two people, which was not directly related to commemorating the Holocaust. What began as the marking of several musicians as a symbol of the cultural gulf, in due course diminished and turned into one anti-Semitic composer loved by the Nazis – Richard Wagner.

Turning Wagner into a symbol was primarily the outcome of an emotional attitude. People living in Germany or Austria in the 1920s and 1930s could not help but hear the music of Wagner, who was the most popular opera composer in those years. Anyone who knew anything about the German culture of the Weimar Republic was aware of the Nazification of Bayreuth and the warm embrace Hitler received from Wagner's widow and family. Those who survived the concentration camps may have heard the tones of his music from the windows of the Nazi commanding officers. Throughout the entire period the Nazis also listened to Beethoven and Liszt, Mozart and Bach. But there is no other composer who publicized his anti-Semitism as blatantly as Wagner, no other composer's family that so warmly embraced National Socialism, and there is no other composer whose music stimulates the senses so strongly, as Nietzsche so well explained. Sounds, perhaps more than any other artistic means, arouse emotions; a horror film without a soundtrack is far less frightening, a romantic film touches the very core our being when the string instruments begin to play. Wagner's sounds stir up the emotions of its lovers and disturb the tranquility of its haters. In the case of Wagner, the circumstances – the music, the timing of his popularity, his personal and familial anti-Semitism – joined hands and made the composer into the symbol of an event that took place light years after his death.

The emotional standpoint toward the composer underlies the politicians' use of the Wagner affair. Most of the politicians who blatantly intervened in the Wagner affair represent the political right and the religious public, but members of the left and the center also expressed their opposition to any public playing of Wagner. The emotions that the politicians mixed into their statements can be divided into three: some of them saw in the artists who collaborated with the Nazis, and particularly in Wagner who was so loved by the Nazis, a sign that could be denounced in public, thus gaining public approval, contrary to the limited public support accorded to politicians who leveled sharp criticism at establishing relations with West Germany. Others employed their rhetorical skills to explain the extent of the horror of listening to the music of one whose works accompanied the Jews on their way to their execution; even if this context had no factual support, the rising popularity of Wagner in the years close to the murder of Jews was sufficient to support the argument. And since the last decades of the twentieth century, opposition to Wagner served as an additional layer in a wider criticism of extreme national and religious groups that oppose Western secular culture, which was adopted by part of the Israeli public.

Analyzing criticism for and against playing Wagner in public also fine-tunes the changes that took place in Israeli society over the years of the boycott. The first time public listening to Wagner was banned was when political dominancy was in the hands of the socialist parties. The first stages of the debate in the 1950s and 1960s took place in a society that was governed by the socialist parties, while the nationalist right and the religious parties were in a minority. The right-wing factors were primarily those who opposed playing the music of composers who were identified with National Socialism. On the other hand, the left-wingers who opposed Wagner, mainly members of Mapam, hardly ever used art to express their anti-German stance; they tended to express their opinions in a direct political context.

From the 1980s the national-religious character of opposition to the German composers was reinforced, and it became clear that Wagner was the only one who aroused soaring emotions. He remained the last sign of a burning hatred of Germany, and became fixed as a clear-cut symbol of the Holocaust. Contrary to reasonable expectations – this fixed place came into being after the market forces made it possible for many Israelis to listen to Wagner's music in their homes or in concert halls abroad, after the number of survivors who were still living in Israeli society gradually dwindled, and when the philharmonic orchestra – perceived as Israel's national orchestra – gave up all attempts to break the Wagner boycott.

An unequivocal call on the part of the Knesset's Education and Culture Committee to refrain from playing Wagner in public was heard for the first time in the 1990s, as a gesture of consideration for the feelings of the Holocaust survivors. Until then all the ministers of education were careful to avoid any direct intervention in the controversy. The new involved approach grew stronger in the early twenty-first century when the Knesset's Education and Culture Committee condemned Daniel Barenboim's attempt to break the taboo. Moreover, at the beginning of the century several Holocaust survivors appealed to the court, requesting it to issue an injunction against the public playing of Wagner and Strauss on the state radio and concert halls. Other survivors protested against this standpoint. Despite the fact that the injunctions were rejected, it is evident that the last decades mark a turning point: the authorities are involved in an issue that in the past was reserved for the decisions of the artistic bodies.

In the early twenty-first century it is hard to judge the controversy, and even harder to foresee the future. The failed attempt to play Wagner's music in Tel Aviv in the summer of 2012 exemplified a toughening of the opposition. It seems that cancelling the event was received as a matter of fact, as if no one believed that this time it would pass without incident. The across-the-board agreement to avoid playing Wagner came about under the initiative of people who were not directly involved in the Holocaust – they were not survivors and many of them have no family ties to those who perished. It seems that years of debate between those for and those against, those who raised the banner of the importance of democracy versus those who protected the feelings of the survivors, and between the left and the right, turned into nothing more than national agreement which only few challenge. Today Wagner serves as a symbol for many members of the general Israeli public, with no correspondence to ethnicity or generation. Does the prohibition of playing Wagner's music – even years after the Holocaust and when Israeli tourism to Germany is booming – mark an end, i.e., will Wagner remain a symbol? Is this far-reaching agreement the outcome of the possibility of listening to Wagner's music in private?

In the past it was possible to interpret the boycott as part of the process of consolidating a national identity. Listening to Wagner was made possible through the mediation of a large orchestra, or over the radio or television – which in Israel were exclusively governed by the state until the 1990s. Today it is easy to listen to Wagner: over the Internet, on CDs, on satellite stations and cables included in Israeli cable packages, and on visits abroad that have become easily available to many Israelis. It may well be that the privatization process, including listening to Wagner's music, has supported the processes that have come into being over decades. Wagner, the darling of the executioners, has turned into a powerful symbol in Israeli society, and not just any symbol – the symbol of the Holocaust.

It is doubtful whether employing Wagner as a symbol leaves room for any significant debate on the role of culture in a nationalistic society, the processes of symbolization, the methods of oppression that a nationalistic society adopts, and the blindness which the great intellectuals and artists develop vis-à-vis the injustices evolving around them. Alongside the super-ficiality of the debate on these crucial issues, Israeli society has created commemoration ceremonies within Israel and at the Holocaust sites them-selves. In other words, the Wagner affair falls in line with the shaping of the ceremonial commemoration in Israeli society as well as with the relinquishment of conducting a debate on the universal – and not only the particular – moral lesson of the Holocaust.

Can one infer anything about Israeli society from the Wagner affair? I am not sure. It seems that Israeli democracy has remained sufficiently open not to leave the decision on playing Wagner to the country's arms of government – in precedential legislation or ruling. Israeli democracy still relies on common sense that knows how to navigate between those for and those against, common sense that will be attentive to feelings and will calm down incitement. Playing Wagner was not censored in Israel. However, the forces that drive society stopped most of the attempts to play his music. Will this statistical item be the last line of this book? Another last line may be the two glaring contradictions with which Israelis live. One is the reverse symmetry between expressing strong feelings about the Holocaust, versus cultivating warm and open relations with the new Germans. The other is more complex: Israelis hold on to Wagner as a symbol, but they have emptied the symbol of the moral lesson it embodies – condemning extreme nationalism of any kind.

Notes

1 "Redefining Attitudes toward Germany: What are Israelis Looking for in Berlin? [Hebrew]," *The Marker [Haaretz]*, 24 April 2010.
2 "Özils Opa war nicht bei der SS," *Der Tagesspiegel*, 8 July 2010.
3 D. Carpi, "The Political Activity of Chaim Weizmann in Italy During the Years 1923–1934 [Hebrew]," *Hazionut* II (1971): 169–207.

Bibliography

Primary Sources

Archives

Archives of the Israel Philharmonic Orchestra (IPO), Tel Aviv.
Archives of the Israel Rishon LeZion Symphony Orchestra, Rishon LeZion.
BBC Archives, London.
Nationalarchiv der Richard-Wagner-Stiftung, Bayreuth.

Newspapers, Online News and Periodicals

ABC News online; Al Hamishmar; Arutz Sheva online; Army Radio (Galei Tzahal); Bama; Beeretz Yisrael; Buenos Aires Herald; Davar; Der Spiegel; Der Tagesspiegel; Deutsche Welle online; Emeth; Guardian online; Globes; Haaretz; Haboker; Hador; Hadashot; Hair; Hamodia; Haolam Hazeh; Hapoel Hatzair; Hashkafa; Hatzofeh; Hayom; Herald Tribune (Paris); Herut; Jediot Hadashot; The Jerusalem Post; Jewish Chronicle; Knesset; Kolbo; Lamerhav; Le Journal d'Orient; Maariv; Mako – Channel 2 News online; The Marker; Moznaim; New York Herald Tribune; New York Post; New York Times online; nrg online; Omer; Sky News (UK) online; Tmura; Turim; Voice of Israel (Israeli state radio); Yedioth Ahronoth; Yedioth Hayom; Yated Neeman; ynet online; Yom Hashishi.

Contemporary Sources

"Reichsminister Dr. Goebbels Huldigt Richard Wagner." *Die Musik* XXV, No. 12 (Sept. 1933): 952–54.

6,000,000 Accusers: Israel's Case Against Eichmann. The Opening Speech and Legal Argument of Mr. Gideon Hausner, Attorney-General. Translated by S. Rosenne. Jerusalem: 1961.

Burk, J. N., ed. *Letters of Richard Wagner: The Burrel Collection.* London: 1951.

Chamberlain, H. S. *Richard Wagner.* Munich: 1896.

Committee of the Eretz-Yisrael Opera Circle, *Booklet of the Eretz-Yisrael Opera.* Tel Aviv: 1935.

Darwin, C. R. *The Descent of Man, and Election in Relation to Sex* (various editions).

—— *The Origins of Species by Means of Natural Selection* (various editions).

Davidon, Y. *Love under Duress* [Hebrew]. Tel Aviv: n.d.

Divrei HaKnesset [protocols of the Israeli parliament].

Führerbotschaft an Volk und Welt: Reichstagrede vom 20. Februar 1938. Munich: Zentralverlag der NSDAP, 1938.

Fenelon, F. *Playing for Time.* New York: 1977.

Filippi, F. "Wagner's Musical Voyage in the Land of the Future." In *The Attentive Listener: Three Centuries of Music*, edited by L. Haskell, 156–60. Princeton, NJ: 1996. Originally published in *Preseveranza* (1870).

Halevy, M. *Stagecraft* [Hebrew]. Tel Aviv: 1946.

Hanfstaengl, E., ed. *Hitler in der Karikatur der Welt*. Berlin: 1935.

Hanslick, E. "Wagner Cult." In *The Attentive Listener*, 170–4. Originally published in *Neue Freie Presse* (1882).

Hinkel, H., ed. *Handbuch der Reichskulturkammer*. Berlin: 1937.

Lahav, D. "Background Document on the Subject: Performing Wagner's Music at the 2001 Israel Festival [Hebrew]," submitted to the Knesset Education and Culture Committee. 7 May 2001.

Mann, T. "The Sorrows and Grandeur of Richard Wagner" (10 Feb. 1933). In *Pro and Contra Wagner*, translated by A. Blunden. London and Boston: 1985.

—— *Wagner und unsere Zeit: Aufsätze, Betrachtungen, Briefe*. Frankfurt a.M.: 1983.

Meroz, Y. *In schwieriger Mission*. Berlin: 1986.

Nietzsche, F. "The Case of Wagner." In *Complete Works*, edited by O. Levy, translated by J. M. Kennedy, vol. 8. New York: 1964.

Ornstein, Y. *In Chains: Memories of a Fighter* [Hebrew]. Tel Aviv: 1973.

Palestine and Jewish Emigration from Germany. Jerusalem: 1939.

Riefenstahl, L. *Memoiren*. Munich and Hamburg: 1987.

Valentin, E. "Richard Wagner politischer Glaube: Eine Beweisführung aus Zeit und Werk." *Bayreuther Blätter* 60, No. 1 (1937): 12–13.

Wagner, C. *Die Tagebücher*. Munich: 1982.

Wagner, F., and P. Cooper. *Heritage of Fire: The Story of Richard Wagner's Granddaughter*. New York and London: 1945.

Wagner, G. *Wer nicht mit dem Wolf heult: Autobiographische Aufzeichnungen eines Wagner-Urenkels*. Cologne: 1997.

Wagner, R. "Judaism in Music." In *Stories and Essays*, translated by C. Osborne, 23–39. London: 1973.

—— *Der Ring des Nibelungen* (various editions).

—— *Gesammelte Schriften und Dichtungen*. Leipzig: 1872.

—— *Richard Wagner: Mein Denken*. Edited by M. Gregor-Dellin. Munich: 1982.

—— "The Art-Work of the Future." In *The Art-Work of the Future and Other Works*, translated by W.A. Ellis, 69–213. Lincoln and London: 1993.

Secondary Literature

Adorno, T. *In Search of Wagner*. Norfolk: 1985.

Altmann, A. *Moses Mendelssohn: A Biographical Study*. Alabama: 1973.

Anderson, B. *Imagined Communities: Reflections on the Origin and Spread of Nationalism*. London: 1990.

Arad-Ne'eman, G. "Israel and the *Shoah*: A Tale of Multifarious Taboo," *New German Critique* 90 (Autumn, 2003): 5–26.

Arendt, H. *Eichmann in Jerusalem* (various editions).

Aschheim, S. E. *Brothers and Strangers: The East European Jew in Germany and German Jewish Consciousness: 1800–1923*. Madison and London: 1982.

Avineri, S. "Comments on the Significance of the Elections to the Thirteenth Knesset [Hebrew]." *Alpayim* 6 (1993): 29–31.

Backes, K. *Hitler und die bildenen Künste: Kulturveständnis und Kunstpolitik im Dritten Reich.* Cologne: 1988.

Balabkins, N. *West Germany and the Reparations to Israel.* New Brunswick: 1971.

Barenboim, D. and Said, E. *Parallels and Paradoxes: Explorations in Music and Society.* New York: 2002.

Bar-Zohar, M. *The Hunt for German Scientists.* London: 1967.

Bauer, O. G. "Das sichtbare und unsichtbare Theater: Zur Geschichte von Funk, Fernsehen und Schallplate im Festspielhaus." In *Bayreuth 1980: Rückblick und Vorschau.* Bayreuth: 1979.

—— "The Nibelungen Saga in the 19th Century." In *Götterdämmerung: Programmheft IV,* 19–25. Bayreuther Festspiele: 1976.

Beers, H. A. *A History of English Romanticism in the Eighteenth Century.* 1899. Reprint, New York: 1968.

Behler, E. *German Romantic Literary Theory.* Cambridge: 1993.

Ben Arzi, Y. *From Germany to the Holy Land: Templer Settlement in Palestine* [Hebrew]. Jerusalem: 1996.

Ben-Joseph, U. *The Watchman Fell Asleep: The Surprise of Yom Kippur and its Sources.* Albany: 2005.

Ben-Natan, A. "The Path to Diplomatic Relations: The Israeli Perspective" [Hebrew]. In *"Normal" Relations: Relations between Israel and Germany,* edited by M. Zimmerman and O. Heilbruner, 24–32. Jerusalem: 1993.

Ben Yoseph, Y. *The Struggle for Hebrew* [Hebrew]. Jerusalem: 1984.

Benevegna, N. *Kingdom on the Rhine: History, Myth and Legend in Wagner's Ring.* Harwich: 1983.

Berg-Pan, R. *Leni Riefenstahl.* Boston: 1980.

Bermbach, U. *Blühendes Leid. Politik und Gesellschaft in Richard Wagners Musikdramen.* Stuttgart and Weimar: 2003.

Bertram, J. *Mythos, Symbol, Idee in Wagners Musik-Dramen.* Hamburg: 1957.

Billig, M. *Banal Nationalism.* London: 1995.

Bondy, R. *Felix: Pinchas Rosen and His Time* [Hebrew]. Tel Aviv: 1990.

Borchmeyer, D. *Drama and the World of Richard Wagner.* Princeton: 2003.

Bracher, K. D. *The German Dictatorship: The Origins, Structure, and Consequences of National Socialism.* 1969. Reprint, Middlesex: 1985.

Brandt, W. "Germany, Israel, and the Jews." Lecture delivered by the Mayor of Berlin at the Theodor Herzl Institute in New York City, 19 March [1961]. Berlin: 1961.

Brock, B. "Der Ring schließt sich – Wahnhaftes Wähnen über Musik und Geschichte." *Tel Aviver Jahrbuch für deutsche Geschichte* XXXI (2003): 401–8.

Brody, E. "The Jewish Wagnerites." *Midstream* 32, No. 2 (Feb. 1986): 46–59.

Busi, F. "Wagner and the Jews." *Midstream* 32, No. 2 (Feb. 1986): 37–42.

Carpi, D. "The Political Activity of Chaim Weizmann in Italy During the Years 1923–1934 [Hebrew]." *Hazionut* II (1971): 169–207

Clyne, M. G. *Language and Society in the German-Speaking Countries.* London: 1984.

Cohen, A. and B. Susser, *Israel and the Politics of Jewish Identity: The Secular-Religious Impasse.* Baltimore: 2000.

Cohen, Y. "Wagner Nonetheless" [Hebrew]. In *Who's Afraid of Richard Wagner,* edited by R. Litvin and H. Shelach, pp. 285–96, Jerusalem: 1984.

Dinur, B. "Yad Vashem's Goals in Researching Holocaust Martyrs and Heroism and the Issues Involved [Hebrew]." *Kovetz Yad Vashem* 1 (1957): 26–7.

Donnington, R. *Wagner Ring and Its Symbols: The Music and the Myth*. London: 1963.

Doron, J. "The Impact of German Ideologies on Central European Zionism: 1885–1914" [Hebrew]. Ph.D. diss., Tel Aviv University, 1977.

Eger, M., *Wagner und die Juden: Fakten und Hintergründe*. Bayreuth: 1985.

Einstein-Barzilay, I. "The Enlightenment and the Jews: A Study in Haskala and Nationalism." Ph.D. diss., Columbia University, 1955.

Eshkoli (Wagman), H. *Silence: Mapai and the Holocaust – 1939–1942* [Hebrew]. Jerusalem: 1994.

Evans, R. J. *Rereading German History: 1800–1996: From Unification to Reunification*. London and New York: 1997.

Evron, B. *Jewish State or Israeli Nation*. Bloomington: 1995.

Feiner, S. "Mendelssohn and Mendelssohn's Disciples: A Reexamination," *The Yearbook of Leo Baeck Institute*, XL, (1995): 133–67.

Feldman, J. *Above the Death Pits, Beneath the Flag: Young Voyages to Poland and the Performance of Israeli National Identity*. New York: 2008.

Feingold, B. *The Theme of the Holocaust in Hebrew Drama* [Hebrew]. Tel Aviv: 1990.

Fischer, J. M. *Richard Wagners 'Das Judentum in der Musik,' Eine kritische Dokumentation als Beitrag zur Geschichte des europäischen Antisemitismus*. Frankfurt am Main: 2000.

Friedländer, S. "Bayreuth und der Erlösungsantisemitismus." In *Wagner und die Juden*, edited by D. Borchmeyer et al. 8–19. Stuttgart: 2000.

Friling, T. *Arrow in the Darkness: David Ben Gurion, the Yishuv Leadership and the Rescue Attempts during the Holocaust* [Hebrew]. Jerusalem and Beersheba: 1998.

Gans, Ch. *From Richard Wagner to the Palestinian Right of Return: Philosophical Analysis of Israeli Public Affairs* [Hebrew]. Tel Aviv: 2006.

—— "Moralische Aspecte des israelischen Wagner-Boykotts." *Tel Aviver Jahrbuch für deutsche Geschichte* XXXI (2003): 385–400.

—— "The Israeli Ban on the Performance of Wagner: Moral Perspectives [Hebrew]," *Zmanim* 79 (2002): 22–32.

Gaull, M. *English Romanticism: The Human Context*. New York and London: 1988.

Geck, M. "Wagner's 'Ring' – The Sum of a Philosophy of Life?" In *Programmhefte der Bayreuther Festspiele 1973*, Heft vii, pp. 13–27.

Geiger, F. "Die 'Goebbels-Liste,' Vom. 1 September 1935, Eine Quelle zur Komposistenverfolgung im NS-Staat," *Archiv für Musikwissenschaft*, 59:2 (2002): 104–12.

Gelber, Y. *New Homeland: Immigration and Absorption of Cultural European Jews: 1933–1948* [Hebrew]. Jerusalem: 1990.

Giladi, D. *Jewish Palestine During the Forth Aliyah Period (1924–1929)* [Hebrew]. Tel Aviv: 1973.

Gilead, I. "Public Opinion in Israel on Relations between the State of Israel and West Germany in the Years 1949–1965 [Hebrew]." Ph.D. diss., Tel Aviv University, 1984.

Gilliam, B., ed. *Richard Strauss and His World*. Princeton: 1992.

Goodrich, N. L. *Medieval Myths*. New York: 1977.

Grey, T. S., ed. *The Cambridge Companion to Wagner*, Cambridge: 2008.

Grossmann-Vendrey, S., ed. *Bayreuth in den deutchen Presse: Beiträge zur Rezeptionsgeschichte Richard Wagners und seine Festspiele. Dokumentenband 3,1: Von Wagners Tod bis zum Ende der Äre Cosima Wagner (1883–1906)*. Regensburg: 1983.

Grout, D. J., and C. V. Palisca. *A History of Western Music*. 1960. Reprint, New York and London: 1996.

Grunberger, R. *The 12-Year Reich: A Social History of Nazi Germany: 1933–1945*. New York, Chicago, and San Francisco: 1971.

Gutman, R.W. *Wagner – The Man, His Mind and His Music*. New York: 1972.

Halbwachs, M. *On Collective Memory*. Chicago: 1992.

Hausner, G. *Justice in Jerusalem*. 1966. Reprint, New York: 1968.

Hein, A. *Es ist viel "Hitler" in Wagner: Rassismus und antisemitische Deutschtums ideologie in den Bayreuther Blättern (1878 bis 1938)*. Tübingen: 1996.

Herf, J. *Divided Memory: The Nazi Past in the Two Germanys*. Cambridge, Mass.: 1997.

Hirshberg, Y. "Music in Little Tel Aviv." In *The First Twenty Years: Literature and Art in Tel-Aviv: 1909–1929* [Hebrew], edited by A. B. Yaffe, 100–55. Tel Aviv: 1980.

Hobsbawm, E. "Introduction: Inventing Traditions." In *The Invention of Tradition*, edited by E. Hobsbawm and T. Ranger, 1–14. Cambridge: 1992.

Hoch, M. *Return from the Inferno* [Hebrew]. Hadera: 1988.

Hollstein, D. *"Jud Süss" und die Deutschen: Antisemitische Vorurteile im nationalsozialistischen Spielfilm*. Munich: 1971.

Holtzman, A. "Trends in Israeli Fiction of the Holocaust in the 1980s." *Modern Hebrew Literature* (new series) 8/9 (Spring–Fall 1992): 23–8.

Horowitz, J. "Wagner und der amerikanische Jude – eine persönliche Betrachtung." In *Richard Wagner und die Juden*, edited by D. Borchmeyer et al. 238–50, Stuttgart: 2000.

Iggers, G. G. *The German Conception of History: The National Tradition of Historical Thought from Herder to the Present*. Middletown: 1968.

Jelinek, Y. A., ed. *Zwischen Moral und Realpolitik: Eine Dokumentensammlung*. Gerlingen: 1997.

Katz, J. *Richard Wagner: Verbote des Antisemismus*. Königstein: 1985.

Kaynar, G. "Das Gesamtkunstwerk ind sein Widerhall bei Hanoch Levin und anderen." *Tel Aviver Jahrbuch für deutsche Geschichte* XXXI (2003): 372–84.

Keren, N. "Preserving Memory within Oblivion: The Struggle over Teaching the Holocaust in Israel [Hebrew]." *Zmanim* 64 (Summer, 1998): 56–65.

Keren, N., and M. Gil, eds. *"I Seek My Brother": Along the Way, Youth Tours in Poland* [Hebrew]. Jerusalem: n.d.

Kimmerling, B. *The Invention and Decline of Israeliness: State, Society, and the Military*. Berkeley: 2001.

Köhler, F. H. "Struktur der Spielpläne deutschsprachiger Opernbähnen von 1896 bis 1966." Lecture delivered at the Schul- und Kulturstatistik conference in Koblenz, 16–17 May 1968.

Köhler, J. *Der letzte der Titanen. Richard Wagners Leben und Werk*. Munich: 2001.

—— *Wagners Hitler: Der Prophet und sein Vollstreker*. Munich: 1997.

Kohn, H. *The Mind of Germany: The Education of a Nation*. New York: 1960.

Kresel, G. *History of the Hebrew Press in Palestine* [Hebrew]. Jerusalem: 1964.

Kroll, E. "Verbotene Musik." *Vierteljahrhefte für Zeitgeschichte* III (July 1959): 310–17.

Large, D. C. "Wagner's Bayreuth Disciples." In *Wagnerianism in European Culture and Politics*, edited by D. C. Large and W. Weber, 72–133. Ithaca and London: 1984.

—— "Ein Spiegel des Meisters? Die Rassenlehre von Houston Stewart Chamberlain." In *Wagner und die Juden*, edited by D. Borchmeyer et al. 144–9. Stuttgart: 2000.

Leshem, S. "The Palestine Theater" [Hebrew]. M.A. thesis, Tel Aviv University: 1991.

Levi, E. *Music in the Third Reich*. London: 1994.

Levy, E. *The Habima National Theater: History of the Theater in the Years 1917–1979* [Hebrew]. Tel Aviv: 1981.

Lipsky, H. "The Term 'SHOAH': Meaning and Modification in the Hebrew Language from its beginning to this day, in the Israeli society" [Hebrew], M.A. Thesis. Tel Aviv University, 1998.

Litvin, R., and H. Shelach, eds. *Who's Afraid of Richard Wagner: Different Aspects of the Controversial Figure* [Hebrew]. Jerusalem: 1984.

Lorenz, A. O. *Das Geheimnis der Form bei Richard Wagner*. Berlin: 1924.

Lowinsky, E., ed. *The Letters of Richard Strauss and Stefan Zweig: 1931–1935*. Berkeley: 1977.

Mackensen, L. *Die Nibelungen: Sage, Geschichte, ihr Lied und sein Dichter*. Stuttgart: 1984.

Mackenzie, D. A. *Teutonic Myth and Legend*. London: 1912.

Mali, Y. "Who's Afraid of Richard Wagner? [Hebrew]," *Zmanim* 20 (Winter, 1986): 93–6.

Markovits, A. S., and S. Reich. "Should Europe Fear the Germans." *German Politics and Society* 23 (Summer, 1991): 1–20.

McCrelless, P. *Wagner's Siegfried: Its Drama, History and Music*. Michigan: 1981.

Meyers, O. and E. Zandberg, "The Sound-Track of Memory: *Ashes and Dust* and the Commemoration of the Holocaust in Israeli Popular Culture," *Media, Culture & Society* 24.3 (2002): 389–408.

Meyers, O., E. Zandberg, and M. Neiger, "Prime Time Commemoration: An Analysis of Television Broadcasts on Israel's Memorial Day for the Holocaust and the Heroism," *Journal of Communication* 59 (2009): 456–80.

Mosse, G. L. *Nazi Culture: Intellectual, Cultural and Social Life in the Third Reich*. 1966. Reprint, New York: 1981.

Motzafi-Haller, P. "A Mizrahi Call for a More Democratic Israel." In *Postzionism: A Reader*, edited by L. A. Silberstein, 275–82. New Brunswick: 2008.

Münkler, H. "Mythischer Sinn: Der Nibelungenmythos in der politischen Symbolik des 20. Jahrhunderts." In *In den Trümmern der Eigen Welt: Richard Wagners "Der Ring des Nibelungen,"* edited by U. Bermbach, 251–66. Berlin and Hamburg: 1989.

Naor, A. *Begin in Power: Personal Testimony* [Hebrew]. Tel Aviv: 1993.

Newman, E. *Wagner as Man and Artist*. New York: 1914.

Niederland, D. *The Jews of Germany – Emigrants or Refugees? An Examination* of Emigration Patterns between the Two World Wars [Hebrew]. Jerusalem: 1996.

Ofer, D. "Linguistic Conceptualization of the Holocaust in Palestine and Israel, 1942–1953," *Journal of Contemporary History* 31.3 (1996): 567–95.

Oren, M. *Six Days of War: June 1967 and the Making of the Modern Middle East.* New York: 2003.

Osborne, C. *The Complete Operas of Wagner.* London: 1992.

Oz-Salzberger, F. *Israelis in Berlin.* Frankfurt: 2001.

Pascal, R. *The German Sturm und Drang.* London: 1953.

Pedhatzur, R. *The Triumph of Embarrassment: Israel and the Territories after the Six-Day War* [Hebrew]. Tel Aviv: 1996.

Perl, B. "Drama and Music in the Work of Richard Wagner [Hebrew]." In *Who's Afraid of Richard Wagner*, edited by R. Litvin and H. Shelach, pp. 170–200, Jerusalem: 1984.

Perris, A. *Music as Propaganda: Art to Persuade, Art to Control.* Connecticut and London: 1985.

Petropoulos, J. *Art as Politics in the Third Reich.* Chapel Hill and London: 1996.

Pinchevski, A. and T. Liebes, "Severed Voices: Radio and the Mediation of Trauma in the Eichmann Trial." *Public Culture*, 22.2 (2010): 265–91.

Porat, D. *An Entangled Leadership: The Yishuv in the Holocaust: 1942–1945* [Hebrew]. Tel Aviv: 1986.

Prieberg, F. K., and C. Dolan. *Trial of Strength: Wilhelm Furtwängler in the Third Reich.* Boston: 1994.

Reichert, H. *Nibelungenlied und Nibelungensaga.* Vienna and Cologne: 1985.

Rein, R. *In the Shadow of the Holocaust and the Inquisition: Israel's Relations with Francoist Spain.* Translated by M. Grenzeback. London and Portland, OR: 1997.

Reinharz, J. *Chaim Weizmann: the Making of a Statesman.* Oxford: 1993.

Rinott, M. *"Hilfsverein der deutschen Juden" – Creation and Struggle* [Hebrew]. Jerusalem: 1971.

Rose, P .L. *Wagner: Race and Revolution.* New Haven and London: 1992.

Rubinstein, A., and B. Medina. *The Constitutional Law of the State of Israel* [Hebrew]. Jerusalem and Tel Aviv: 1997.

Saalfeld, L. von. "Die ideologische Funktion des Nibelungenliedes in der Preussisch-Deutschen Geschichte: von seiner Wiederentdeckung bis zum Nazionalsozialismus." Ph.D. diss, Freie Universität Berlin: 1977.

Sachs, H. *Toscanini.* New York: 1988.

Schweid, E. "The Expulsion from Spain and the Holocaust" [Hebrew]. *Alpayim* 3 (1991): 69–88.

Segev, T. *1967: Israel, the War, and the Year that transformed the Middle East.* New York: 2007.

—— *The Seventh Million: The Israelis and the Holocaust.* New York: 1993.

—— *1949: The First Israelis.* London: 1986.

Shafir, S. *An Outstreched Hand: German Social Democrats, Jews, and Israel 1945–1967* [Hebrew]. Tel Aviv: 1986.

Shapira, A. *Israel: A History.* Lebanon: 2012.

—— "The Holocaust: Private Memory and Public Memory." *Jewish Social Studies* 4, No. 2 (Winter, 1998): 40–58.

—— "The *Yishuv* and the Survivors of the Holocaust." *Studies in Zionism* 7 (1986): 277–301.

Shapiro, Y. *Chosen to Command: The Road to Power of the Herut Party – A Socio-Political Interpretation* [Hebrew]. Tel Aviv: 1989.

—— *Politicians as a Hegemonic Class: The Case of Israel* [Hebrew]. Tel Aviv: 1996.

Shavit, Z. "The Formation of the Literary Center in Eretz-Yisrael in the Institutionalization of *Yishuv* Society [Hebrew]." *Catedra* 16 (June, 1980): 207–33.

Sheffi, N. *Vom Deutschen ins Hebräische: Übersetzungen aus dem Deutschen im jüdischen Palästina 1882–1948*. Göttingen: 2011.

—— "Between Germanophobia and Germanophilia: Israelis read German Literature," *Trumah* (forthcoming).

—— "Jews, Germans and the Representation of Jud Süss in Literature and Film," *Jewish Culture and History* 6, No. 2 (Winter, 2003): 25–42.

—— "The Jewish Expulsion from Spain and the Rise of National Socialism on the Hebrew Stage." *Journal of Jewish Social Studies* (Fall, 1999): 82–103.

Shenhav, Y. *The Arab Jews: A Post Colonial Reading of Nationalism, Religion and Ethnicity*. Palo Alto: 2006.

Shoham, H. *The Drama of "A Generation in Israel"* [Hebrew]. Tel Aviv: 1989.

Skelton, G. *Wagner at Bayreuth: Experiment and Tradition*. London: 1965.

Smith, A. D. *National Identity*. London: 1991.

Soley, L. C. *Radio Warfare: OSS and CIA Subservice Propaganda*. New York, Westport, and London: 1989.

Storch, W., ed. *Die Nibelungen*. Munich: 1987.

Tal, U. *Christians and Jews in Germany: Religion, Politics and Ideology in the Second Reich: 1870–1914*. Ithaca and New York: 1974.

Tammuz, B., ed. *Tenth Anniversary Book of the Cameri Theater 1944–1954* [Hebrew]. Tel Aviv: 1954.

Toeplitz, U. *The History of the Israel Philharmonic Orchestra Researched and Remembered* [Hebrew]. Tel Aviv: 1992.

Tomburg, F. "Faschismusverständnis im Schatten Richard Wagners." *Dialektik, Beiträge zu Philosophie Wissenschaften: Antisemitismus* 7 (1983): 202–23.

Toury, G. *Translational Norms and Literary Translation into Hebrew: 1930–1945* [Hebrew]. Tel Aviv: 1977.

Vaget, H. R. "Wieviel 'Hitler' ist in Wagner: Anmerkungen zu Hitler, Wagner und Thomas Mann," in *Wagner und die Juden*, ed. D. Borchmeyer et al. pp. 178–206. Stuttgart: 2000.

—— "Anti Semitism, and Mr. Rose Merkwurd'ger Fall!" *The German Quarterly*, 66:2, (Spring 1993): 222–36.

Viereck, P. *Metapolitics: The Roots of the Nazi Mind*. New York: 1961.

Vogel, R., ed. *The German Path to Israel*. Chester Springs: 1969.

Wagner, G. "On the Need to Debate Richard Wagner in an Open Society: How to Confront Wagner Today Beyond Glorification and Condemnation." In *Richard Wagner for the New Millennium*, edited by M. Bribitzer-Stull, A. Lubet and G. Wagner, 3–24. New York: 2007.

Waite, R. G. L. *The Psychopathic God: Adolf Hitler*. New York: 1978.

Weiner, M. A. *Richard Wagner and the Anti-Semitic Imagination*. Lincoln and London: 1997.

Weiss, Y. *Deutsche und polnische Juden vor dem Holocaust: jüdische Identität zwischen Staatsbürgerschaft und Ethnizität, 1933–1940,* translated by M. Schmidt. Munich: 2000.

Weitz, Y. "Changing Conceptions of the Holocaust: The Kasztner Case." *Reshaping the Past: Jewish History and the Historians,* edited by J. Frankel. *Studies in Contemporary Jewry,* Vol. X (1994): 211–30.

—— "The Herut Movement and the Kasztner Trial." *Holocaust and Genocide Studies* 8, No. 3 (1994): 349–71.

—— "Political Dimensions of Holocaust Memory in Israel during the 1950's." *Israel Affairs* 1, No. 3 (1995): 129–45.

Windell, G. G. "Hitler, National Socialism, and Richard Wagner. In *Penetrating Wagner's Ring: An Anthology,* edited by J. L. DiGaetani, 219–38. New Jersey and London: 1974.

Wistrich, R. S. *Weekend in Munich: Art, Propaganda and Terror in the Third Reich.* London: 1995.

Wolffsohn, M. *Keine Angst vor Deutschland!* Erlangen: 1990.

Wunderlich, W. "Der Schatz des Drachentänders: Materielen zur Wirkungsgeschichte des Nibelungenliedes." *Literatur-wissenschaft-Gesellschaf-twissenschaft* 30 (1977): 11–22.

Yablonka, H. "The Formation of the Holocaust Consciousness in the State of Israel: The Early Days." In *Breaking Crystal: Writing and Memory after Auschwitz,* edited by E. Sicher, 119–36. Urbana and Chicago, IL: 1998.

—— "The Law for the Punishment of Nazis and their Collaborators: Another Aspect of the Issue of Israelis, Survivors, and the Holocaust [Hebrew]." *Cathedra* 82 (Jan. 1997): 135–52.

Yadgar, Y. "From the particularistic to the universalistic: national narratives in Israel's mainstream press, 1967–97," *Nations and Nationalism* 8.1 (Jan. 2002): 55–72.

Yehil, L. "The Wanderings of Jews from Germany, Austria and Czechoslovakia (1933–1939): Basic Issues and Main Outlines" [Hebrew]. In *History Conference Lectures* [Hebrew], 103–23. Jerusalem: 1973.

Yovel, Y. "'Nietzsche contra Wagner' und die Juden." In *Richard Wagner und die Juden,* edited by D. Borchmeyer et al., pp. 123–43. Stuttgart: 2000.

Zandberg, E. "The Right to Tell the (right) Story: Journalism, Authority and Memory." *Media, Culture and Society,* 32 (2010): 5–24.

—— "Critical Laughter: Humor, Popular Culture and Israeli Holocaust Commemoration," *Media, Culture & Society* 28.4 (2006): 561–79.

Zelinsky, H. "Richard Wagner 'Kunst der Zukunft' und seine Idee der Vernichtung." In *Von kommenden Zeiten: Geschichtsprophetien im 19. und 20. Jahrhundert,* edited by J. A. Knoll and J. A. Schoeps, 84–105. Stuttgart and Bonn: 1984.

Zertal, I. *Israel's Holocaust and the Politics of Nationhood.* Cambridge: 2010.

Zuckermann, M. "Richard Wagner, the Revolutionist and Reactionist [Hebrew]." *Zmanim* 12 (Summer, 1983): 60–73.

—— *Shoah in the Sealed Room: The "Holocaust" in the Israeli Press during the Gulf War* [Hebrew]. Tel Aviv: 1993.

Index

Printed and bound by CPI Group (UK) Ltd, Croydon, CR0 4YY

09/06/2025

14685805-0002